Educational Research and Policy-Making

The worlds of educational policy and research are acknowledged to be very different from each other, with potential for mutual misunderstanding. This book provides a fascinating insight into this sometimes troubled relationship, showing how each of these areas is in a state of dynamic change and how, as a result, they are posing increasingly complex problems for each other. It suggests a number of scenarios for the future development of the relationship and throws down some challenges for both communities.

Much has been said and written in the last ten years about the need for – or else the impossibility and undesirability of – 'evidence-based education' in principle. There has been rather less said about what might be involved, practically and intellectually, in creating environments where research can have a realistic and beneficial influence on the development of particular policies. This book is unique in bringing together writers who have had a major effect, through their research efforts, on the way policy initiatives have evolved, and contributors who have helped to build policy capacity to appreciate and use research intelligently. The book focuses on the dilemmas and opportunities faced by academic researchers who work in the research–policy 'border country', and gives a view from inside the policy environment as described by some of the people who mediate research for their policy colleagues.

With contributions from eminent academics and influential individuals, the book offers an unusual combination of scholarly knowledge and practical wisdom. It helps to demystify structures, organisations and processes that can often seem remote or closed-off, and will be helpful for researchers wanting to understand the policy environment more deeply and/or engage more closely with policy in their specialist areas.

Lesley Saunders works for the General Teaching Council (England) as their Senior Policy Adviser for Research. She has been engaged in developing and implementing a research strategy that draws on high quality scholarship and research to support the breadth of the GTC's remit and aspirations. She is also Visiting Professor at the Institute of Education, London.

Educational Research and Policy-Making

Exploring the border country between research and policy

Edited by Lesley Saunders

Routledge
Taylor & Francis Group

NEW YORK AND LONDON

First published 2007
by Routledge
2 Park Square, Milton Park, Abingdon, Oxon OX14 4RN

Simultaneously published in the USA and Canada
by Routledge
270 Madison Ave, New York, NY 10016

Routledge is an imprint of the Taylor & Francis Group, an informa business

© 2007 selection and editorial matter Lesley Saunders; individual chapters the contributors

Typeset in Times New Roman by Keyword Group Ltd
Printed and bound in Great Britain by the Cromwell Press, Trowbridge, Wiltshire

British Library Cataloguing in Publication Data
A catalogue record for this book is available
from the British Library

Library of Congress Cataloging in Publication Data
A catalog record has been requested for this book

ISBN 10: 0-415-41174-2 (hbk)
ISBN 10: 0-415-41175-0 (pbk)
ISBN 10: 0-203-93979-4 (ebk)

ISBN 13: 978-0-415-41174-5 (hbk)
ISBN 13: 978-0-415-41175-2 (pbk)
ISBN 13: 978-0-203-93979-6 (ebk)

'The situation was so bizarre, so totally unlike her usual environment, that there was a kind of exhilaration to be found in it, in its very discomfort and danger, such as explorers must feel, she supposed, in a remote and barbarous country'.

David Lodge, *Nice Work* (Penguin Books, 1989)

i.m. Carol Adams, 1948–2007

Contents

Contributors   ix
Foreword   xi
ANDREW POLLARD
Editor's introduction   xiii
LESLEY SAUNDERS

1   **Education(al) research and education policy-making:
    is conflict inevitable?**   1
    GEOFF WHITTY

2   **Schools research in the English Ministry of Education:
    an inside view**   19
    VICTORIA WHITE

3   **The interplay between policy and research in relation
    to ICT in education in the UK: issues from
    twenty years of programme evaluation**   35
    BRIDGET SOMEKH

4   **Exploring literacy policy-making from the inside out**   55
    GEMMA MOSS AND LAURA HUXFORD

5   **Negotiating policy space for teachers' continuing
    professional development: a view from the higher
    education institution**   74
    HAZEL BRYAN

6   **Learning from the work of the National Educational
    Research Forum**   92
    ANDREW MORRIS

7   Go-betweens, gofers or mediators?: exploring the
    role and responsibilities of research managers
    in policy organisations   106
    LESLEY SAUNDERS

8   Enhancing impact on policy-making through
    increasing user engagement in research   127
    JUDY SEBBA

9   Protecting the innocent: the need for ethical
    frameworks within mass educational innovation   144
    TIM OATES

    Notes   175
    Index   177

Contributors

Hazel Bryan is Director of the MA Framework in the Department of Professional Development, Faculty of Education, at Canterbury Christ Church University. Her research interests include constructs of teacher professionalism, education policy and continuing professional development.

Laura Huxford is Senior Research Fellow at the Department of Education, University of Oxford. She was the Director of Professional Development in the National Literacy and Primary Strategies and continues to advise government on issues relating to literacy.

Andrew Morris was, until 2006, Director of the National Educational Research Forum. He was originally a teacher in post-16 education and later worked as a Vice Principal in Islington Sixth Form Centre/City and Islington College and then as a Research Manager at the Learning and Skills Development Agency.

Gemma Moss is Reader in Education in the School of Educational Foundations and Policy Studies, Institute of Education, University of London. Her main research interests are in the areas of literacy and education policy, including gender and literacy; children's informal literacy practices and their relationship to the English curriculum; and the role of policy-makers, practitioners and the research community in re-shaping the literacy curriculum.

Tim Oates is Group Director of Assessment Research and Development at Cambridge Assessment. In 1993 he joined the National Council for Vocational Qualifications (NCVQ) in England, as head of Research and Development. On the merger of NCVQ and the schools curriculum and assessment authority (SCAA) to form the Qualifications and Curriculum Authority (QCA), he was appointed Head of Research, a position he held from 1997 to 2006. He was a member of the Education sub-panel for the UK Research Assessment Exercise 2004, was co-author with Mike Coles of the new pan-European Qualifications Framework, and has advised a number of governments and agencies on qualifications strategy.

Lesley Saunders has been the Senior Policy Adviser for Research at the General Teaching Council for England since its inception in 2000. She holds a Visiting Professorship at the Institute of Education, University of London, and is serving on the Education sub-panel for the UK Research Assessment Exercise 2008. Previously she was a principal research officer at the National Foundation for Educational Research for England and Wales, where she headed the School Improvement Research Centre, and she was one of the original members of the National Educational Research Forum.

Judy Sebba is Professor of Education at the Sussex Institute where she leads the teaching, learning and assessment research. She is a member of the Education sub-panel in the UK Research Assessment Exercise 2008. Previously, she was Senior Adviser (Research) in the Standards and Effectiveness Unit of the English government's Department for Education and Skills, where she was responsible for developing the research strategy and quality of research, including the development of systematic reviewing. Prior to that she was a researcher and lecturer at the universities of Cambridge and Manchester on special educational needs, inclusion and school improvement.

Bridget Somekh is Professor of Educational Research and leads the ICT, Pedagogy and Learning research group in the Education and Social Research Institute at Manchester Metropolitan University. She is the author of *Action Research: A Methodology for Change and Development* (Open University Press 2006) and *Pedagogy and Learning with ICT: Researching the Art of Innovation* (Routledge 2007). Since 1992 she has been an editor of the international journal, *Educational Action Research*.

Victoria White is Research Manager for the Chief Adviser on School Standards at the Department for Education and Skills. This role involves improving the access and uptake of research evidence by field and policy staff at the DfES and by practitioners. Prior to that she was part of the DfES team with responsibility for providing strategic support to the National Educational Research Forum and for managing the contract for the Evidence for Policy and Practice Information and Coordination Centre.

Geoff Whitty is Director of the Institute of Education, University of London. His main areas of teaching and research are the sociology of education and education policy. He has led evaluations of major educational reforms in the UK, including changes in initial teacher education and, most recently, provision for pupil voice in schools. He has also assisted schools and local authorities in building capacity for improvement. He is currently President of the College of Teachers and President of the British Educational Research Association and a member of the General Teaching Council for England. He also acts as a specialist adviser to the House of Commons Education and Skills Select Committee.

Foreword

This important volume represents yet another step forward as educational researchers progressively rethink the relationship of educational research and policy-making.

The main focus is on the challenges, dilemmas and opportunities faced by those researchers who commit to work in the research-policy 'border country'. Such intrepid pathfinders engage with the assumptive worlds of policy-makers and practitioners knowing of the considerable differences in the daily experiences, cultures, priorities, accountabilities and incentivisation systems of each party. In such circumstances the potential for misunderstandings is high – as is the risk of raising suspicions and failing tacit loyalty tests from colleagues in one's own home community. Working in the border country is thus to accept a degree of vulnerability.

And yet, histories of the evolution of disciplines and of knowledge often show the fertility of the spaces where one set of ideas and practices rub up against another. If engagement can be conducted constructively, these can be sites for rapid innovation, reappraisal and development.

In my view, contemporary educational research is seeing just such a move forward. From the mutual incomprehension of a decade ago there have been many attempts to develop new understandings. Some have generated considerable controversy and debate, but it is arguable that we are gradually arriving at a new settlement – to which this book contributes significantly.

A classic question has been whether social scientists should 'take' or 'make' the problems they study. Should they respond to the agendas and priorities of others (such as funders or governments), or position themselves to develop more independent analyses of social issues? What, to put it other ways, should be the role of the university in a free society, the intellectual in a democracy, or the social scientist in his or her community?

There are many answers to the question. One builds on the old Enlightenment commitment to the application of 'reason' for social improvement – and, indeed, I have associated the Teaching and Learning Research Programme (TLRP) with this position. In that instance, a value commitment to 'improving learning' provides a generalised rally point for such applied research. There are also equally strong and valid arguments for studies which focus more exclusively on particular analytic issues or use single disciplinary lenses to highlight dimensions which might otherwise have been overlooked. In cumulation, such work may contribute to theorised understandings of enduring challenges and factors in learning and education more generally. However, whatever such distinctions, there is growing appreciation of how different forms of research endeavour can complement each other – or even be combined in sophisticated research designs. At this point, the issue therefore becomes one of fitness for purpose. One of the things which this collection helpfully demonstrates is that such approaches are compatible – and deserve the mutual respect which they are increasingly getting.

The form of the book is interesting. Its combination of major overviews of issues and case studies of experiences at the research-policy interface is reminiscent of collections of narrative accounts by ethnographers. Such personal and grounded texts provide insights into the messy realities of facing practical dilemmas – and offer a rich starting point for understanding. Further, they illuminate something of the struggles of the personnel involved, from policy-makers, civil servants, researchers and practitioners alike. This is very important because it demystifies and personalises structures, organisations and processes which can often seem remote or closed. Although UK education systems are characterised by incredible scale and complexity, my work with TLRP rapidly showed that they are sustained by the integrity and expertise of literally thousands of professionals. We make contributions in many different ways and share the discursive spaces which underpin provision. In such circumstances however, we don't get far without a degree of openness, respect for the expertise of others and appreciation of their structural position and constraints.

The editor and contributors to this book are to be congratulated for presenting and analysing so many of the issues which arise when exploring the relationship between educational research and policy-making – and it is excellent that BERA and its Special Interest Group have been instrumental in bringing it about.

Professor Andrew Pollard
Director, Teaching and Learning Research Programme
January 2007

Editor's introduction

Lesley Saunders

This book is dedicated to the memory of Carol Adams who, among her very many outstanding achievements as Chief Executive of the General Teaching Council for England from 2000 to 2006, appreciated, promoted and in every way encouraged the flow of ideas and evidence from research into policy, in order to improve and sustain the cogency of the decisions made and positions taken by the Council. She was exemplary in the way she supported her research staff, valued their professionalism and argued for the continuing importance of a broad-based research programme even when there were so many other demands on the budget. I am proud to have been part of that effort under her resolute and dynamic leadership.

The epigraph from David Lodge's novel satirising the state of relationships between industry and the university could, *mutatis mutandis*, equally well refer to the seemingly mutually incomprehensible worlds of policy and research. The metaphor of a 'remote and barbarous country' is treated quite literally in a brilliant study by the cultural historian, Marina Warner (2002), where she explores the transmigration of stories from one culture to another, and the surprising ways in which they travelled,

> circulating via … the diplomatic bags of early empire-builders and proselytizers, specimen-hunters and cartographers, figures who are themselves often situated at turning points in culture and at moments of clash and conflict between one intellectual hegemony and another: it is characteristic of metamorphic writing to appear in transitional places and at the confluence of traditions and civilizations.
>
> (p. 18)

Warner goes on:

> I was looking for 'congeners', materials through which one culture interacts with and responds to another, conductors of energies that may themselves not be apparent or directly palpable in the resulting transformations.
>
> (ibid.)

I venture to hope that the wealth of ideas, essays and stories so expertly articulated by the authors of the chapters in this book will act as energetic 'congeners' in and for our contemporary local context, not least by creating some distinctive and habitable intellectual border country that is contiguous with both policy and research territories – which may thereby become less estranged and remote from each other.

It is worth mentioning that the book arose from, and reflects, a very particular set of circumstances. At the 2004 annual conference of the British Educational Research Association (BERA), papers presented in one of the symposia triggered a heated discussion amongst the large audience. The debate turned into a more general one that was, directly or indirectly, about the disputed – some would say endangered, others might say inflated – role and status of educational research.

Since the criticisms of educational research made in the mid to late 1990s, a succession of Secretaries of State for Education, starting with David Blunkett, had been urging research to come forward with more attractive propositions for helping to address, in Charles Clarke's words (THES 2003), *some of the key challenges we face in public policy*.[1] The response of some researchers was to attempt to remind politicians of the serious contributions to policy already made by – and of the uses that could and should have been made of – educational research, and to insist upon the need for politicians and policy-makers to read, listen and memorise more carefully. Others believed the whole enterprise of producing research that could speak to policy concerns was bound to founder in practice and/or was theoretically flawed.

It was evident that the BERA session had lifted the lid on a difficult and surprisingly emotive set of issues that had been simmering away for some years; and that BERA itself needed to host some kind of forum where they could be discussed more fully and constructively. A special interest group (SIG) was exactly the right kind of structure and process for this, so I made a proposal to convene a new SIG on the broad theme of educational research and its relationship with education policy: it seemed to me that this was where the apparently intractable difficulties lay (rather than in the relationship between research and the practice of teaching) (see Saunders 2004). The intention of convening the group was to bring together a range of philosophical, conceptual and empirical understandings – including in the field of research utilisation and 'impact'[2] – to explore a variety of infrastructures, processes and institutional arrangements as a basis for further developing and influencing research-informed policy-making. Would it then be possible to make some headway on how and under what conditions educational research can and should seek to inform the processes of policy-making at different levels within the system?

There were also some quite specific objectives for the group, namely:

- to identify key areas of policy which may be particularly supported, or contraindicated, by current research evidence;

- to identify and strengthen processes, environments and institutional arrangements for the mediation and 'translation' of research knowledge for decision-making;
- to explore a range of methodologies for synthesising research knowledge into 'bodies of evidence';
- to identify new substantive areas, new research models and modes, and/or insufficiently understood issues for policy-relevant research;
- to deepen researchers' understandings of policy-making systems and processes.

This all seems to have touched a nerve: the SIG was launched at the 2005 annual conference with a double symposium attended by a large number of obviously engaged participants (and the 2006 conference went on to attract many individual papers and several symposia). This book brings together, in fuller versions, all but one of the 2005 symposium papers, and adds two further chapters contributed by influential figures in educational research. Before introducing each of the contributions, I will sketch out a little of the general context for their work without – I hope – going over too much of the ground which has already been covered in many excellent journal articles and books with which readers are no doubt already familiar.

My starting point is that one might rather expect to take for granted that in a mature democratic polity the decisions that are made about the use of public resources should be, and generally are, informed by a combination of some kind of empirical evidence and intelligence, and of what are recognisable as underpinning concepts or mid-range theories, as well as by all the other influences and pressures on political decision-making. This is hardly a new or particularly contentious notion.[3] But, for various historical, political and epistemological reasons, 'evidence-based policy' in English education is currently not an unexceptionable aspiration, a neutral ascription. It has instead become a highly charged and polarising idea, with different factions in the educational research community taking strongly contrasting, even oppositional, stances. These have resulted not only in some distancing of educational research from education policy, and *vice versa*, but also in theoretical and methodological stand-offs, paradigm and turf wars; and there are people who have felt hurt and angry, misunderstood or misjudged. What has made a fairly mundane fact of public policy-making the subject of so much controversy and the object of feelings of hostility, contempt and betrayal in recent years clearly continues to need different sorts of explanation, especially since the Rhind report on the social sciences (op. cit.) showed that education has not been alone.

This book in the main does not seek theoretical or systemic explanations but instead offers – from different viewpoints – an analytical and illuminative account of some actual circumstances and key relationships between educational research and policy at a particular juncture in the educational reform movement that began in England in the fourth quarter of the last century. In that time, there have been some fundamental shifts in the balance of power and responsibility, epochal reversals in what central government holds tight and what it keeps loose in public service sectors like education (as between, say, governance and power-to-spend on the one hand, and the professional domains of curriculum, pedagogy and assessment on the other), and in how educationists of all kinds are consequently meant to conceive of, and enact, accountability for the public resources invested. These shifts were initiated by the Education Reform Act of 1988, and the political direction of travel has continued much the same since, with research and evaluation increasingly seen as the servants of accountability.

Moreover, since 1997 there was a rhetorical turn towards 'evidence-based' policy, which was intended to signal the end of ideology as the key determinant of decision-making. This was a disingenuous gesture, of course, since ideology, for instance in the form of talk about the superiority of 'consumer choice' as an organising principle in public services, has gone from strength to strength in politicians' semantic apparatus. But, in a competitive market place for knowledge – and let us not forget that the 'evidence' mantra brought with it a large injection of government cash to support educational research – the basic idea sounded persuasive enough to many buyers and some producers of research that, in effect, they colluded with each other to permit some assumptions to flourish: for example, that policy should attend to evidence above all else, that it is the principal job of research to produce that evidence, and even that the methods that will produce results that can count as evidence can and should be tightly prescribed. There are various different vantage points from which such assumptions, particularly the first, can be attacked – for example:

All governments and parties are operating in an environment where there is far more evidence, where the public are far more attuned to the idea that you test things, you measure them, and then some work and some don't. But it's very hard really to drive a government solely based on evidence; and it's values which determine what are your non-negotiable lines you won't cross.
(Geoff Mulgan, Director of the Young Foundation and former government adviser, speaking in the BBC Radio 4 programme Analysis: 'Politics for Plumbers?', broadcast 13 April 2006)

I wouldn't for a minute suggest that all education policy should have to be rooted in research – politics and government don't work like that.
(Baroness Morris, former Secretary of State for Education, writing in *The Guardian,* 26 September 2006).

… knowledge and expertise are socially constructed and … the utilisation of research-based knowledge is driven as much by political expediency and broader social and political factors as it is by standards of objective truth and epistemological certainty …
(Burton 2006, p. 191)

To take an obvious case: what a newly elected administration believes it needs by way of evidence to support policy evolution is very different from the intelligence which the same administration might require about the efficacy of its existing policies in the run-up to the next election. One thing is certain, that policy never will be able to be read off in a linear and straightforward fashion from research; as the authors of a Demos pamphlet argue (Stilgoe *et al.* 2006, p. 72), 'The political legitimacy of policy does not increase with more evidence or more expertise. In the sorts of areas in which expert wisdom is useful – unbounded, uncertain, complex – policy is not a line from evidence to execution, it is a complex system'.

Interestingly, however, educational research has also been pressed over the same period to provide the basis for the professional practice of teaching – not least through the Teaching and Learning Research Programme (TLRP), funded by the UK's Economic and Social Research Council (ESRC) and now under the expert and creative leadership of Andrew Pollard – and I find it intriguing that the affordances of research for teaching are in general well understood and appreciated by teachers and expressed with enthusiasm and nuance by many academics. The way many teachers now talk about the significance of research for their practice – as 'an island waiting to be discovered' in one teacher's memorable phrase – no doubt owes much to the efforts of teacher educators and scholars like Professors Michael Fielding, John Elliott, Jean Rudduck and many others to ensure that the inspirational work of Lawrence Stenhouse remains vivid. He taught us to think of research and pedagogy as dialectically connected in and through the day-to-day reflexive expertise of teacher-scholars. This idea is, I think, quite different from that of 'evidence-based' practice. Part of the difficulty with 'evidence-based' as distinct from 'research-informed' lies in its apparent definitiveness, its implied certainty. But as Hagger and McIntyre (2006, pp. 24–25) argue:

> … research-based knowledge about teaching can take us only a limited way towards an understanding of good practice .… The idea of a 'technology of teaching', with scientifically established rules of good practice which teachers would be obliged to follow, is not attractive … it is also wrong. Its success would have to depend on there being a body of totally reliable and generalizable scientific laws by which one could predict the effects upon pupils' thinking and learning of whatever teachers did. Not only would this body of scientific knowledge have to be immense … ; it would also have to be as precise and reliable as … Newtonian physics .… .

Eraut (2004, p. 97) put the issue slightly differently but with equal force: 'the chances of the expert being already familiar with the system-based knowledge will be high, the chances of the system capturing most of the expert-based knowledge near to zero'.

So there may be something valuable for policy environments to be inferred, possibly transferred, from the ways in which many teachers and researchers understand, and engage in and with, knowledge-in-action, research-for-teaching. That is, we might try to think of research as a form of specialised knowledge which is created, not as a product made elsewhere and then disseminated to and applied by the 'users' of research, but through a process which is collaborative, reflexive and discursive, is wholly comfortable with provisionality and can make room for the contribution of different kinds of expertise. Research might then have a better chance of fulfilling what Engeström (2007) calls its capacity to 'evoke and support human agency'. (Flyvbjerg [2001] has some exciting things to say about this kind of approach to knowledge creation in the social sciences generally.)

My sense is that there have recently been some significant initiatives which are moving us towards this more realistic and complicated understanding of research and its relationship to policy. As well as the burgeoning of useful research-based communications – all the various bulletins, newsletters, e-mail alerts, web-based and other on-line summary materials – I would include such activities as the project conducted by Furlong and Oancea (culminating in their 2005 report) on assessing the quality of applied and practice-based research; the seminar series funded by the TLRP titled 'Making a difference: collaborating with users to develop educational research', which forms the subject of Judy Sebba's chapter in this book (see also http://www.tlrp.org/themes/seminar/edwards/index.html for working papers); the recently begun work, again under the aegis of the TLRP, on the epistemological bases of educational research (being led by Professor David Bridges); and the research seminars for policy-makers at the DfES coordinated by Victoria White and described in her chapter for this book.

These are all useful not least because – being constructed around conversations between mixed groups of academic researchers, policy staff and advisers, and teacher-researchers – they take us away from dualities and polarities, and further into complexities and pluralities. And they are complemented by new ways of conceptualising research for a policy context that are being developed by, for example, Pawson (2006) who compares policy mechanisms and their evaluations across different public policy sectors, to powerful effect. One issue that emerges with great clarity is that education – like all other public sector services – is imbued with, founded upon, values of one colour or another, about which there will probably be lasting argument. Researchers as much as policy-makers hold their values dear, and what start or appear as disagreements over theory or method or interpretation of evidence may turn out to be, or be the result of, equally profound and important disputes about values.

Of course, not all the running is to be made by researchers and the academic community; there is much self-development work to be done by the policy and political communities as well. A commentary by Hagger and Furlong (2006) on their recent report for the Welsh Assembly on teachers' pre-service training and education appears to betoken, in this instance, a more open and pragmatic partnership between researchers and policy-makers than perhaps we have been accustomed to in England; it is not beyond the bounds of possibility that some of the features of the English political-cultural terrain which we assume to be generic and intrinsic could in fact be parochial and even transient.

Nonetheless, I agree with Burton (op. cit., pp. 191 and 174) when he says 'the relationship between policy research, the evidence it generates and the policy process remains complex and not well understood ... in these debates, less attention has been paid to how we conceptualise the demand side of the equation – the nature of policy-making'. There is much still to explore and explain.

Significantly, the majority of the contributors to this book have been closely connected with, and several have been employed in, the policy environment in education – and the DfES, like other government departments and agencies, is becoming increasingly permeable to 'outsider' perspective and input (see, for example, Levitt and Solesbury 2005). Some of these writers have had a major effect, through their research efforts, on the way policy initiatives have developed and been modified; others have been extraordinarily influential in shaping the national landscape of educational research and/or the national policy capacity to generate, appreciate and integrate research. These are writers who have lived with the issues, and not just as bystanders or commentators. This means that they have not on the whole been inclined to adopt *a priori* positions, nor particularly tempted to pathologise the state of either policy or research, preferring rather to interrogate what they have done, witnessed and experienced in their service to education, and on that basis provide substantive insights and arguments that considerably deepen our comprehension of what is happening and what we should make of it. In summary, they are fulfilling the defining purpose of scholarly research, that is, to strengthen our collective intellectual grip on themes and claims of public interest. A few of them go further and make explicit recommendations for improving the circumstances, infrastructures and philosophies upon which better relationships can flourish.

One consequence of the writers' direct engagement in the policy issues of the day from their own standpoints is that readers will encounter more than one reading of the same critical stimuli and initiatives (such as the decision to establish the National Educational Research Forum [NERF]). I hope this will be another way in which the book encourages full and open debate.

Andrew Pollard was kind enough to act as our discussant for the launch symposium of the SIG referred to above, and I am now extremely grateful for his generous foreword, which also manages in its brief space to be panoptic and agenda-setting.

The book itself opens with a challenge from Geoff Whitty, in his role as then president of BERA, and closes with a polemic from Tim Oates, until recently Head of Research at the Qualifications and Curriculum Authority in England (QCA). The arc created by their texts ensures readers will be in no doubt about the big picture, the overarching issues, with which this book is concerned. Both chapters are grounded in a broad foundation of scholarly knowledge and practical wisdom, and derive their authority from an enviable degree of influence, both public and behind-the-scenes. Whitty, in patiently reinstating the right of educational research in England to be acknowledged, as the ESRC recently has done, as being on a par with the best of the rest of the world, unpicks the history and implications of recent research-policy relations; he re-asserts the responsibility of research to be concerned in the main with improving education provision and therefore to be sometimes more or less aligned with government policy and also, on occasions, be explicitly opposed to it; or even – in some cases and in the interests of eschewing narrowness and fixity – be entirely lacking in current policy relevance. Whitty ends with a judicious call for the universities to defend the multifaceted and 'inclusive' nature of research in and for education, as they best can practise it.

Next comes a chapter from Victoria White, Research Manager for the Chief Adviser on School Standards, who gives us a detailed account of the research strategy and activity of the Schools Division of the DfES in England, which cannot fail to show how seriously the function and use of research are taken, whatever judgements one may choose to make about particular government policies. In keeping with her status as a civil servant, White has needed to receive clearance for putting this material in the public domain and I am grateful to her for making the time to attend to these internal accountabilities as well as to write a chapter which gives readers a wealth of important information and insights that would have been hard for most readers to get by any other means. White currently convenes the Schools Research Liaison Group, an informal but very active group of senior research advisers and managers in the DfES, its non-departmental public bodies and other national policy agencies, who meet regularly together, and annually with representatives of key organisations like BERA, TLRP and the Universities Council on the Education of Teachers (UCET).

The following two chapters dig deeper into some of the issues raised by Whitty and their *realpolitik*, by providing highly nuanced narratives of encounters between researchers and policy-makers in the process of bringing research and evaluation to bear upon the development of particular national government policies in education. Bridget Somekh tells a balanced but personal and highly intriguing story of how research and evaluation shaped and informed the development of government policy and strategy on information and communication technology (ICT) in schools over a span of some 20 years, of several different political administrations (Conservative and New Labour) and of enormous growth and change in the technology itself. This depth of experience means that she is able to explain how and why research and evaluation of ICT were sidelined or ignored in some specific circumstances – including errors of judgement on the part of the researchers as well as peremptory abandonment of out-of-date policies by politicians – thus helping readers towards a more differentiated analysis of 'what works' for research uptake and impact. She concludes that – especially but not exclusively in the case of ICT – research can and should do more to help shape future policy and strategies in education. This is no mere wishful thinking on her part, since she is held in great respect, and listened to, by policy staff in different organisations; she speaks eloquently about the relationships between her team at Manchester Metropolitan University and professional staff at the British Educational and Communications Technology Agency (Becta) that have started to be built which are enabling theoretical insights to feed into the policy process. The next step must be, she argues, for the key players to create new social identities that transcend fixed roles (such as 'producers' and 'users' of knowledge).

The events recounted by Gemma Moss (a Reader at the Institute of Education, London) and Laura Huxford (then the Director of Professional Development in the National Literacy and Primary Strategies) were enacted within a shorter but equally critical time-frame, that of the introduction and evolution of the national literacy strategy. One of the many achievements of this chapter is to show how complex the process of policy-making has become and how long the chain of implementation is, with an amazing number and variety of intermediary links – including the meticulous and authoritative input of Moss's and Huxford's academic scholarship – between the originating idea and what emerges as classroom practice. These many layers and levels of decision-making serve to extend or elasticise the whole notion of 'policy', and the chapter helps us see vividly how policy is made in and through the *practice* of different groups of players. The chapter not only contributes new knowledge about, for example, the way some important technical issues involved in the teaching and learning of literacy to a generation of school children were handled, it also means there is no longer any excuse for us to oversimplify what we mean by 'policy'!

Teachers' own professional learning and practice have been deeply implicated in, and entailed by, most of the recent national policies in education; so it is fitting that Hazel Bryan's chapter confronts head-on the development of government policy on teachers' in-service or continuing professional development (CPD) since it was first thought to be worthy of political attention. Bryan takes us on a thoughtful and thought-provoking journey from the early 1970s to the present day, pointing out interesting features and contentious changes, and drawing attention to the recent wealth of research and evaluation studies of CPD which have found their way into policy and strategy – not least those of the General Teaching Council (the professional and regulatory body for teachers in England). She argues strongly for the role of universities, as co-constructors of professional learning, to be strengthened rather than weakened, though she ends not at some grand rhetorical terminus but with the serious thought that the environment within which teachers practise continues to be complex and contested, not least because it is the underlying question of teachers' professional identity that is at stake.

By contrast, Andrew Morris's chapter, grounded in his work as Director of the NERF from 2002 to 2006, takes a particular 'moment' in the evidence-based education movement in England (the creation of the Forum) and draws out the generic issues and lessons to be learned from what Morris rightly calls 'a unique experiment at the level of a whole country' – how the organisation was set up, its aims and functions, its strengths and weaknesses, its lasting innovations and achievements, and its failures (largely attributable to circumstance and context), but above all its symbolic importance as a visible bridge between communities.

Morris's efforts have ensured that this intention endures in the minds and plans of many, despite the decision by the DfES not to continue NERF's funding after the end of the 2006 financial year. At the time of writing, proposals are being firmed up to take forward aspects of NERF's varied and practical programmes of work, and perhaps some of its strategic functions may also find new sponsors, though there seems no desire nor need to establish a body which would try to replicate NERF. Morris's synoptic and acutely analytical chapter should provide colleagues with much to think about and also with some excellent intellectual scaffolding to support and guide this new enterprise, in whatever forms it is manifested.

In his diagnosis of the issues, Morris highlights the importance of translation, facilitation, mediation, catalysis, in the process of research-policy engagement. There are many ways of thinking about, and organising, such processes: for example, a forthcoming study by OECD/CERI (2007) on the challenges of using research and evidence in educational policy-making is to have a whole section on 'mediating the research/policy interface: the role of brokerage agencies' – this is advertised as a series of accounts of the work of organisations that deal in knowledge synthesis and management. My own chapter addresses the theme from a different point of view, that of the somewhat invisible and dispersed group, research advisers and managers in policy organisations. In some senses, of course, this is a *parti pris* piece of writing, though I believe it is justified on the grounds that it is this group of people who are charged, *de facto* if nothing else, with the task of bringing research and policy together, often in unpropitious situations. I raise the question of how such people can create for themselves or be offered (for example, through their professional research association) a stronger sense of professional identity, professional development and professional community not least in order to be able to fulfill more confidently the ethically and intellectually demanding responsibilities that fall on them.

Judy Sebba used to discharge that mediating role – exceptionally well, it has to be said – when she was Senior Adviser for Research in the Standards and Effectiveness Unit of the Department for Education. Now, having returned to the university, she has co-designed and led (with Professor Anne Edwards and Dr Mark Rickinson) the TLRP seminar series exploring partnerships between researchers and users of educational research to develop new forms of research and research use. Her chapter clearly summarises the diverse, challenging and extremely engaging issues raised during the five sessions, and sets out a realistic agenda for the future. This chapter also provides a much-needed scholarly grounding in the research and evidence about notions of 'use' and 'impact' of research, terms often rather freely bandied about.

As I indicated earlier, Tim Oates's chapter, which closes the book, is another *tour de force* which traverses huge terrain, not only of content – a range of curricular reform initiatives and attempts over the past couple of decades – but also of the issues raised by such reforms that really have not been given enough room for discussion and scrutiny. These are issues which Oates sees in starkly ethical terms, and the presentation he gave at the BERA symposium, on which his chapter is based, was received in a way that showed how much delegates needed and wanted such an exposition. Oates's previous position at the QCA qualifies him to speak with certainty rather than speculation on these matters; and the fact that he expounds an explicitly theoretical position in doing so can only help to ensure that this supremely important discussion is taken up and continues beyond that single occasion.

This is not entirely the last word by way of introduction, however. As I intimated near the beginning of this introduction, there is a chapter I dearly hoped would make the book even richer than it is; it could not be included, owing to the dreadfully sad and sudden death of Professor Ray Bolam before he had a chance to complete it. It was to be based on a heroic commission that he undertook, with Dr Dick Weindling, on behalf of the GTC – a synthesis of some 20 very diverse research and evaluation studies on teachers' CPD that had each been contracted or funded in direct response to national policy developments, particularly the national strategy for CPD launched by the DfES in 2001. In fulfilling their brief (which was under my direction), Bolam and Weindling developed and tested a new methodology for research synthesis, which was in some ways the opposite of the conventional 'systematic review'. In the GTC's view, it was very successful and the outcomes of their labour can be viewed at http://www.gtce.org.uk/research/commissioned_res/cpd1/, as well as traced through numerous policy statements and strategies. The chapter would have told, with Bolam's characteristic humour and frankness, I am sure, the story of the process from the researchers' point of view. I sorely regret its absence, but not one iota as much as I, and so many colleagues, friends and associates, miss the man.

Acknowledgements

I am grateful to the author and the editors of the *British Educational Research Journal* for their kind permission to reproduce Geoff Whitty's presidential address at the British Educational Research Association annual conference 2005 (first published in *BERJ* Vol. 32, No. 2, 159–176) as the opening chapter of the book.

References

Burton, P. (2006). 'Modernising the policy process: making policy research more significant?', *Policy Studies*, **27**(3), 173–195.

Commission on the Social Sciences. (2003). *Great Expectations: the Social Sciences in Britain*. Downloadable from: http://www.the-academy.org.uk/

Engeström, Y. (2007). 'Studying learning and development as expansive phenomena.' Paper presented at a public seminar, Oxford University Department of Educational Studies, Oxford, 15 January.

Eraut, M. (2004). 'Practice-based evidence.' In: Thomas, G. and Pring, R. (eds.). *Evidence-Based Practice in Education*. Conducting Educational Research series. Maidenhead: Open University Press.

Flyvbjerg, B. (2001). *Making Social Science Matter. Why Social Inquiry Fails and How it can Succeed Again*. Cambridge: Cambridge University Press.

Furlong, J. and Oancea, A. (2005). *Assessing Quality in Applied and Practice-based Educational Research: a Framework for Discussion* (ESRC Report RES-618-25-6001). Oxford: Oxford University Department of Educational Studies.

Hagger, H. and McIntyre, D. (2006). *Learning Teaching from Teachers: Realizing the Potential of School-Based Teacher Education*. Maidenhead: Open University Press.

Hagger, H. and Furlong, J. (2006). '"Taking the evidence": comparing a national policy review with policy research: the Review of Initial Teacher Training Provision in Wales.' Presentation at Oxford Department of Education Studies, 30 October.

Levitt, R. and Solesbury, W. (2005). 'Evidence-informed policy: what difference do outsiders in Whitehall make?' ESRC UK Centre for Evidence Based Policy and Practice: Working Paper 23.

Organisation for Economic Co-operation and Development, Centre for Educational Research and Innovation. (2007). Draft outline for the forthcoming CERI publication 'Research and Evidence in Educational Policy-making: New Challenges'. Downloadable from: http://www.oecd.org/document/31/0,2340,en_2649_35845581_37813919_1_1_1_1,00.html

Nutley, S. (2003). 'Bridging the policy/research divide: reflections and lessons from the UK.' Keynote paper presented at 'Facing the future: engaging stakeholders and citizens in developing public policy', National Institute of Governance Conference, Canberra, 23 April.

Nutley, S.M. and Davies, H.T.O. (2000). 'Making a reality of evidence-based practice.' In: Davies, H.T.O., Nutley, S.M. and Smith, P.C. (eds.). *What Works? Evidence-based Policy and Practice in Public Services*. Bristol: The Policy Press.

Nutley, S.M., Percy-Smith, J. and Solesbury, W. (2003). *Models of Research Impact: a Cross-Sector Review of Literature and Practice*. London: Learning and Skills Development Agency.

Nutley, S.M. and Webb, J. (2000). 'Evidence and the policy process.' In: Davies, H.T.O., Nutley, S.M. and Smith, P.C. (eds.). *What Works? Evidence-based Policy and Practice in Public Services*. Bristol: The Policy Press.

Pawson, R. (2006). *Evidence-Based Policy: a Realist Perspective*. London: Sage.

Saunders, L. (2004). *Grounding the Democratic Imagination: Developing the Relationship between Research and Policy in Education. Professorial Lecture*. London: Institute of Education.

Stilgoe, J., Irwin, A. and Jones, K. (2006). *The Received Wisdom: Opening up Expert Advice*. London: Demos. Downloadable from: http://www.demos.co.uk/files/received-wisdom.pdf

Times Higher Education Supplement. (2003). 'Social science failing its users, report says', No. 1582, page 6; and Leading Article, No. 1582, page 14; 28 March.

Warner, M. (2002). *Fantastic Metamorphoses, other Worlds: Ways of Telling the Self*. Oxford: Oxford University Press.

Young, M. (1981). 'The Second World War.' In: Pinder, J. (ed.). *Fifty Years of Political and Economic Planning: Looking Forward 1931–1981*. London: Heinemann.

Chapter 1

Education(al) research and education policy-making

Is conflict inevitable?[†]

Geoff Whitty

Introduction

As British Educational Research Association (BERA) members well know, the relationship between research, policy and practice in education has been high on the agenda of the research and policy communities for a number of years now. In the UK it was highlighted in the mid-1990s, when a succession of commentators questioned the value and quality of much of the work of our community. It then became a particular issue for New Labour with its proclaimed commitment to evidence-informed policy and its emphasis on finding out and disseminating 'what works'. But it is also an issue in other countries. For example, BERA has been active in fostering dialogue with education researchers in the USA, where the education research community is facing similar scrutiny in terms of the quality, relevance and impact of its work (See, for instance, the What Works Clearinghouse. See also Center for Education, 2004). Some of our Australian colleagues have been grappling with these same issues (see Yates, 2005).

Much of my own time in recent years has been spent in meetings discussing this issue – whether as Dean and then Director of the Institute of Education, as Vice-President and now President of BERA, as a member of the first Teaching and Learning Research Programme steering committee, as a member of the General Teaching Council for England and, most explicitly, as a member of the reconstituted National Educational Research Forum.[1] I have also addressed it more reflectively in my 2002 publication, *Making Sense of Education Policy,* and in papers I have given to the Higher Education Academy's Education Subject Centre (ESCALATE) (Whitty, 2003) and to the Scottish Executive Education Department (Whitty, 2005).

While I shall draw on this work, in this paper I am going to focus specifically on relations between education researchers and government policy makers. I shall explore the extent to which that relationship is inherently one of conflict or at least a site of mutual misunderstanding and even suspicion, but also suggest some ways in which we ourselves might help to minimise the misunderstandings.

Ministerial views on the research–policy relationship

David Blunkett, Secretary of State for Education and Employment from 1997 to 2001, looked at the research–policy relationship in detail in his 2000 Economic and Social Research Council (ESRC) lecture entitled 'Influence or irrelevance?'. In this he threw down the gauntlet to the social science community to contribute more directly and 'productively' to policy-making. But some academics read his lecture as a sinister demand that research should support government policy. After all, on taking office, he had told head teachers that the 'cynics' and 'energy sappers' should move aside rather than 'erode the enthusiasm and hope that currently exists' (Gardiner, 1997) – and it sometimes seemed that he felt that was all education researchers ever did.

Similarly, his successor, Charles Clarke, was wont to complain that education research never gave him anything useful, though his own characterisation of his perspective as a 'saloon bar' view suggests that even he recognised that his complaint was not itself securely evidence-informed. Nevertheless, throughout his period of office there were rumours that he wanted to do something drastic about the quality and relevance of education research.

The current Secretary of State, Ruth Kelly,[2] actually cites research in her speeches more often than her predecessors (e.g. Kelly, 2005a, 2005b). However, the potential tension between government and education researchers was recently highlighted again when the *Times Educational Supplement* ran a story about Peter Tymms's work at Durham University under the title 'Why this man scares Ruth Kelly' (Mansell, 2005). It described what they called his 'bitter row' with government over his analysis of the National Curriculum Key Stage 2 performance data, which seemed to demonstrate that the government's much proclaimed success in raising standards in primary schools was no such thing.

So now seems an opportune time to reflect again on the nature of the relationship between education researchers and government – and to consider the implications for BERA.

The abuse of education research

The election of New Labour was not, of course, the start of the affair. Throughout the 1990s there had been a whole series of reviews and criticisms of research in education. In 1991 and 1995 reviews were undertaken for the ESRC and a few years later another review was undertaken for Leverhulme, which considered the quality, funding and uses of research in education (see Rudduck & McIntyre, 1998). But the debate became dominated by a range of seemingly damning, albeit sometimes contradictory, criticisms made – for example, by David Hargreaves (1996) for the Teacher Training Agency (TTA), Tooley & Darby (1998) for the Office for Standards in Education (OFSTED), and by Hillage *et al.* (1998) for the then Department for Education and Employment (DfEE) itself.

Although the overall picture was not entirely bleak, politicians reading the headlines and press reports could perhaps be forgiven for believing that UK education research as a whole was characterised by the following features:

- lack of rigour
- failure to produce cumulative research findings
- theoretical incoherence
- ideological bias
- irrelevance to schools
- lack of involvement of teachers
- inaccessibility and poor dissemination
- poor cost-effectiveness

Part of the problem is that subsequently all education research has tended to be tarred by the same brush and judged as wanting against the policy priorities of particular ministers. But this is neither fair nor a good evidence base for decisions about the future funding of education research. I will make just a few points about this now, but will return to the issue later.

First, with regard to quality, no one who regularly reviews papers and research proposals could deny that there is some poor-quality research in education, but then so there is in medicine and other fields with which education is often unfavourably compared. Yet education is one of the social sciences that the ESRC currently regards as meeting world-class quality criteria, notwithstanding its disappointing Research Assessment Exercise (RAE) grade profile in 2001 (Diamond, 2005a). Clearly, there is some excellent research going on in education departments and it is galling that this is so rarely acknowledged.

Second, with regard to relevance, not all research in education has the same focus or purpose. So the frequent charge from politicians of our irrelevance to schools and classrooms in terms of helping to raise achievement is surely both inaccurate, if one looks at the long history of classroom ethnography or action research (Hammersley, 1993), and anyway irrelevant to much of our work. While we may applaud the government's focus on raising achievement and may even see it as the key agenda for most education departments in universities, it would make little sense to judge the birth cohort studies or our work in the history of education on their contribution to improving Standard Assessment Task results – at least directly.

Third, even research that is centrally concerned with improving practice and supporting teachers – in whatever phase of education – needs to be more diverse in its nature than the rhetoric of 'what works' sometimes seems to imply. Research defined too narrowly would actually be very limited as an evidence base for a teaching profession that is facing the huge challenges of a rapidly changing world, where what works today may not work tomorrow. Some research therefore needs to ask different sorts of questions, including why something works and, equally important, why it works in some contexts and not in others. And anyway, the professional literacy of teachers surely involves more than purely instrumental knowledge. It is therefore appropriate that a research-based profession should be informed by research that questions prevailing assumptions – and considers such questions as whether an activity is a worthwhile endeavour in the first place and what constitutes socially just schooling (Gale & Densmore, 2003).

So, while we must always take the criticisms of education research seriously, and be prepared to contribute to evidence-informed policy and practice, we must beware of inadvertently accepting the assumptions underlying them and allowing inappropriate assumptions, on the part of ministers and others, to define our field. And, while seeking to improve the quality of all UK research in education, we must resist attempts to impose inappropriate quality criteria. In my view, education research, and BERA as a professional association and learned society needs to be a broad church, and the assessment of quality must take into account fitness-for-purpose.

This means that, while some of our work will be aligned in various ways to the government's agenda, some of it will necessarily be regarded by government as irrelevant or useless. Furthermore, some of it may well be seen as oppositional. Such a range of orientations to government policy is entirely appropriate for education research in a free society.

In practice, though, and perhaps even in principle, most members of BERA would probably agree with Paul Black & Dylan Wiliam (2003) that:

> We do not believe that all educational research should be useful, for two reasons … [Firstly] there should be scope for some research in education to be absolutely uninterested in considerations of use. [Secondly] it is impossible to state, with any certainty, which research will be useful in the future. Having said this, we believe strongly that the majority of research in education should be undertaken with a view to improving educational provision
>
> (p. 632).

To that extent, there may be less actual conflict between government priorities and researcher priorities than is sometimes suggested. This makes it important to look in more detail at how the relationship works out in practice. It is certainly not straightforward, either in general terms or in relation to the particular governments we have now, bearing in mind that we have different governments responsible for education in the different devolved administrations of Scotland, Wales and Northern Ireland. Even where the priorities of governments and researchers are broadly similar, there may well be conflicts in practice.

New Labour and education research

To explore this, I will look at the New Labour government's treatment of education research in more detail. In this section, I shall be largely referring to the UK government, which is responsible for education in England.

The first thing to acknowledge is that, while the election of New Labour in May 1997 did not bring in a golden age for education, there were some important and positive contrasts with the previous Conservative administrations, not least for research in education. In rhetorical terms at least, the emphasis on evidence-informed policy was a welcome change. And, as John Furlong (2005) has pointed out, it also brought resources. For example, in the party's first three years in government, annual research expenditure in the English Education Department doubled from £5.4 million to over £10.4 million. Several major research programmes and centres have been established, such as the Centre for the Economics of Education and the Centre for Research on the Wider Benefits of Learning. The major budgets associated with key government programmes have also funded significant research operations, for example, the National Research and Development Centre for Adult Literacy and Numeracy (NRDC). The Department, and its equivalents in the devolved administrations, along with the Higher Education Funding Council for England (HEFCE) and others, have also been involved in the ESRC-managed Teaching & Learning Research Programme, which is the largest programme of research in education in UK history. The programme is committed to the application of its findings to policy and practice and, more specifically, to conducting research with the potential to improve outcomes for learners.

As well as targeted programmes of research, there has been an attempt to bring greater coherence to education research – both in terms of synthesising research that is already available and coordinating future projects. From 2000, the Department for Education and Skills (DfES) funded a five-year programme of systematic reviews of education research supported by the Evidence for Policy and Practice Information and Coordinating Centre (EPPI) (see Oakley, 2002). The National Educational Research Forum (NERF) was set up in 1999 with the aim of better coordinating research efforts. The Schools Research Liaison Group, which pre-dates NERF, serves a similar purpose, being a mechanism by which the DfES and non-departmental public bodies share research agendas and devise strategies for addressing common problems such as priority setting.

But greater funding and public visibility have not been without their costs for education research. New Labour's founding commitment to the 'Third Way' brought with it a mantra of 'what works', often interpreted in a rather narrow and mechanistic way. Under this commitment, and as the main funder of research and initiatives, the government has been increasingly explicit about the type of research that it sees as best fulfilling its aims. This was evident in David Blunkett's aforementioned ESRC lecture and his call for a 'revolution in the relations between government and the research community' to support the government's modernising agenda, which was coupled with an emphasis on research that demonstrates what types of policy initiatives are likely to be most effective (2000, p. 21).

The model against which research is most often judged in politicians' minds seems to be what Sharon Gewirtz (2003) has characterised as the 'hyper-rationalist technicist' approach. This is epitomised by David Hargreaves's call for research that:

> (i) demonstrates conclusively that if teachers change their practice from x to y there will be a significant and enduring improvement in teaching and learning and (ii) has developed an effective method of convincing teachers of the benefits of, and means to, changing from x to y
>
> (1996, p. 5).

While I think David Hargreaves's position is actually more sophisticated than Gewirtz suggests, something closer to her caricature was implicit in the draft of the first consultation paper produced by NERF (2000), which seemed to advocate a particularly limited and instrumental view of research. Indeed, this view of education research was seen as highly sinister by my colleague Stephen Ball, who claimed that it treated research as 'about providing accounts of what works for unselfconscious classroom drones to implement' and that it portended 'an absolute standardization of research purposes, procedures, reporting and dissemination' (Ball, 2001, pp. 266–267). Similar criticisms have been levelled at systematic reviewing (e.g. MacLure, 2005).

I am sure that most BERA members would resist such a view of education research, both in terms of its narrow focus and its engineering model of the way in which research relates to improvement. I imagine they would be particularly outraged if this became the only sort of research in education that was supported by public funds. However, it is surely difficult to claim that academics should have more rights than elected governments in determining priorities for public expenditure, so we need to argue the case for public support of a broader view of what research in education is about and the criteria against which it should be judged.

Although the NERF consultation exercise actually led to the acknowledgement of the need for a pluralist view of research, it also argued for a means of prioritising resources based on research making a 'worthwhile contribution' to education and 'maximising impact' (NERF, 2001). We need to establish what this might mean in our case and whether this is an appropriate test for all education research. ESRC, for example, values relevance to the development of a discipline as well as to policy and practice, as Ian Diamond made a point of stressing in his lecture at this year's BERA conference (Diamond, 2005b).

Some of the criteria for public support of medieval history, to take Charles Clarke's favourite scapegoat, are different from those for business studies, even if there is another set of criteria that applies to both. Much the same surely applies to the different components of education studies and we should not be cajoled into accepting that the only research in education that is worthwhile is research that has immediate pay-offs for policy and practice.

That said, and at the risk of seeming to narrow the field myself, I want to focus now on the sort of work that fits New Labour's apparent preference for research on issues which are (to use David Blunkett's words) 'central and directly relevant to the policy debate' (Blunkett, 2000, p. 2).

Understanding the use and misuse of education research

At this point, it should be noted that, in his ESRC lecture, David Blunkett did at least recognise that relevance to the government's agenda did not imply unconditional support for government policy and that there had been misunderstandings on both sides:

> sometimes, when [research] does try to be directly relevant to the main policy and political debates, [it seems to be] driven by ideology paraded as intellectual inquiry or critique, setting out with the sole aim of collecting evidence that will prove policy wrong rather than genuinely seeking to evaluate or interpret impact. A number of studies have tried to claim evidence of poor outcomes when policies have barely been implemented. I acknowledge that previous criticisms I have made of particular studies have been interpreted by some as denial of evidence which conflicts with policy but we must move forward now—government in its capacity to give serious consideration to 'difficult' findings and researchers in their capacity to remain open minded [about our policies]
>
> (Blunkett, 2000, p. 2).

But how realistic is this in practice? Even if it were of the highest international quality and clearly demonstrated what works, would governments consistently seek out the best research and make good use of it? Would they submit research to rigorous evaluation before using it to inform or justify policy? And if they did, how would this fit with the timescale of policy-making and implementation? I will start with the negative cases, where research has been ignored or where it has been used selectively.

One well-known example is the use that was made in England of evidence on class size during the 1997 general election. Evidence on the effects of class size is notoriously contentious and difficult to interpret, and the controversies continue to this day (see Blatchford *et al.*, 2004). Even so, New Labour's commitment in the 1997 election to cut class sizes at Key Stage 1 traded quite consciously on research findings accepted by most researchers and most teachers – evidence that, if smaller classes have an unambiguously positive impact anywhere, it is most marked in the very early years of schooling and in the most socially disadvantaged areas. So, the manifesto commitment to cut class sizes at Key Stage 1 to below 30 using monies that had formerly been used to send able children to private schools[3] looked like a socially progressive policy based on robust research findings. Yet, as a policy it was probably driven as much by the findings of election opinion polling as those of education research, given that most classes over 30 were in marginal suburban constituencies, not in inner-city areas where classes were already below that level. Some even more robust findings on the beneficial effects of cutting infant class size to 15 in disadvantaged areas did not influence the policy at all, presumably because it would have been extremely expensive, but possibly also because additional votes in these inner-city constituencies would not swing the election (Whitty, 2002).

One could argue that as far as New Labour was concerned, 1997 had to be all about getting into power, and only then could things be different thereafter. Yet, even in power, New Labour has sometimes used research quite selectively and has not appeared particularly concerned about the quality of research as long as it serves its policy purposes. One notorious example of this that I have cited before is the way in which research was used in the English White Paper of 2001, *Schools: achieving success* (DfES, 2001). One paragraph stated bluntly: 'There are those who have said that specialist schools will create a two-tier system. They won't' (p. 40). In making its case on specialist schools the White Paper unashamedly used research carried out for the Specialist Schools Trust, which at the time had not been submitted to peer review and was regarded as flawed by key researchers in the field (e.g. Goldstein, 2001). This particular example is even more striking given that, at the very same time, the Department of Health was publicly rejecting some potentially damaging research on the measles, mumps and rubella vaccine and autism on the grounds that it could not be taken seriously because it had not been subjected to scientific peer review. In neither case am I making any judgement about the actual quality of the research, merely noting the different terms on which government was prepared to use it, motivated presumably by considerations other than the robustness of the research.

A current example of problematic use of research evidence is provided by the Academies programme. Although we do not yet have the data against which to assess Tony Blair's claim that Academies are working (e.g. Smithers *et al.*, 2005), the use of evidence to date has been less than convincing. Quite apart from the way in which the government has spun the critical PriceWaterhouseCoopers report (DfES, 2005) and the critical report by OFSTED on Unity City Academy in Middlesbrough (e.g. see Ford, 2005), Stephen Gorard (2005) has demonstrated that there are serious questions about the way in which the government has used performance data to justify continuing with the policy. His own analysis of early results indicated that claims that these schools were, in general, performing better for equivalent students than the schools they had replaced could not be sustained on the basis of the evidence then available. In a carefully worded conclusion, he says:

> any improvement may take time and will be very challenging, and it would be hasty to condemn the programme as a whole on the [limited data available so far]. On the other hand, it is quite clear that it would be equally hasty and far less warranted to credit the programme with success at this stage. Yet this is

what the government and the Academies are doing. To point this out is not to make a criticism of the individuals involved or their practice, but of the way in which policy is being made on the basis of little useful evidence, and is seldom allowed to be seen to fail for electoral reasons. To expand the [Academies] programme on the basis of what has happened so far is so removed from the evidence-based policy-making that is a mantra of government today that it is scarcely worth pointing out

(p. 376).

This parallels concerns expressed by the Education and Skills Committee (2005), which used both the specialist school and Academies programmes to argue that:

Despite the government's proclaimed attachment to evidence-based policy, expensive schemes seem to be rolled out before being adequately tested and evaluated compared to other less expensive alternatives

(p. 17).

Gorard argues that a more equitable policy than the Academies programme would be one targeted at individuals for as long as they remain disadvantaged and in whichever area or institution they move to. My final example of the complex relations between research and policy also relates to this issue and is one that touches me personally in a number of ways.

In July 2005 an article in the *Times Educational Supplement* commented on the relative influence on policy of consultancy companies, think tanks and the higher education research community (Slater, 2005). It began as follows:

If you want to influence Labour's education policy, you could do worse than target a think tank and a management consultancy. More than London University's Institute of Education, the teaching unions or even the Labour Party, the Institute for Public Policy Research and McKinsey have the ear of people in high places

(p. 15).

My initial defensive reaction, as Director of the Institute, was that this claim was somewhat misleading, not least because the influential new recruit to McKinsey that the article cited, Michael Barber, was formerly a professor at the Institute. Furthermore, two of the only four university-based educationists mentioned as having any ongoing influence at the DfES, David Hopkins and Tim Brighouse, are actually based at the Institute. However, the following week, I came to realise that the article's central claim about our lack of influence was unfortunately true.

Ruth Kelly made a keynote speech – as it happens, at the Institute for Public Policy Research (IPPR) – in which she acknowledged that the gap between poorer and richer children's results in primary schools had not been reduced by New Labour policies. The DfES's own research had apparently shown that, while all pupils did better in 2004 than in 1998, those pupils from higher income families made more progress than those on free school meals, even though schools in deprived areas improved more than those in wealthier neighbourhoods. She also advocated more use of individual interventions, singling out Reading Recovery[4] for special mention and support (Kelly, 2005b).

I was not surprised either at this finding or the proposed remedy. But I was puzzled that New Labour should have been surprised. After all, nearly eight years previously, just as New Labour was coming to power, along with Peter Mortimore, I published a paper entitled 'Can school improvement overcome the effects of disadvantage?' (Mortimore & Whitty, 1997), which predicted this very outcome. In it, we warned that a careful reading of the school effectiveness research (of which Peter was one of the leading UK exponents) indicated that, if all schools were brought up to the level of the best, the social class gap in performance would be even starker than it was then – unless, that is, positive action were to be taken to provide extra support for disadvantaged pupils, including, incidentally, Reading Recovery.

So I couldn't help but ask, isn't there a lesson for New Labour in all this? If they had listened more openly to the academic research community back in 1997, they might not have spent eight years pursuing policies with such perverse consequences for a supposedly progressive political party. While New Labour certainly listened to research on school improvement, it did not take seriously the research on the limitations of such an approach. As Denis Lawton put it in his recent book on Labour Party education policy, 'Research evidence as well as the views of education theorists have too often been ignored in favour of the quick - fix bright ideas of spin doctors and advisers at No. 10' (Lawton, 2005, p. 142).

But should we really be too surprised or shocked at this? Often the implication of both the critique of research and the response to it is that once the right sort of research evidence is in place and communicated clearly, it will always – or should always – have an influence on policy or practice. But I would suggest that this is, first, to take New Labour's rhetoric at face value and, second, to ascribe to the government greater control over policy than it might actually have. New Labour contradictions aside, should we not recognise that, in reality, policy is driven by all sorts of considerations, of which the findings of education research are likely on some occasions to be pretty low down? As the Canadian commentator, Ben Levin, outlines, these factors include the vicissitudes of the moment, the requirements of staying in office and the beliefs and commitments of policy makers and their advisers. More fundamentally, we have to acknowledge that politics is substantially shaped by symbolic considerations that may have little to do with the real effects of policies, and that the focus sometimes has to be on what can be done, instead of on what might really make a difference (Levin, 2005, p. 23).

It is for these kinds of reasons that we cannot always expect policy makers to be scrupulous in their use of education research or adopt the same canons concerning its use as education researchers themselves. When I made this point at the aforementioned Scottish Executive Education Department conference (Whitty, 2005), at least one of those present was shocked that I should appear so accepting of this situation. Her response was that, as most research was paid for from public funds, governments had a duty to act on it, otherwise they were effectively squandering public resources. Now I think this is a good campaigning point, and one that BERA might want to make use of. But I nevertheless remain of the opinion that no one, let alone the social scientists we claim to be, can realistically expect governments to act on every piece of research we produce, regardless of other such considerations – and this applies even to research in the 'hyper-rationalist-technicist' tradition.

The use of education research: some (more) hopeful examples

However, that does not mean that there are not times when researchers' and policy makers' interests and timescales coincide. So, in the interests of balance, I will now look at a selection of more positive cases, where there is at least some prima facie evidence that education research has had an impact in various places and at various levels.

A frequently cited example is the research on assessment, carried out across the UK and elsewhere in the world, which has challenged prevailing political orthodoxies by demonstrating the importance of formative assessment and the concept of assessment for learning. The synthesis of this research by colleagues based at King's College, London (Black & Wiliam, 1998) has been particularly influential. In England, it could be argued that the research has influenced teachers' practice more than it has policy. At the policy level, although it has informed the government's Secondary National Strategy, the demands of accountability require that assessment is used for multiple purposes and this means that it often takes forms that are not conducive to deep learning. On the other hand, Jane Davidson, Welsh Assembly Minister for Education and Lifelong Learning, reported that this same work has influenced policy in Wales to move away from National Curriculum tests and the publication of league tables (Davidson, 2005). It has also had some influence on the Scottish Executive's recent consultation on Assessment, Testing and Reporting 3–14.

Then, at classroom level, there are examples of how teachers undertaking classroom action research have changed their practice in response to their own research and their exposure to a wider research literature (e.g. Torrance & Pryor, 2001). This is particularly important for the development of teaching as a research based profession. Ironically, in England, the government decided to phase out its Best Practice Research Scholarships designed to encourage and enhance this process before it had received the results of an evaluation designed to consider its effectiveness (Furlong et al., 2003). However, this work is actively encouraged under the General Teaching Council for Scotland (GTCS) Scotland's Teacher

Researcher Programme aimed at helping to enhance teachers' professional practice and development. There is a similar initiative in Wales (Davidson, 2005). It may be that, in England, its importance will again be recognised in the General Teaching Council for England (GTCE) Teacher Learning Academy and the Chartered London Teacher scheme.[5]

At the other extreme in terms of scale, the third example concerns early childhood education, where large-scale studies on the effectiveness of different forms of provision appear to be influencing policy on the nature of provision, as well as current moves towards integrating education and other children's services. This seems to have been confirmed by Ruth Kelly when in her first major education speech she said:

> There is considerable evidence … that sustained investment in early years support and education works. The most important ongoing study is probably the Effective Provision of Pre-school Education (EPPE) study. This exciting new evidence means we can now say definitively … that high quality pre-school experiences have lasting effects and continue to make a real difference to how well children do and how they develop soundly throughout the early years of primary school. This is especially so for those children from disadvantaged backgrounds
>
> (Kelly, 2005a).

As some of this evidence has been around for some time, it could be argued that this case is similar to my earlier negative example of research being ignored until it suited the government. But, in a sense, I use it against myself, as it demonstrates that whether research is used constructively in policy or not depends on us as well as them. Kathy Sylva, director of the EPPE project, herself makes this point when she uses the project to demonstrate that 'it is possible to influence government policy at national and local level through a combination of rigorous research methods, user friendly dissemination, the combining of quantitative and qualitative approaches, and adequately funded research activity' (Sylva, 2004, p. 1).

Implications for the research community

While these examples, both negative and positive, are interesting, it is not my main intention to produce a balance sheet of pluses and minuses in policy makers' use of evidence. Rather, I want to consider what lessons there are in all this for us as the research community and the different ways in which we might relate to policy.

Clearly, if we want to influence policy there are things that we can do to facilitate this. Part of this involves responding to criticisms, and working with the government's agenda, though not at the expense of our values as researchers. It is notable that both the early years and assessment examples acknowledge some of the criticisms of education research that have been made, and seek to work with some aspects of the government's approach to research and its agenda for education. For example, Sylva (2004) highlights the importance of improving the accessibility of research reporting. Gewirtz (2003), meanwhile, shows how the positive influence of the assessment studies has been achieved in part by demonstrating that formative assessment can raise attainment according to official indicators. That, in turn, has allowed the other benefits, which the researchers perhaps value more highly, to be realised in some contexts. Thus, although the 'engineering model' of the research–policy relationship is problematic in many ways, it can sometimes be used to further progressive and emancipatory ends.

Importantly though, as Gewirtz herself notes, such 'concessions' should not be allowed to undermine the credibility of research that seeks to work against or to disrupt the engineering paradigm, or inform policy and practice in more subtle and modest ways, by feeding into public debate and the discursive milieux within which policy makers operate. One could even argue that this is a more democratic mode of action – attempting to influence public debate rather than seek privileged access to policy (MacDonald, 1974).

We should remember that we do not always have to be close to government to influence policy. Levin (1998) uses the notion of 'policy epidemic' as a tool for thinking about cross-national policy sharing. He also asks whether 'prevention' could be a similarly useful idea to apply to education – in terms of preventing unfavourable policy epidemics. He suggests that there may be ways of strengthening the public mind on education to increase 'resistance' to superficial but seemingly attractive policies. In this respect, building partnerships among different stakeholders and making use of a range of opportunities to disseminate research findings is crucial.

So, research can influence policy and practice in different ways – often indirectly and sometimes in ways that were not intended. Rather than seeing impact as only likely to arise from research conceived in the engineering mode, we should welcome the sometimes serendipitous nature of the relationship between research and policy. Carol Weiss, herself one of the strongest US advocates and exponents of evidence-based policy-making, has helpfully set out the varied ways in which research can achieve impact:

> It takes an extraordinary concatenation of circumstances for research to influence policy directly ... [rather] research helps people reconsider issues, it helps them think differently, it helps them re-conceptualise what the problem is and how prevalent it is, it helps them discard some old assumptions, it punctures old myths
>
> (Weiss, 1991).

This suggests that a diversity of research purposes and approaches within the field of education research needs to be encouraged, partly because we cannot know which will ultimately influence policy.

However, although research in the disciplines of education may impact upon policy, and policy-oriented research may impact upon the disciplines, their core purposes are somewhat different. There needs to be a place for 'blue skies' research, which is significant in disciplinary terms but whose impact on policy is an unpredictable bonus that cannot reasonably be made a condition of funding. The education research community must continue to make this point in its relations with government and funding bodies.

As part of this, we need to ensure that we use appropriate quality criteria for each approach. In the UK, the Research Assessment Exercise (RAE) is a crucial, perhaps even *the* crucial element in shaping the balance of the research that is carried out in universities. If we are to establish a truly mixed economy of research we must get the criteria right. The recent ESRC project in Oxford (Furlong & Oancea, 2005) has contributed to this process by suggesting quality criteria that can embrace different research approaches in advance of the next RAE in 2008. Only by having appropriate criteria can we begin to establish the value of different types of education research. This may even mean having diverging sets of criteria, although this is not so far the route that Furlong and Oancea have proposed. My own view is that we probably need to develop overlapping ones, with some core criteria applicable to all forms but others used in the evaluation of particular approaches.

On the matter of the RAE, it is interesting to look to Australia, which is currently in the process of introducing an equivalent – the Research Quality Framework – and where, consequently, these issues are particularly live. As one commentator there, Lyn Yates, points out, it is best for the education research community to help develop the criteria against which they will be assessed than have them applied by external bodies (Yates, 2005). In the UK context, it is gratifying to know that the Chief Executive of the ESRC, Ian Diamond, has committed it to working with the respective research communities in its efforts to benchmark quality across research outputs in the social sciences (Diamond, 2005b).

Concluding remarks

In thinking about the research-policy relationship and the points I have raised in this chapter, I looked again at the stated aims of BERA. The current overarching aim of BERA is to sustain and promote a vital research culture in education. It seeks to achieve this by:

- encouraging an active community of educational researchers
- promoting cooperation and discussion – with policy makers and practitioners, as well as national and international associations in education and related subject areas
- encouraging and supporting debate about the quality, purpose, content and methodologies of educational research
- developing and defending an independent research culture committed to open inquiry and the improvement of education

- enhancing the professional service it provides for its members – through communication, training and representation for educational researchers.

These are entirely worthy aims, but some of them are more relevant to some aspects of research than others – and the effect is often to present all education research as being of a kind and even speaking to the same audiences. So I do wonder whether there needs to be more clarity and public acknowledgement that education research is multifaceted. Much of the debate, and indeed this chapter, has been about research that seeks to influence policy and practice. Sometimes the dispute is not about whether this is desirable but whether the research supports one policy approach or another. Indeed, some of the critics of New Labour's engineering model are themselves in effect proposing an alternative engineering solution based on a different diagnosis of the engineering 'problem'. Some people even suggest that *all* research should serve an emancipatory interest and that all researchers have a responsibility at least to reflect on the practical effects of their work. Gewirtz, for example, therefore rejects 'any absolute distinction between analysis *of* and analysis *for* policy' (2003, p. 12).

Although I have some sympathy with this position, I now think that it may be important, for both principled and tactical reasons, to make a distinction between studies *of* education and studies *for* education. We certainly need to reiterate the importance of basic research and scholarship and recognise that education researchers are not necessarily under an obligation to make their research explicitly useful, any more than researchers in many branches of the social and natural sciences. With the current focus of debate around the 2008 RAE on the need for quality criteria for applied and practice-related research and ways of assessing impact that go beyond citation counts, we should beware of going to the opposite extreme and disadvantaging research that follows traditional academic models. This would be ceding too much to those who argue that all research, or at least all publicly funded research, should be able to demonstrate practical utility.

One way of handling the distinction might be to use the terms 'education research' and 'educational research' more carefully. In this paper, I have so far used the broad term 'education research' to characterise the whole field; but it may be that within that field we should reserve the term 'education*al* research' for work that is consciously geared towards improving policy and practice. In its early days, NERF used both terms in its title, depending on what document you read, but it now seems to have decided upon 'educational research', which may prove helpful in demarcating its responsibilities. I still have an open mind about whether self-consciously education*al* research needs an additional and new funding stream to put to bed altogether charges that there is insufficient policy- and practice-related research in our field. The Applied Educational Research Scheme in Scotland is an example of this.

A specific problem for us with my distinction between 'education research' as the broad term, and 'educational research' as the narrower field of work specifically geared to the improvement of policy and practice, is that it would mean that

BERA, as the British Education*al* Research Association, would have to change its name or be perceived as only involved with the latter activity. So, trying to make the distinction clearer would also involve BERA in a rebranding exercise, which may not necessarily be the best way of spending our time and resources. But it is at least worth considering.

Whether or not we pursue this, I believe it is particularly important that universities defend an inclusive conception of education research. Although there are now many other players than higher education in our field, including private consultants and think tanks, universities in the UK are still well placed to foster this broad notion of education research, including – but not limited to – educational research. Even if it does not always seem that way, universities remain relatively free to pursue lines of enquiry that are marginalised in those state agencies that are more thoroughly embedded in an instrumentalist culture.

In January 1997, on the fiftieth anniversary of the death of Karl Mannheim, one of my predecessors as a professor of education at the Institute of Education, I cited with approval his assertion that educationists should resist the growing tendency 'to discuss problems of organisation rather than ideas' and 'techniques rather than aims' (Mannheim, 1951, p. 199, in Whitty, 1997). I also mentioned that Fred Clarke, the Director of the Institute who appointed him, justified the appointment of Mannheim, a social theorist, on the grounds that educational theories and policies that took no account of wider social forces were 'not only blind but positively harmful'. Some of the developments under the New Labour government that was elected later that year have made this even more important today, so I hope that, while BERA will respond constructively to legitimate criticisms of our field from government and others, it will also resist any pressure to restrict what counts as research in education.

References

Ball, S. J. (2001) You've been NERFed! Dumbing down the academy. National Educational Research Forum 'a national strategy—consultation paper': a brief and bilious response, *Journal of Education Policy*, **16**(3), 265–268.

Black, P. & Wiliam, D. (1998) *Inside the Black Box: raising standards through classroom assessment* (London, King's College London).

Black, P. & Wiliam, D. (2003) 'In praise of educational research': formative assessment, *British Educational Research Journal*, **29**(5), 623–638.

Blatchford, P., Bassett, P., Brown, P., Martin, C. & Russell, A. (2004) *The effects of class size on attainment and classroom processes in English primary schools (Years 4 to 6) 2000–2003*. Research Brief, Department for Education and Skills, December.

Blunkett, D. (2000) *Influence or irrelevance: can social science improve government?* (London, Department for Education and Employment).

Center for Education (2004) *Advancing scientific research in education* (Washington, DC, National Academies Press). Available online at: http://www.nap.edu/books/ 030909321X/html/

Davidson, J. (2005) Welcoming speech, *British Educational Research Association annual conference*, Glamorgan, 14–17 September.

Department for Education and Skills (DfES) (2001) *Schools: Achieving Success* (London, The Stationery Office).

Department for Education and Skills (DfES) (2005) *Academies Evaluation—2nd Annual Report* (London, The Stationery Office).

Diamond, I. (2005a) Science and technology and international collaboration in higher education. *Lecture to the meeting of the UUK International and Longer-term Strategy Groups*, March.

Diamond, I. (2005b) Keynote lecture, *British Educational Research Association annual conference*, Glamorgan, 14–17 September.

Education and Skills Committee (2005) *Secondary Education—fifth report of session 2004–05* (March) (London, The Stationery Office).

Ford, L. (2005) Ofsted fails academy school, *Guardian*, 27 May.

Foster, P. (1999) 'Never mind the quality, feel the impact': a methodological assessment of teacher research sponsored by the Teacher Training Agency, *British Journal of Educational Studies*, **47**(4), 380–398.

Furlong, J. (2005) 'New Labour and teacher education': the end of an era, *Oxford Review of Education*, **31**(1), 119–134.

Furlong, J. & Oancea, A. (2005) *Assessing Quality in Applied and Practice-Based Educational Research: a framework for discussion* (Oxford, Department of Educational Studies, University of Oxford).

Furlong, J., Salisbury, J. & Coombes, L. (2003) *Best Practice Research Scholarships: an evaluation* (Cardiff, Cardiff University School of Social Sciences).

Gale, T. & Densmore, K. (2003) *Engaging Teachers: towards a radical democratic agenda for schooling* (Maidenhead, Open University Press).

Gardiner, J. (1997) Marriage of maximum inconvenience? *Times Educational Supplement*, 6 June.

Gewirtz, S. (2003) Enlightening the research–policy relationship: issues and dilemma for educational researchers. Paper presented at the *European Conference on Educational Research*, University of Hamburg, 17–20 September.

Goldstein, H. (2001) The 2001 Education White Paper and evidence-based policy: a commentary. Available online at: http://www.mlwin.com/hgpersonal/educationwhitepaper2001.pdf

Gorard, S. (2005) Academies as the 'future of schooling': is this an evidence-based policy? *Journal of Education Policy*, **20**(3), 369–377.

Hammersley, M. (Ed.) (1993) *Controversies in Classroom Research* (2nd edn) (Milton Keynes, Open University Press).

Hargreaves, D. (1996) *Teaching as a Research-Based Profession* (London, Teacher Training Agency).

Hillage, J., Pearson, R., Anderson, A. & Tamkin, P. (1998) *Excellence in Research in Schools* (London, Department for Education and Employment).

Kelly, R. (2005a) Speech to *North of England Education Conference*, Manchester, 6 January.

Kelly, R. (2005b) Education and social progress, Keynote speech, *Institute for Public Policy Research*, July.

Lawton, D. (2005) *Education and Labour Party Ideologies: 1900–2001 and Beyond* (London, RoutledgeFalmer).

Levin, B. (1998) 'An epidemic of education policy': (what) can we learn from each other? *Comparative Education*, **34**(2), 131–141.

Levin, B. (2005) *Reforming Education: From Origins to Outcomes* (London, RoutledgeFalmer).

MacDonald, B. (1974) Evaluation and the control of education. Reprinted in R. Murphy & H. Torrance (Eds.) (1987) *Evaluating Education: Issues and Methods* (London, Harper & Row).

MacLure, M. (2005) 'Clarity bordering on stupidity': where's the quality in systematic review? *Journal of Education Policy*, **20**(4), 393–416.

Mannheim, K. (1951) *Freedom, Power and Democratic Planning* (London, Routledge & Kegan Paul).

Mansell, W. (2005) Why this man scares Ruth Kelly, *Times Educational Supplement*, 26 August.

Mortimore, P. & Whitty, G. (1997) *Can School Improvement Overcome the Effects of Disadvantage?* (London, Institute of Education).

National Educational Research Forum (NERF) (2000) *A National Strategy*. Consultation paper issued by the National Educational Research Forum (London, NERF).

National Educational Research Forum (NERF) (2001) *A Research and Development Strategy for Education: developing quality and diversity* (London, NERF).

Oakley, A. (2002) 'Social science and evidence-based everything': the case of education, *Educational Review*, **54**(3), 277–286.

Rudduck, J. & McIntyre, D. (Eds.) (1998) *Challenges for Educational Research* (London, Paul Chapman).

Slater, J. (2005) Meshed in web of power, *Times Educational Supplement*, 22 July.

Smithers, R., Curtis, P. & Taylor, M. (2005) Academies claim boost for GCSEs, *Guardian*, 26 August.

Sylva, K. (2004) Briefing note from Effective Provision of Pre-school Education (EPPE) Project for ESRC/OUDES Working Day on Applied and Practice-Based Research, 16 July.

Tooley, J. & Darby, D. (1998) *Educational Research: a critique* (London, Office for Standards in Education).

Torrance, H. & Pryor, J. (2001) Developing formative assessment in the classroom: using action research to explore and modify theory, *British Educational Research Journal*, 27(5), 615–631.

Weiss, C. H. (1991) Policy research: data, ideas or arguments? in: P. Wagner, C. Weiss, B. Wittrock & H. Wollmann (Eds.) *Social Sciences and Modern States: National Experiences and Theoretical Crossroads* (Cambridge, Cambridge University Press).

Whitty, G. (1997) Social theory and education policy: the legacy of Karl Mannheim, *Karl Mannheim Memorial Lecture*, Institute of Education, University of London.

Whitty, G. (2002) *Making Sense of Education Policy: studies in the sociology and politics of education* (London, Sage).

Whitty, G. (2003) Trends in educational research and policy formation in England. Paper to ESCALATE, November.

Whitty, G. (2005) Research, policy and practice: a crucial but complex relationship. *Keynote address to the Scottish Executive Education Department's Schools Research Conference*, January.

Yates, L. (2005) Is impact a measure of quality? Producing quality research as producing quality indicators of research in Australia. *Keynote address for AARE Focus Conference on 'Quality in Educational Research: directions in policy and practice'*, Cairns, July.

Chapter 2

Schools research in the English Ministry of Education

An inside view

Victoria White[1]

Introduction

This chapter describes how England's education ministry, the Department for Education and Skills (DfES), plans, commissions and uses education research, and discusses various resulting issues and current debates particularly on access and uptake of research. The focus for the chapter is on schools research and the programme of work to support 'evidence informed policy and practice', since this is the author's own background, although readers should note that the Department's policy brief covers the whole education system, from pre-school to higher education. It also has responsibility for general child welfare issues, including aspects of health and social work located in the Children, Young People and Families Directorate which has oversight of the government's 'Every Child Matters' agenda: a wide-ranging set of principles, programmes and activities that are intended to improve the well-being of children and young people from birth to age 19.

England has a relatively centralised education system in the sense that there is a national curriculum and national system of assessment and testing. The DfES also has extensive powers to regulate and intervene in the working of schools. It provides the great bulk of public funding in education and hence most school funding since private provision and funding is a small proportion of the total: for example, only around seven per cent of secondary pupils are in private or independent schools.

It is worth pointing out that, while the UK is constitutionally a unitary state, the national government has increasingly been devolving power to the three non-English nations, Scotland, Wales and Northern Ireland, so that all three now have their own education ministries with independent policy-making power and this includes the conduct of their own research, based on their priorities. The commentary in this chapter is therefore specific to England.

The chapter is in two broad sections: first, a fact-based account of the research activity in, and for, the schools division of the DfES; this is followed by a more discursive discussion of the main issues and challenges in the uptake and use of research in schools as well as government.

Facts and figures

Broad purpose of DfES research

The Department undertakes research largely to inform its policy-making, with the aim of meeting its current and readily foreseeable needs for evidence and information. The Department expects to use its research to assess how well its current policies are working and to develop and justify new policies. Sometimes the Department undertakes research to respond to issues raised in the outside world, and so the choice of what to research reflects questions of the wider public interest in addition to ministerial accountability.

As well as needing to have readily applicable findings for these purposes, the DfES also has an expectation that all research will be published, with the underlying data being made available, if appropriate and possible, for further analysis.

DfES funding for research

A key document is the Department's 2006 analytical strategy (DfES 2006a) which is in the public domain and provides an overview of the wide range of analytical work that the Department planned to undertake to meet its policy priorities as well as its future challenges. It also recorded the Department's expenditure on research as well as its recent and forthcoming publications.

As noted in the analytical strategy (op. cit.) the total funding committed to all analytical work externally commissioned by the DfES underway in financial year 2005–06 was approximately £139 m. (However, this figure included funding committed to projects whose lifetime stretched over a number of years, so this figure is not an indication of actual spend on research and evaluation solely in that year.) Of this total, £13.7 m was related to newly approved or contracted analytical work funded through the research budget.

For 2006–07 some £4.5 m was available to spend on new externally commissioned research, with around £0.5 m of this (slightly over ten per cent) being allocated to schools research.

Composition of schools research funded by DfES

Over the last ten years or so, there has been an increased focus on commissioning large-scale and longitudinal work – a deliberate response to one of the recommendations made by 'Excellence in Research in Schools' (Hillage et al. 1998) – the findings of which emphasised the need for a more robust and cumulative evidence base to support education policy. This Hillage report was commissioned by the former Department for Education and Employment – see later for a more detailed account of this work and its consequences. Recently published examples of studies which tracked cohorts of pupils and/or staff over time include the four-year mixed-methods study on variations in teachers' work, lives and effectiveness

(Day *et al.* 2006). Longitudinal studies in progress include one investigating citizenship education (2001–09) (being conducted by the National Foundation for Educational Research; see project website for list of publications to date: www.nfer.ac.uk/nfer/index.cfm?3C0E0ACF-D713-2E82-923A-CB224986C2AC), which is examining the short- and long-term effects of the introduction of citizenship education as a national curriculum subject in schools; and another groundbreaking study which is tracking the effects of effective provision of pre-school and primary education on pupils aged 3–11 years. The report of the first phase of the project which focused on pre-school provision (1997–2003) has been published (Sylva *et al.* 2004). Phase 2 of the project which focuses on primary education is due for completion in 2008. Studies from phase 2 include Sammons *et al.* (2006a, 2006b).

The establishment of dedicated research centres was another recommendation in the Hillage review, conceived of as a way to enhance research capacity in the system as a whole, as well as to build a cumulative evidence base which could inform policy development. The Department has provided core funding for a number of dedicated research centres, including the Centre for Economics of Education (based at the Centre of Economic Performance in partnership with the Institute for Fiscal Studies and the Institute of Education, London (http://cee.lse.ac.uk), and the Centre for Research on the Wider Benefits of Learning (based at the Institute of Education, London www.learningbenefits.net) Of particular interest to, and practical use by, the DfES Schools Directorate has been the Evidence for Policy and Practice Information and Coordinating Centre (EPPI Centre) which the Department set up with the aim of developing systematic reviews of research in education. Since its inception in 2000, more than 40 reviews covering the school phase of education have been published. These encompass a range of 'impact-related' issues in school subject areas, in assessment and pedagogy, in school workforce issues including leadership, and in professional development for teachers.

As part of the Department's commitment to improving access and uptake of research by users – and particularly school staff – it works with the Innovation Unit, the General Teaching Council for England and the National College for School Leadership to collaboratively fund the National Teacher Research Panel (NTRP) (www.standards.dfes.gov.uk/ntrp). Comprising around 20 practising teachers and head teachers, the NTRP aims to increase practitioners' engagement in and with research, and to ensure a practitioner perspective within the national educational R&D effort. One of the National Teacher Research Panel's major activities has been to hold a biennial conference on best practice in practitioner enquiry for around 500 teachers and heads. These events provide an opportunity for practitioners to learn how to access and use research as well as to find out from other practitioners how to undertake robust action research.

There are various ways one might classify the kinds of research which the Department commissions, for example, according to whether it is pure research in the sense of information gathering, such as exploring aspects of teaching or school governance or even the physical fabric of the schools; or whether it is an evaluation of a policy programme or initiative; or whether it has a specific policy aim, such as raising pupil attainment, improving pupil welfare and/or behaviour. The analytical strategy document for 2006 (already cited) breaks down the budget allocation by education phase and also by the Department's current Strategic Research Priorities, which were, in 2006:

- Demography
- Globalisation
- Technology
- Horizon scanning
- Social mobility
- Focusing on users
- Role of demand in shaping services
- System reform
- Value for money
- Metrics

An in-depth description of the strategic priorities for 2006 can be found in the strategy document.

In terms of research methods, the Department employs a wide range of research designs governed by fitness for purpose. These include for example, large-scale questionnaires, informed by a review of the literature, and then frequently supplemented with case studies. Other examples include intervention studies, for instance, the raising boys' achievement project (Younger *et al.* 2005) which involved researchers working with primary and secondary schools which had already narrowed the gap between girls' and boys' attainment to develop and refine these strategies further so that they could be taken up with confidence by other schools. Of course, research is not the only source of evidence and information on schools and the Department has long undertaken extensive and regular national statistics data gathering on schools, pupils and teachers. More recently, it has created the National Pupil Database, a longitudinal school pupil record which allows linkage of pupils' personal, school and attainment characteristics from age 5 to 18.

Furthermore, the English national examinations at ages 16 and 18 together with national tests at ages 7, 11 and 14 mean that the Department can draw on what is probably the best pupil attainment-related information of any country. Since this is based on near 100 per cent 'population samples' of pupils and schools, this allows for extensive disaggregation in terms of pupil groups and school types as well as geographically and over time. The Department devotes considerable in-house resources to gathering and analysing this statistical information and the data are also available for academics and others to analyse.

The Department's schools research in the national context

The most recent estimate of the total national spending on educational research in the UK was £75 m (NERF 2000). This exercise looked at expenditure by funder and not by educational phase. While the Department is likely to be the most significant single commissioner, it nonetheless has a minority share because the bulk of spending is accounted for in terms of individual university academic departments (mainly, but not necessarily always, of education).

The Organisation for Economic Cooperation and Development (OECD) in its review of education research and development in England (OECD/CERI 2002) noted that total national education 'R and D' in 2001 represented around 0.5 per cent of total education spending, 'far less than the average spent on R and D in the business sector or other knowledge-dependent organisations' (ibid. p. 8). On the other hand, it also cites a 1995 OECD study which found that the equivalent figure for six western countries where data were available was 'under 0.3 per cent' (ibid. p. 8).

It is not intended here to review the totality of schools research but it is useful to mention the research undertaken and commissioned by other national public bodies in education. There are three bodies which are funded by, and report to, the DfES as agencies: the National College for School Leadership (NCSL), the Qualifications and Curriculum Authority (QCA) and the Training and Development Agency for Schools (TDA). Two other statutory bodies with responsibility for the inspection of schools and the regulation of the teaching profession, respectively, the Office for Standards in Education (OFSTED) and the General Teaching Council for England (GTC), report directly to Parliament.

These five organisations have specific and distinct policy remits and undertake their research autonomously. Nonetheless, they seek to keep each other informed about key research outputs and future research plans. This is effected primarily through meetings of an informal schools research liaison group, comprising representatives of the five bodies and of the DfES Schools Directorate. Its purpose is to try to avoid unnecessary duplication of data gathering as well as to raise awareness of individual and collective research priorities. It may also seek to collaborate where appropriate; so, for example, the GTC and TDA have each funded systematic reviews through the EPPI Centre, which is funded by DfES; the DfES, GTC and TDA are funding a longitudinal study of trainee and early career teachers; and the DfES Innovation Unit and NCSL are collaborating on a 'next practice' project on system leadership.

Determining research priorities in the DfES

The DfES operates with an annual programme of research, the broad timetable for which is as follows: between September and November, individual policy directorates discuss and agree their key research questions for the coming year, which need to take account of the Department's overall strategic research priorities (those for 2006 have been set out above) as well as of particular issues relating to the responsibilities for their Directorate. The Schools Directorate, for example, holds meetings with senior officials to review its existing research questions and set new ones. 'Analytical programmes' are then developed to answer these questions, a process which typically begins with analytical staff reviewing existing evidence against each question and identifying the critical gaps in knowledge or evidence. These gaps indicate what new research, if any, needs to be commissioned in future. Early in the new following year, the Department's Research Approvals Committee (RAC – and see below) considers all the proposals being submitted for research that would be externally commissioned. Agreed proposals are then submitted to the Secretary of State for approval.

The research-based questions for 2006–07, listed below, build on the previous year's questions and are designed to provide a research framework to underpin the continuing delivery of the Department's five-year strategy for children and learners (2004) and recently updated (2006). The questions are:

- What are the most effective ways of closing attainment gaps?
- What forms of personalisation are most effective in enhancing pupils' chances of success?
- What are the most productive and effective ways of mobilising the 'pupil voice'?
- What measures improve practitioners' access and uptake of research evidence as a vehicle for improving teaching and learning?
- What in-school practices support staying on and training after school?
- What changes to the accountability system will be most effective in raising standards, particularly with regard to targets, incentives and funding?
- How can we optimise the levers of school choice, competition, contestability and new governance arrangements to yield improved outcomes for pupils?
- How are the energies and skills of the workforce best harnessed to raise standards?
- Which forms of school intervention and rescue work best and in what conditions?
- Which emergent models of school leadership work best and under what conditions?
- Which interventions and approaches work best for groups of pupils who persistently under perform?
- How do effective teachers plan a lesson or sequences of lessons?
- What curriculum and assessment measures are most effective in accelerating the progress of pupils in core subjects?
- What methods of curriculum organisation work best for lower-attaining pupils?
- What parental support is most effective for pupils struggling to progress at school, and how is this best harnessed?
- Where is best practice on parenting in LAs and how can we share it?

This relatively new 'high level' approach to determining analytical work replaces a more 'bottom-up' approach where individual policy divisions used to bid for research funding to undertake specific projects. This is essentially in response to the Department's drive to be more strategic and to ensure that research should be commissioned not just to meet immediate and easily identifiable needs for information, but that it is also focused on providing a sound knowledge base for deciding and evaluating its longer-term priorities. These include taking account of wider issues that impact on education (such as the implications of globalisation). The Department's publication of its analytical strategy in conjunction with its various consultations – including with scholars and experts – on the 'broad strategic questions' aims to engender a greater public awareness about its research choices.

The establishment of the RAC is also part of the Department's drive to be more strategic. The purpose of the RAC is to scrutinise all new research and evaluation proposals to be funded by the Department that will be carried out under a contract with an external organisation. The RAC is chaired by the Department's Chief Economist and comprises senior analysts and policy officials. The main aims of the RAC are to: quality assure new proposals and help avoid duplication of research and evaluation effort across the Department; help make links between otherwise disparate research and evaluation activities; ensure that the Department's research is undertaken in the most cost-effective way; and ensure that ministers are aware of the totality of research and evaluation commissioned by the Department (taken from DfES Analytical Strategy op. cit.).

It is also worth noting that this formal research planning round still leaves flexibility for commissioning *ad hoc* research at any time of the year and part of the research budget is left uncommitted to allow for such contingencies. As with the general research round and with evaluation projects, all such *ad hoc* research has to be agreed at a senior official level and finally by the Secretary of State. The Department also considers unsolicited research proposals, although in practice these are fairly rarely received, probably because of (largely correct) perception amongst research providers that the Department generally has scarcely any unallocated funds for such work.

Two constraints on DfES research activity: burdens on schools and response rates

By sponsoring schools research the Department accepts that completing survey questionnaires, participating in interviews, etc., is a legitimate use of the time of school staff and pupils. Naturally, however, there has been growing concern about information-seeking burdens of all kinds (not just research) on schools. This led, some six years ago, to the setting up of a standing committee within the DfES to review all schools research proposals, called the 'Star Chamber', to assess whether they were likely to impose undue burdens on schools in providing the information requested. The Star Chamber is primarily concerned with issues of survey and interview efficiency (for example, deciding whether the information is gathered elsewhere and/or is really necessary). In principle Star Chamber could oppose a whole research proposal. This issue of burdens points to a real policy dilemma: the effective conduct of policy requires good research information (and the number of schools policies has increased markedly over the past ten years) and yet schools are not explicitly funded to provide these data; moreover, almost all research surveys are voluntary so it is left to the schools to decide whether they regard their participation as worth their while.

Related to this, the Department has been interested in improving response rates to its schools surveys and it recently commissioned and published a review of its performance with regard to response rates in surveys of schools, teachers and pupils (Sturgis *et al.* 2006). This study found that there had been a definite and marked downward trend over the past ten years, with an average of a two per cent per annum decline across 73 surveys. However, it also found that it was still possible to achieve a very high response to a given survey. In other words, many schools seemed to be acting as discerning non-respondents, deciding on a case-by-case basis whether a particular survey justified their staff taking part. Here too this is a concerning trend where there is no ready answer. It would be very expensive to pay schools for every survey and the response rates study mentioned above suggested that schools would be unlikely to be influenced by the sort of sums that it would be feasible to offer even on a case-by-case basis. Furthermore, the study showed that schools perceived the survey burden as a mix of requests not just from the DfES but also from academics and commercial organisations, and that they did not necessarily give greater weight to DfES surveys. So there would be no guarantee that cutting the volume of DfES research would have any material effect on response.

It is worth mentioning in this context that the NTRP (already mentioned) has produced guidelines for schools on hosting research (NTRP 2003). The guidelines comprise a series of questions designed to inform dialogue between teachers, schools and research teams about how to make the processes of large-scale research activities, as well as the eventual outcomes, mutually beneficial. (The Panel suggested that the research community would develop similarly high expectations of the potential benefits of the research process by developing a parallel set of questions that researchers can ask of schools.)

Improving the usefulness of schools research to policy-makers, intermediaries and practitioners

It is important to begin by explaining what we mean by 'usefulness' of research and particularly to define this in terms of 'useful to whom'. The current view at the DfES distinguishes three broad groups of users: first policy-makers, that is to say, DfES Ministers and officials; second 'practitioners', that is, school staff and teacher educators; and third the broad group of 'intermediaries' and particularly field staff – people who have liaison, coordinating and/or delivery roles between government and schools or local authorities and schools.

The role of intermediaries in helping to get the messages across from research and 'best practice' is recognised by the DfES as being important. For example, the intermediary role was highlighted in the DfES-funded study on 'Factors affecting the transfer of good practice' (Fielding et al. 2005), which noted that practitioners benefit from outside support which can help them learn and adopt new practices. Although the Department does not see it as its particular role to undertake research designed primarily for practitioners, the Schools Directorate has a small but influential programme of work designed to increase practitioners' and field staff access to, and uptake of, research as well as to promote practitioners' engagement in research. Specific initiatives in this programme include rewriting recent relevant journal articles into user-friendly summaries for teachers (The Research Informed Practice Site or TRIPS: www.standards.dfes.gov.uk/research sponsored by the Innovation Unit) and providing online dialogue opportunities for practitioners to discuss the implications of recently published academic research in facilitated discussion forums called 'talk2learn'.

In addition, the majority of schools research projects funded by the Department which are contracted to outside organisations usually include a research-informed practitioner on project steering groups. The role of practitioner steering group members is to comment on the research design, conduct, instruments and draft reports, to ensure resonance with schools, and also to help consider in what ways the outcomes from the research may be of direct interest to teachers, and if so how the messages might be communicated. The National Teacher Research Panel (see above) has been working with research funders and managers, including DfES officials, and with practitioners who have recent and current experience on steering groups to develop guidance on how to get best value from practitioner members.

While social science research in general and education research within this have long been established as making a central contribution to the policy-making process there has also been a call for the quality and relevance of research to improve in order to maximise its contribution (e.g. Hillage 1998). The OECD examiners' report of Educational Research and Development in England (op. cit.) suggested that over the last 20 years the status of educational research and development in England has suffered a low point and also reached a high point. The low point occurred during the 1980s during an era of educational reform which culminated in the Education Reform Act of 1988, when, according to the OECD report, 'educational R and D was unnecessary' because 'government officials believed that they already knew what they had to do to improve the quality of education' (p. 9). The reformers expected the education system to improve continuously using assessment and accountability as the feedback mechanism to correct for failure. However, as the OECD report goes on to suggest, by the mid-1990s government officials found that implementation of the reforms had been more complex than expected, particularly in the area of classroom instruction.

One solution was to expect teachers (as distinct from policy-makers) to pay more attention to research. In 1995, the then Teacher Training Agency (now the TDA) publicly pressed the case for teaching to become an evidence-informed profession. Professor David Hargreaves spoke at the TTA conference the following year arguing that, whilst teaching needed to be evidence-informed like medicine, educational research – unlike medical research – was not up to the job.

This was not a view that won universal support, but it did lead to some interesting changes at policy level. Reflecting on these concerns, Professor Michael Barber who was appointed head of the new Standards and Effectiveness Unit (within Schools Directorate) under the incoming Labour (Tony Blair-led) government in 1997, together with Professor Judy Sebba, seconded to act as senior adviser on research, were responsible for commissioning the wide-ranging review of schools research mentioned earlier (Hillage *et al.* 1998). The report was based partly on a literature review and partly on extensive interviews with researchers, policy-makers and practitioners. The report made clear that there was a wide divergence of views, noting for example that 'Most of the researchers contacted felt that the balance (of current research) was too skewed towards policy and practice, while the practitioners and policy-makers generally thought the opposite' (p. x).

The report recommended, in very summary terms, that:

- there should be a national education research strategy and a new, government-funded, but independent body to run this (the National Education Research Forum, NERF);
- there should be a publicly-funded system to enable the production of 'systematic reviews' of existing education research (the EPPI-Centre mentioned above);
- that there should be a drive to raise the quality of research by means of explicit quality standards and better training of researchers;
- there should be a much greater emphasis on research dissemination both to policy-makers and to practitioners;
- the Department should establish dedicated specialised education research centres (again, see above). Finally and without being specific about any institutional or practical implications, the report called upon policy-makers to 'commit to ensuring that wherever possible, policies are developed on the basis of, and/or related to publicly available research evidence and encompass clear and independent evaluation strategies'.

As is obvious throughout this chapter, the Hillage report proved to be highly influential with the Department and all of its institutional recommendations were quite quickly implemented, although it must be acknowledged that they have varied in how far they have achieved their hoped-for aims.

Given that it is ten years since the report was published, and that most of the recommendations were acted on within a short time after that, it is worth providing an update on the delivery and impact – from the DfES' point of view – of the recommendations.

The National Educational Research Forum[2] (NERF www.nerf-uk.org) was formed in 1999 by the then Secretary of State for Education, David Blunkett, to develop a national strategy for educational research. In the first few years NERF had an intensive consultation and discussion phase, and from 2002 to 2006 it focused on collaborative and developmental action to improve the quality and impact of research for the education sector. Although NERF came to an end as planned in March 2006, a number of its projects are still continuing with funding from other organisations, notably the CfBT education trust. Continuing projects include the development of a UK Educational Evidence Portal (www.eep.ac.uk) which is designed to enable access to quality-assured research across all education sectors and topics for educationists through a central portal.

The OECD examiners report (op. cit.) suggested that 'NERF was a somewhat vulnerable body, with few resources and no direct decision-making competencies which depends very much on the enthusiasm of its members and its contributions'. However, its large number of reports and resources, e.g. on systematic reviewing, setting research priorities, and assessing research impact, have been useful to a range of individuals in education, if personal testimony is anything to go by. Probably a lasting contribution of NERF has been its brokering role in getting different organisations together to work collaboratively on projects, including encouraging more dialogue between different parts of the education research community. The current EEP project above is an example of this.

The Department continues to fund the dedicated research centres and the EPPI Centre for systematic reviews – these are now established features of the education research landscape and are internationally recognised. For example, the EPPI Centre has worked with the Canadian government and the University of Colorado to offer advice on systematic reviewing techniques. However, it is also fair to say that, while systematic reviewing has substantially improved the efficiency of how to use research, it has also highlighted – in some areas – the paucity of good-quality studies related to the precise question a given review seeks to address – thus highlighting gaps for further research. In terms of impact, there have been some notable and fairly conclusive findings from the reviews which have been taken up by policy. These include, for example, strong indications of what works to support sustained and collaborative professional development for teachers (CPD EPPI Review Group 2003, 2005a, 2005b); and of what strategies in classrooms work well in motivating pupils to learn mathematics between the ages of 14 and 16 (Mathematics EPPI Review Group 2006).

Studies such as the CPD and mathematics EPPI reviews have perhaps been particularly successful in informing policy development due to a number of factors. These factors include: senior policy officials working closely with the review teams from the beginning of the project to shape and define the question ensuring it remained pertinent to policy; policy officials providing up-to-date information and thinking on policy developments to researchers on a regular basis; flexible reporting – with researchers providing emerging findings at critical times to feed into policy decisions; a commitment from both policy officials and researchers to generate a useful and robust output for policy.

Research and practice: the current situation

The DfES would, of course, be interested to know how these reforms are seen by the research community and by practitioners. A MORI Teachers' Omnibus survey (commissioned by the Department on behalf of NERF in 2004) which investigated teachers' attitudes towards research showed that 93 per cent of teacher respondents used research findings at least occasionally to inform their classroom practice or as part of their professional development. Although this result seems encouraging, other sources suggest that teachers have a pretty broad interpretation about what constitutes research. Another question in the same MORI poll showed that 88 per cent of respondents who said they used research reported that they would find a hard copy bulletin of educational research findings useful – hence indicating a desire for 'harder' evidence than anecdote and hearsay.

More generally, there is very little evidence to help us know on just what beliefs and ideas teachers base their practice and how far they assess its effectiveness and adapt their behaviour accordingly (which is one definition of what it means to be 'reflective practitioners'). Education research is certainly not alone in this, however. A report by Walter and Nutley (Walter *et al.* 2004) examining the use of research in social care practice, prompted this response on the Social Care Institute for Excellence (SCIE) website, the commissioning organisation for the study:

> Evidence-informed policy and practice demands increasing recourse to research as a key source of knowledge about how to improve practice. However, there is little point in simply turning up the rate at which research flows to the social care workforce – little research in fact has direct applicability, many practitioners are not equipped to digest research, and appropriate support systems are lacking. What we need is a better understanding of the relationship between social care research and the work of social care practitioners, including what organisational structures are needed to realise the aim of using research to improve practice.
>
> (Preface to 'Improving the use of research in social care practice', op. cit. 2004).

Research and policy: the current situation

There has been much debate over the years on how far research can and does influence policy and what the mechanisms might be for achieving this. However, it is clear from the substantial sums that government spends each year on its own research that it expects to use research in the conduct of its business, and bids to the research budget often exceed the amount available. The current government's commitment to evidence was affirmed by Alan Johnson, Secretary of State for Education and Skills, who in 2006 wrote:

> We are committed to raising the aspirations of learners and to help them develop confidence skills and knowledge they need to realise their full potential. To this end we shall base our policies to reshape the systems for delivering education, training and children's services on the best available evidence.
>
> (DfES analytical strategy, op. cit.)

Furthermore, the ability for civil servants to demonstrate 'Use of evidence and analysis of data' has been identified as one of four core skills which every civil servant needs. The core skills form part of the Professional Skills for Government (PSG), which is a major, long-term change programme designed to ensure that civil servants, wherever they work, have the right mix of skills and expertise to enable their Departments or agencies to deliver effective services. An initial analysis on the extent to which PSGs had been embedded within the Senior Civil Service across all Government Departments suggested that the majority of senior civil servant respondents thought they had successfully demonstrated the 'use of evidence and analysis of data' core skills (Sector Skills Council for Central Government, Cabinet Office 2006).

Improving access and uptake of research: lessons learned and what next?

The drive to improve further access to, and uptake of, research on the part of field staff, policy officials and practitioners is now the responsibility of the Office of the Chief Adviser on School Standards, which works in close collaboration with social researchers and analysts in Schools Directorate. The Directorate has undertaken a range of activities to improve the research service for policy and field staff and practitioners. In 2006, it reviewed its activities and reconfigured these into a focused action plan with ongoing evaluation.

The action plan to some extent captures existing research activities (though serves to make them more accountable) including for policy officials, the provision of a regular supply of robust evidence including topic papers and bespoke briefings, as well as a monthly research newsletter with key findings of national and international research written in plain English.

The action plan also includes new strands of work notably a dedicated research service for field staff. This first involved compiling a list of names and e-mail addresses of school phase field staff, interested in being kept up to date with research, from the DfES as well as partner organisations. These field staff are sent on a monthly basis the 'schools research news', available at www.standards.dfes.gov.uk/research which comprises user-friendly summaries of UK and international schools research drawn from reports published on a wide range of websites as well as academic journals. Field staff are also able to request subject specific compilations of research on topics including English, mathematics, information and communications technology (ICT) and science. Although primarily written for field staff subject specialists, these updates have frequently been requested by field staff working in other areas, as well as by practitioners. A research induction pack for field staff with information on where to access evidence, a list of the Schools Directorate research priorities, and a programme of research events has also been produced.

A key commitment in the action plan has been to invite field staff and policy officials to participate in a regular research seminar series. These events provide participants with the opportunity to discuss research findings from emerging studies and/or across different studies, and consider the implications in their own contexts. The design of these events has largely been informed by NERF's evaluation of an earlier series of research seminars (Norman 2004). At the end of each event policy officials and field staff are invited to complete an evaluation form. An analysis of completed forms has indicated that field staff and policy officials have found the events useful, have said they would like to attend future events – and indeed many have already signed up for future seminars. Participants have also reported that they often set themselves follow-up actions to take back to their organisations. The researchers who present their work at the seminars have reported that they find the events useful too – as the discussions help to articulate current policy issues as well as areas of future research interest.

It is worth pointing out that in order to make the events work well considerable planning and background work has been required. This includes identifying the topics policy officials and field staff are most interested in having presented at a seminar; involving relevant policy teams in the design of events; briefing the researchers on the current policy context and possible questions participants may ask; as well as providing researchers with examples of user-friendly presentation slides; and keeping the momentum going in terms of planning future events in the series. At least as important as the content of the action plan has been the commitment to deliver and monitor it. Learning from the previous evaluations of research in England (Hillage 1998; OECD 2002) for the action plan to work, i.e. if it is to realistically improve access and uptake of research, it has to be regularly monitored to ensure that what it is doing is relevant to the intended beneficiaries, i.e. policy officials, field staff and practitioners. Monitoring is kept light touch, e.g. in terms of seeking feedback to the field staff service, they are requested to reply to a few short questions by an e-mail reply. Similarly evaluation forms for the research seminar series are kept brief to one side of paper. Although 'light touch' to reduce burdens of staff, monitoring is undertaken fairly frequently to ensure that the action plan remains relevant to the needs of policy officials and field staff.

The next task will be to produce an impact report on the outcomes from the action plan. The early signs that it is working are: seminars are often over-subscribed; field staff provide unprompted feedback on how they have made use of evidence; and there has been an increased interest from various sectors of the research community to share their emerging work with policy.

So what next after the impact report? In the words of many of the field staff – 'keep it going'.

References

CPD EPPI Centre Review Group. (2003) *How does collaborative Continuing Professional Development (CPD) for teachers of the 5–16 age range affect teaching and learning?* Evidence for Policy and Practice Information Co-ordinating Centre. Available online at: http://eppi.ioe.ac.uk/cms/Default.aspx?tabid=364

CPD EPPI Centre Review Group. (2005a) *The impact of collaborative continuing professional development (CPD) on classroom teaching and learning – Review: How do collaborative and sustained CPD and sustained but not collaborative CPD affect teaching and learning?* Evidence for Policy and Practice Information Co-ordinating Centre. Available online at: http://eppi.ioe.ac.uk/cms/Default.aspx?tabid=364

CPD EPPI Centre Review Group. (2005b) *The impact of collaborative continuing professional development (CPD) on classroom teaching and learning — Review: What do teacher impact data tell us about collaborative CPD?* Evidence for Policy and Practice Information Co-ordinating Centre. Available online at: http://eppi.ioe.ac.uk/cms/Default.aspx?tabid=364

Day, C., Stobart, G., Sammons, P., Kington, A., Gu, Q., Smees, R. and Mujtaba, T. (2006) *Variations in Teachers' Work, Lives and Effectiveness.* Nottingham: DfES Publications.

Department for Education and Skills. (2004) *Five Year Strategy for Children and Learners.* Nottingham: DfES Publications.

Department for Education and Skills. (2006a) *Analytical Strategy 2006.* Nottingham: DfES Publications.

Department for Education and Skills. (2006b) *The Five Year Strategy for Children and Learners: Maintaining the Excellent Progress.* Nottingham: DfES Publications.

Fielding, M., Bragg, S., Craig, J., Cunningham, I., Eraut, M., Gillinson, S., Horne, M., Robinson, C. and Thorp, J. (2005) *Factors Influencing the Transfer of Good Practice.* Nottingham: DfES Publications.

Hillage, J., Pearson, R., Anderson, A. and Tamkin, P. (1998) *Excellence in Research in Schools.* London: DfES Publications.

Market and Opinion Research International (MORI). (2004) *MORI Teachers' Omnibus 2004 (Wave 2).* London: MORI.

Maths EPPI Centre Review Group. (2006) *Strategies to raise pupils' motivational effort in Key Stage 4 Mathematics.* Evidence for Policy and Practice Information Co-ordinating Centre. Available online at: http://eppi.ioe.ac.uk/cms/default.aspx?tabid=714

National Educational Research Forum. (2000) *Research Funding – Sub Group Report (2000).* London: National Educational Research Forum.

National Teacher Research Panel. (2003) *Hosting Research in Schools – NTRP Consultation 2003.* Available online at: www.standards.dfes.gov.uk/ntrp/ourwork/hostingresearch/

Norman, L. (2004) *Research – Policy Interaction. A study of a Series of DfES Convened Seminars.* London National Educational Research Forum. Available online at: www.nerf-uk.org/word/Eightpointone.doc?version=1

OECD/CERI. (2002) *Educational Research and Development in England – Examiner's Report.* OECD.

Sammons, P., Melhuish, E., Romaniuk, H., Sylva, K., Siraj-Blatchford, I. and Taggart, B. (2006a) *The Effectiveness of Primary Schools in England in Key Stage 2 for 2002, 2003 and 2004.* Nottingham: DfES Publications.

Sammons, P., Taggart, B., Siraj-Blatchford, I., Sylva, K., Melhuish, E. and Barreau, S. (2006b). *Variations in Teacher and Pupil Behaviours in Year 5 Classes.* Nottingham: DfES Publications.

Sector Skills Council for Central Government, Cabinet Office. (2006) *Professional Skills for Government: an Initial Analysis.* Available online at: http://psg.civilservice.gov.uk/

Sturgis, P., Smith, P. and Hughes, G. (2006) *A Study of Suitable Methods for Raising Response Rates in School Surveys.* Nottingham: DfES Publications.

Sylva, K., Melhuish, E., Sammons, P., Siraj-Blatchford, I. and Taggart, B. (2004) *Effective Provision of Pre-School Education (EPPE) Project: Final Report – Findings from Pre-school to End of Key Stage 1.* Nottingham: DfES Publications.

Walter, I., Nutley, S., Percy-Smith, J., McNeish, D. and Frost, S. (2004) *Knowledge Review 07: Improving the Use of Research in Social Care Practice.* London: Social Care Institute for Excellence. Available online at: www.scie.org.uk/publications/knowledgereviews/kr07.asp

Younger, M., Warrington, M., Gray, J., Rudduck, J., Mclellan, R., Bearne, E. and Bricheno, P. (2005) *Raising Boys' Achievement.* Nottingham: DfES Publications.

Chapter 3

The interplay between policy and research in relation to ICT in education in the UK

Issues from twenty years of programme evaluation

Bridget Somekh

Introduction

This chapter engages with the central issues of the book. What is the relationship between research and the making of policy? How can the knowledge generated by academics through, in this case, research into innovative information and communication technology (ICT) projects be communicated to policy-makers in ways that are meaningful and therefore useful? At the heart of these questions lie the reality of two very different life views, each with their own embedded assumptions about what counts as valid 'knowledge'/'evidence' and how we can judge its reliability. It is commonplace to remark on the difference in the language used by researchers and policy-makers and there is a tendency for each group to be impatient of the language of the other. These different discourses reflect different values and understandings of the world. What policy-makers value – the evidence about 'what works' – may appear to university-based researchers to be at a superficial, technical level; researchers are likely to be more concerned with understanding the deeper social and political processes involved in human beings' *attempts to make something 'work'*. In relation to the use of ICT in education these differences translate into two habitual postures: policy-makers have a tendency to see ICT as a high-profile, system-wide means of 'transforming' learning, and social science researchers have a tendency to see ICT as a distraction from the core educational business of teaching and learning. In their concern to 'speak truth to power' (Wildavsky 1993), they often dismiss policy-makers' aspirations as a futile search for 'magic solutions' (House 1974, pp. 213–214).

My own career, first as a teacher who used a computer to teach writing in 1984, later as part of a team developing software and supporting other teachers learning to use computers in their classrooms, and for the last 20 years as a researcher and evaluator of innovative ICT programmes, has placed me both within and across these two worlds. I have sometimes found myself uncomfortably positioned between them – classed by the academic community as too much of an advocate and by those with an entrepreneurial vision as too distanced, even cynical. In this chapter I want to argue for the importance of inhabiting both worlds and moving between them, adopting participatory research methods to explore prototypes of innovative practice; and finding ways of using powerful theories to inform the process of policy development and its translation into new kinds of teaching and learning with ICT. Writing a chapter for this book provides me with the opportunity to reflect back on my attempts to work at the boundaries between these two communities, and to argue for a new kind of partnership between policy-makers and researchers.

My transitional position can be seen in the following quotation from a keynote presentation to a conference organised in 1990 by the Computers in Teaching Initiative Support Service. In arguing for evaluation as an essential component of development work I was speaking both as an advocate leading the process of change and as an evaluator of one of the first projects in the Higher Education Funding Council for England (HEFCE) Teaching and Learning Technology Programme (TLTP).

> Those of us at the forefront of an innovation lead extraordinarily busy lives. (...) That is the typical social context which leads to simply going for it, getting things done, being hands-on people, getting into action, operating. The problem is that without evaluation and reflection, we may find in ten years time that we are disappointed with what has happened as a result of our efforts.
>
> (From 'The Evaluation of Teaching with Computers', Somekh 1990)

Looking back it is interesting to ask what has happened in the innovation of 'teaching with computers' since I gave that keynote. After 15, rather than 10 years should we be celebrating the achievements of many people's hard work or looking back with regret?

This chapter reflects back on 20 years' experience of carrying out evaluation work of initiatives aimed to embed ICT in education for various departments of the British government, including the Scottish Office prior to Scottish devolution. Its first focus is on the inter-relationship of researchers with policy-makers, and on the extent to which evaluators have been able to play a significant role in shaping policy and practice. This undoubtedly depends on three, inter-related factors: first the quality and relevance of the knowledge and understandings that emerged from the research which are in part dependent upon the nature of the contract; second, the extent to which policy-makers have wished to learn from the outcomes of the evaluations they commissioned; and third the extent to which those commissioning the evaluations have had the power to develop new policies that built on research knowledge. The second focus of this chapter is on new forms of reporting evaluation research that build scenarios of possibility for the future, in addition to identifying and analysing the intended and unintended outcomes of innovative ICT initiatives.

The chapter draws on six sponsored evaluation projects, starting with a retrospective report on the Department of Trade and Industry's (DTI) Micros in Schools Schemes of the early 1980s (MacDonald *et al.* 1988), spanning the evaluation of the Education Departments' Superhighways Initiative (EDSI), otherwise known as 'the Superhighways Evaluation' in the mid 1990s (Somekh *et al.* 1999). In addition, the ImpaCT2 evaluation of the National Grid for Learning around the turn of the century (Somekh, Lewin *et al.* 2002), and the Evaluation of the GridClub Website for 7–11-year-old children (Somekh *et al.* 2003), as well as two contracts still current at the time of going to press, the evaluations of the ICT Test Bed Project and of the Primary Schools Whiteboard Initiative (Somekh *et al.* 2007a; Somekh *et al.* 2007b).

All this work has been carried out within a coherent methodological framework. This casts evaluators as providing a public service with a duty to identify and judge the worth of the impact of educational initiatives financed with public money; while at the same time contributing to the effectiveness of policy-making by maximising learning from both its intended and unintended outcomes (Patton 1986). Evaluation research is understood to be engaged and purposeful rather than neutral, and inevitably operating within a politicised context in which a range of different stakeholders are likely to attempt to influence the evaluators' judgements and thereby *de facto* undermine their independence. Evaluators, therefore, have a duty to balance the interests of all stakeholders and resist being co-opted by any group (Stake 1998, pp. 203–204). They must ensure that those who are responsible for policy development understand the implications of their decisions and the complexities of the process of policy implementation; and that those who are tasked with implementing policy in practice or supporting its implementation are not held to account for factors which are beyond their control. The starting point for this approach, deriving from the work of the Centre for Applied Research in Education (CARE) at the University of East Anglia (UEA), where I was a senior research associate from 1987 to 1995, was MacDonald's 'democratic evaluation' (MacDonald 1974; Ryan and DeStefano 2000), and Stake's responsive evaluation (Stake 2003). This was later developed into a new model of *supportive evaluation* to meet the needs of ICT initiatives, many of which are not led by experienced project managers and require collaboration between partners from diverse backgrounds, such as technology, school teaching, the business world and universities. *Supportive evaluation* incorporates a more explicit role for evaluators to contribute knowledge from their previous experience of innovative ICT programmes, and assist in brokering inter-cultural understanding between different participating groups (Somekh 2001).

The relationship between policy and research – insights from analysis

There is currently a recognition from both sides of the divide that research and policy need to be drawn into better alignment. In this section I will first explore how thinking on this issue developed among policy-makers and then discuss the contributions made by several papers in a special issue of the *British Journal of Sociology* in 2004.

From the policy perspective

One of the main criticisms findings of the Hillage Report on Excellence in Research on Schools, commissioned by the Department for Education and Employment (DfEE) in England (Hillage *et al.* 1998), which was not however as widely disseminated as were its other findings, was that poor communications between policy-makers and researchers were a major factor in the fragmentation of research effort: in effect Hillage said that educational research was irrelevant to policy-makers largely because policy-makers did not pay it serious attention or fund it properly. Arguably, evaluations commissioned during the 18 years of Conservative Government prior to 1997 had a largely 'cosmetic' purpose, their main importance consisting in being seen to be done rather than in the learning that emerged from them. For example, Philip Lewis, the senior civil servant with oversight of policy for IT in education, argued in a presentation to the World Conference for Computers in Education in Sydney in 1990 that he knew of no research that had had any impact on practice. By contrast, during the last 10 years, as part of the Labour Government's commitment to 'education, education and education', policy on ICT in education has been much more closely aligned with evidence. There has been a considerable increase in government funding for ICT initiatives, across all sectors of education, sustained over time and evaluated by commissioned research studies. While the evidence of impact on schooling has remained somewhat disappointing, the radical changes in other areas of society and human activity, the influx of computers and the internet into homes, and the enthusiasm for and expertise of young people in using them in out-of-school settings, indicate that it is the culture and structures of the education system which are the problem, rather than the vision that ICT has the potential to transform students' learning. I have argued elsewhere that the education system is experiencing the 'culture lag' which McLuhan identified as characteristic when new technologies are introduced into out-dated infrastructures (McLuhan 1964), and that it is time for research in the social sciences to go beyond exposing to ridicule the mismatches between vision and practice and re-orientate itself towards describing scenarios in which radical new structures enable real change in both culture and practice (Somekh 2004).

From the research perspective

Lauder *et al.* (2004) have recently put forward similar arguments, inspired by what they see as 'the emergence of a renewed belief in the power of the social sciences to inform policy after a long period in which faith in social development was placed in the hands of the 'free' market and its theorists' (ibid. p. 4).

They make two important points: first, that sociologists have the capability to make an important contribution to policy development, and second that they have a duty to become much more pro-active in engaging with policy-makers and seeking to communicate the outcomes of their research through channels, such as the media, where it will have impact. They argue that it is sociologists' 'theoretical insight' which enables human behaviour to be understood in terms of 'the way societal power structures are constructed and sustained' (p. 6) and that 'unless social researchers take an active role in the dissemination of findings, their work will be "reinterpreted" or ignored especially if it is "off message"' (p. 19). However, this motivation to engage with, almost perhaps to assist, policy-makers is in tension with a central tenet of sociological work – what Lauder *et al.* call 'the key role' of 'hold(ing) governments to account' (p. 20). It remains a central purpose of social scientists 'to discover the unintended consequences of purposive, political action' (p. 11).

It is, perhaps, the fact that social scientists have traditionally seen this latter function as more important than the provision of constructive advice, that has sometimes made politicians and policy-makers resentful and bred mistrust between them and researchers. (I am reminded of David Blunkett's angry outburst, as Secretary of State for Education, when the *British Educational Research Journal* published an article showing that primary school children's attainment in tests was not improved by doing homework – which at the time was a key policy initiative to build greater involvement of parents in their children's education.) In a response to the article by Lauder *et al.*, in the same issue of the *British Journal of Sociology*, Johnson, a senior civil servant and policy-maker at the Department for Education and Skills (DfES), points out that identifying social problems without at the same time giving constructive advice leads only to a confusing proliferation of policy initiatives since 'when they know there is a problem, inaction is rarely an option for policy makers, particularly for politicians' (Johnson 2004, p. 25). He goes on to say that discovering the unintended consequences is insufficient: 'it is also rather important to determine whether the purposive action has had the intended consequences' (ibid. p. 26).

These issues are complicated by the fact that researchers and policy-makers are both operating in a world where the old rules have been swept away by new information and communication technologies. Castells (2004, p. 370) suggests that the media is now so central to the process of political activity and policy formation that both only function at all within the media spotlight: 'Outside the sphere of the media there is only political marginality'. This is why Wiles (2004), in another article responding to Lauder *et al.* says that he doubts the ability of sociologists to engage effectively in public policy debates: 'the more directly popularist nature of contemporary politics, together with a polycentric mass media, have speeded up political debate and made it more difficult for specialist and nuanced voices to be heard' (ibid. p. 33). This is an age in which almost all policy initiatives are subjected to negative media 'spin', either in the polemical thrust of the tabloid newspapers or through the BBC's convention of giving equal time in discussions of policy to both points of view. Thus the media spotlight has been a major factor in generating a blame culture in UK society, in which politicians and policy-makers have become far too vulnerable to allow them to enjoy engaging with researchers whose priority is to find the 'unintended consequences' rather than seeking for the gains resulting from policy implementation.

The relationship between policy and research – reflections on practice

So, now when I look back on 20 years of occupying the contested space of programme evaluation, what can I learn? How have the relationships between researchers and policy-makers been constructed in the performance of evaluating ICT in education initiatives? How much attention has been paid by the researchers to uncovering the unintended consequences and have policy-makers learnt from them? Have we paid due attention to identifying and publicising the intended outcomes? And how effectively have both parties – policy-makers and researchers – between us managed the public communication of the evaluation outcomes?

Evaluation of the DTI micros in schools support

When in 1988 I worked with colleagues at CARE/UEA on the evaluation of the DTI's Micros in Schools Schemes of 1981–84, the relationship with DTI civil servants was pretty *ad hoc*. An evaluation of this initiative to put microcomputers into secondary and primary schools had never been planned at the time it was implemented and, by the time a new Secretary of State took office in 1988 and began to ask questions about its effectiveness, all the civil servants who had been responsible for implementing the scheme had moved on to other posts. There was no institutional memory left. The DTI had probably, in actuality, conceived of the scheme as a mechanism for kick-starting the British computer industry, by creating an immediate educational market, which was intended in the longer term to spearhead the move of computers beyond schools and 'grow' a market in British homes and businesses. However, in response to our direct request, we were told – after a delay – that the aims of the schemes had been:

- to promote awareness among school children of information technology;
- to encourage the use of computers in education not just for computer studies, but as an aid to the teaching of all subjects;
- and to do this in a cost-effective way.

It was clear from both the emphasis on using computers for the 'teaching of all subjects' and from the discourse of 'IT' (a term used between 1987 and the advent of 'ICT' in the mid 1990s) rather than 'microcomputers' (the terminology used in the title of the initiative) that these aims had been invented because no one at the

DTI could find any statement of the original aims. The comment from one of our key informants was 'inventing history beautifully – if these had been stated objectives from the beginning things might have been different'. Nevertheless, as we said in our report, these were aims which our respondents were agreed should be the *current* aims (i.e. in 1988) of using computers in schools, so already, by 1988, an educational vision was beginning to emerge, sustained by a community of local education authority (LEA) workers, software developers and innovative teachers. The schemes had been a major factor, together with the work of the Microelectronics in Education Programme (MEP, 1980–86) (of which there had been no evaluation), in establishing computers as equipment which all schools should possess and use in teaching and learning: 'the scheme forced the pace and direction of change' (MacDonald *et al*. op. cit. p. 4). It also helped to create a community of skilled personnel to carry IT in education forward. Many of these people are still actively engaged in continuing this effort today.

Much was also learnt from this evaluation about what to avoid in IT initiatives in the future – for example that 'cascade' training where two teachers are trained and go back to train their colleagues, does not occur 'naturally' just because teachers are working together; and that provision of inferior equipment (e.g. tape-recorders rather than floppy disc drives) is a big 'turn off' for teachers. The key unintended consequence, which was not to emerge clearly until a few years later, was the creation of a perception in the minds of parents and employers that British computers were 'for children', and that something else – the personal computer (PC) – was what was needed for the work place.

I was a new researcher at the time, and so it is likely looking back that I would not have been involved in direct discussions with DTI civil servants. Nevertheless, my impression is that there probably was little contact apart from telephone conversations (little use of email in those days): we conducted this evaluation very remotely. There was certainly no Steering Group. The evaluation was a three-month contract commissioned in a hurry and carried out with greater injection of resources by CARE than the funding justified, because as Barry MacDonald said at the time, 'This is an area of work in which we want to establish a track record'. This was a period when there was little perceived need for evaluation as noted earlier in this paper in the quotation from Phillip Lewis's presentation to the WCCE conference in 1990. Policy-making for ICT in education was fraught with difficulty at the time and characterised by the search for new people who would deliver what those entrusted with the previous project had failed to deliver. There was an assumption of incompetence brought about by extremely unrealistic policy aspirations, such as the commissioning of the Interactive Video in Schools Project to produce the discs (including making the videos and materials for them), get them working on computers (design, encode and trial the software) and pilot them in use in schools, all within a two-year period (Norris *et al*. 1990). In sheer frustration in 1990 the DES sponsored an evaluation of the Impact of IT in schools with a prescribed research design involving comparisons between 'high IT' and 'low IT' schools which proved (all too predictably) to be unworkable in the rapidly shifting context of IT provision and use in schools at the time (Watson 1993).

Evaluation of the EDSI

By the time of the EDSI (Superhighways) evaluation in the mid 1990s, I was working in Scotland and relationships between the researchers and sponsors were greatly complicated by the fact that I was responsible to the Scottish Office and managed by the Scottish Council for Educational Technology (SCET), while at the same time being required to work as part of a very large team of evaluators across the whole of the UK, responsible to the DfEE in England and managed by the National Council for Educational Technology (NCET). This was my first experience of working with a 'synopter' whose role was to write a succinct summary of the findings from a group of evaluation studies, thereby allowing the four Education Departments of England, Wales, Scotland and Northern Ireland to commission a very large evaluation without giving too much funding or responsibility to any one group. The result was that relationships became fraught, with two or three levels of communication separating the evaluation teams on the ground from those who had commissioned the evaluation in London and Scotland. Disagreements between the Scottish Office and London were sufficient to necessitate my colleagues at the Scottish Council for Research in Education (SCRE) (I had moved to Huddersfield before the work was completed) writing a separate report for Scotland in addition to the one submitted to the synopter to go into the main report (Scrimshaw 1997). The precariousness of those involved in the development of policy for ICT in education was strongly indicated by the 'early retirement' of the civil servant with overall responsibility for ICT at the DfEE, shortly after the EDSI evaluation was finalised. Three Chief Executives of NCET and its predecessor the Microelectronics in Education Support Unit (MESU) also fell from office over the period 1988–1997 and, arguably, in the case of the last one the rupture was caused by adverse DfEE reactions to an evaluation of the integrated learning system (ILS) software which had been managed by the British Educational and Communications Technology Agency (Becta) NCET and had come up with unwelcome findings (Underwood *et al.* 1994; Wood 1998). ICT seemed to be a catalyst for unleashing naked power struggles.

In many ways, EDSI was a very effective evaluation which had a considerable impact on policy development. A comparative examination of Scrimshaw's synoptic report (op. cit.) and the consultation document put out by the new Labour government closely following their election (DfEE 1997), suggests considerable carry-over of learning had taken place. As an initiative, however, EDSI had peculiarities which made our position as evaluators ambivalent and even potentially untenable. The initiative was launched in 1995 with a publication called *Superhighways in Education* and rapidly became very high profile because of public interest in the internet at the time (DfEE 1995). There was an invitation to tender for a series of evaluations of the initiative, focusing respectively on the school curriculum, vocational training, home-school links, professional development/training and the two Scottish projects. Meanwhile, projects were invited to put themselves forward for evaluation on condition that they had already secured some commercial sponsorship. What was not clear, however, from the Superhighways document was that projects that were successful in being selected to be evaluated would not receive any government funding – the commercial sponsorship was actually the *only* funding they would have, not, as all the teams in Scotland assumed, a minor additional source of funding. Introducing our team to the two selected Scottish projects was not a happy experience as we found ourselves having to explain the anomaly that we were being paid to evaluate projects which were not themselves funded. Understandably, both project teams needed some persuasion that they should give up time to work with us. One thing that emerged very clearly from the EDSI evaluation was that commercial sponsorship is not available to schools and education authorities equally in all areas of the UK, but is invested differentially between north and south and between urban and rural areas. The level of funding that a project based in the highlands and islands of northern Scotland could raise from commercial companies could never be adequate, whereas projects sited around London or other major conurbations in the south of England could secure comparatively lavish funding. This was an important message at a time when a central tenet of the then government's education policies was to find levers to draw commercial companies into investing directly in schools.

Transition to new relationships

The change of government to a New Labour administration in 1997 brought a new approach to the funding of ICT in education. After the flurry of initiatives in the 1980s – MEP, Micros in School Scheme, the Technical and Vocational Education Initiative (TVEI) – the Conservative government had ceased to put sustained funding into IT (this refers to the pre-ICT time during the 1980s) in education projects. For several years in the late 1980s and early 1990s there had been a series of suddenly announced initiatives from the DTI at the end of the financial year, to 'use up' surplus money (e.g. providing British-made modems for secondary schools which notoriously lurked for years in cupboards) and there were some one-off initiatives such as the Initial Teacher Education and New Technology project (INTENT, 1990–1992) of which I was the Coordinator. However, after 1997 there was a new continuity of policy, initiatives were comprehensive rather than focused on small-scale 'pilots' and were sustained from one to the next, so that the NGfL (National Grid for Learning, 1999–2002), merged seamlessly into ICTIS (ICT in Schools, 2003–2006). For me personally, coinciding with my move to Manchester Metropolitan University at the end of 1999, this made it possible to start building a very different kind of relationship with civil servants at the DfES and with officers and managers at Becta. Involvement in two less high-profile evaluations – ICT and Home-School Links (2002) (Somekh, Mavers and Lewin, 2002) sponsored by Becta, and the Evaluation of the

GridClub Edutainment Website (2002–03) (Somekh *et al.* 2003) sponsored by the DfES and managed by Becta, gave us the opportunity to engage with children's learning out of school. It was clear that those involved in managing the GridClub evaluation did not feel themselves under stress and were able to engage in discussions about what we were learning without anxiety about its outcomes. Early Steering Group meetings were lively events focused on mutual learning. But, as the reason for these stress-free relationships emerged, attendance at the meetings declined – the GridClub report would not be formally published by the DfES and therefore there would be no press release and no active promotion of the report. It was not 'high stakes' and would attract no media coverage. We could and did publish it ourselves at MMU, but without formal endorsement it could have little or no impact other than among the academic community (Somekh *et al.* 2003).

The ImpaCT2 evaluation of the National Grid for Learning

Between 1999 and 2002 I was involved in the evaluation of the National Grid for Learning, known as ImpaCT2 (Harrison *et al.* 2002) because, in part, it was intended as a follow-up to the 'Impact' study by King's College commissioned by Philip Lewis 10 years previously (Watson, op. cit.). In this evaluation I was not the lead director but co-director working with Colin Harrison from the University of Nottingham. Our relationship with the DfES was one-step removed, through a manager at Becta. This had both advantages and disadvantages: on the one hand we had close, personal contact with a manager who had real interest in our research activities, but on the other hand we sometimes felt we were trying to 'second-guess' what was required from the information coming to us through a filter. A clear phenomenon in ImpaCT2 was the raising of the stakes over time. The first year was relatively stress free and our interim report was well received. During the second year the relationship between the evaluation team and Becta became rather more fraught, creating stress for the ImpaCT2 Director and we believe also for our manager at Becta. The English parliamentary elections in 2001 were probably a factor, coupled with the policy decision after the elections to wind down the NGfL programme and replace it with the ICTIS strategy in 2002. Publication of the final report became a matter of urgency once the programme had ended. The scenario for the DfES was clearly demanding – large amounts of public money had been spent on the NGfL and had to be accounted for to the Treasury. Future funding for ICTIS depended on making a good case for the positive outcomes of the NGfL investment. In ImpaCT2 we had identified a considerable body of positive outcomes, but the focus for the DfES, driven by the Treasury, had to be on the so-called 'hard' evidence of improved attainment as measured by national test scores and GCSE results. The fact that no definite link could ever possibly be established between improved test scores (should we find them) and the NGfL initiative, because of the many other factors in the course of pupils' education which must be influencing their attainment, was unwelcome news for the DfES civil servants. Their anxiety was passed on to us through Becta, which itself experienced considerable pressure from civil servants with consequent stress for staff.

As time went on, the ImpaCT2 evaluation ran into a further, classic problem of unintended outcomes. We had been contracted to measure the impact on learning outcomes in English, mathematics and science in primary and secondary schools, but when we asked pupils to tick a box indicating the frequency with which they had been using computers in these subjects, in most age groups, and across all three subjects, many ticked the 'never' or 'hardly ever' boxes. What emerged from the qualitative evidence, but not at all through the quantitative evidence, was that the IT equipment purchased with NGfL funding was being used overwhelmingly to teach ICT skills, rather than to teach subjects across the curriculum. Moreover, the guidelines for using ICT produced by the Qualifications and Curriculum Authority (QCA) *de facto* encouraged schools to adopt this approach because they consisted of a series of lessons focused on the acquisition of ICT skills, embedded in other activities but mainly consisting of short sequences of activities which could most easily be taught by an ICT specialist. Even when the ImpaCT2 data went beyond the three core subjects specified in the evaluation contract it covered only geography, history, modern foreign languages and design and technology (Harrison *et al*. op. cit. p. 31). There was not a single graph in the report showing the use of ICT in ICT lessons, yet this was the area of the curriculum in which pupils were using the NGfL equipment. The positive gains in test scores in English, mathematics and science were disappointingly small, yet the very low levels of ICT use in these subjects meant that this did not provide valid evidence of the impact or otherwise of ICT on learning. There was some evidence of statistically significant small gains in English for 11 year olds where pupils reported slightly higher levels of use, and in science at age 14 and 16, and, given the way that the equipment had mainly been used, it was a very positive indication that we found any evidence of gains at all. The problem was greatly compounded, however, by the special importance placed by the DfES on the quantitative results, and the fact that the effort to get the reporting of these quantitative data 'right' led to complex and protracted negotiations, and ended by the publication of the outcomes from the quantitative data separately from those of the qualitative data. This was a major error of judgement – which the evaluators should have foreseen and warned about – but through oversight we were complicit in a gross, unintentional mismanagement of the media. The quantitative report received fairly extensive, negative coverage in the newspapers, whereas when the qualitative report was subsequently published, providing an explanation which might have mitigated the negativity, it received no media attention whatever – ImpaCT2 was by then yesterday's news. This experience has certainly constituted major learning for me. To ensure that the evaluation is conducted and reported in a manner that is 'democratic, fair, and ultimately based upon the moral values of equality, autonomy, impartiality, and reciprocity' (House 1980, p. 256) I now try to ensure that negative findings are presented alongside any explanatory discussion which may be relevant.

Building new kinds of relationships in current evaluation projects

Since April 2003 our Centre for ICT, Pedagogy and Learning (CIPL) at MMU has been carrying out, in collaboration with Jean Underwood and her team at Nottingham Trent University, the evaluation of the ICT Test Bed project, funded by the DfES and managed by Becta. In April 2004 CIPL also started work on the evaluation of the Primary Schools Whiteboard Project, funded by the DfES and directly managed by civil servants. In my role as Director of these two studies I have had considerable opportunity to reflect on the inter-relationships between researchers and policy-makers and their agents. A very positive factor has been the continuity of relationships that we have established over the last five years. Some of the key people we are working with were involved in managing the ImpaCT2 evaluation and we have been able to build new relationships with others within a framework of existing mutual expectations and understandings. I hasten to say that this does not mean that there is no stress in the relationship. Once again we are experiencing the phenomenon of the raising of stakes over time. Inherently, evaluation is concerned with the judgement of worth of an initiative and those responsible for managing us at both the DfES and Becta have a vested interest in seeing such a key initiative succeed. Unavoidably, they would like us to produce an evaluation which carries good news. However, as employees of universities – and with the support of a strong research group experienced in carrying out evaluation work – we are well placed to remain independent and ensure that to the best of our ability our reports are fair and balanced.

Several features of these current relationships seem to me to be of special interest in enabling us, as researchers, to provide policy-makers with knowledge that can feed into future planning. One is that we are aware of the need to shift the focus of the evaluation over time, in order to keep track of changes in policy and provide knowledge needed to support ministers in promoting new initiatives. This shift in focus is, of course, something that is generally considered unacceptable in research, and indeed distinguishes evaluation as an activity which has distinct differences from other forms of research. In the ICT Test Bed Evaluation this process was specified in the original invitation to tender and written into our proposal to the DfES as an aspiration of the research design: 'We welcome the need for flexibility in research design and look forward to drawing up revised plans annually for approval by the Steering Group to keep abreast of changes in policy and developments in technology'. It is not, however, a process that can be dealt with solely by means of annual planning in January. The BETT exhibition in January is a key moment when new government policies are launched, but the policy development work of course takes place earlier in the year. Ideally, ministers might like to see the previous year's Annual Report of the Evaluation flagging up issues which will be carried forward in the new policies. To meet this need, and to ensure that reports provide information directly relevant to our stake-holders (both managers and those responsible for implementing the initiative), in both the ICT Test Bed and Whiteboard evaluations we are developing with our managers an additional process of collecting their current and burning questions at key points in the year and giving these as much priority as we can while we are collecting data and writing reports. This has to be balanced, however, with the need to provide a coherent evaluation of the initiative's work in the light of the aims that participants on the ground were asked to work towards. Shifting the goal posts by which we judge the worth of the work carried out by practitioners would certainly be unethical.

A second feature of the relationship is to remain aware that those who manage us, both in the DfES and Becta, are primarily working *for* policy-makers and/or *taking part in* the policy-making process rather than actually being policy-makers themselves. They can be imagined, perhaps, as resembling puppeteers who need to make us perform in ways that will fulfil the needs of a more remote audience. My former colleague, Barry MacDonald, used to say that the problem for evalu-ators was that we are often restricted to talking to 'middle grade civil servants'. Several interesting factors arise from this. One is the need to be aware that a top priority for the evaluators should be to assist our managers in disseminating the work of the project to others within the Department or Agency itself. If knowl-edge from the project is to have an impact on policy development for the future it must be brought to the attention of senior civil servants and agency directors. The evaluators, coming from an external, independent and credible institution – in this case, a university – can command attention in a different way from those internal to the Department or Agency. However, extremely careful planning of such events is essential, since the evaluators need to understand enough of the internal politics and current policy concerns to be able to capture and sustain attention. Knowledge about the project needs to be contextualised for the policy audience, just as its construction has already been necessarily bound up in the contexts of the project's activities. Another factor is that evaluators have a role to remind all concerned about the larger policy concerns which led to an innovative programme being set up. Otherwise there can be slippage in the process of judg-ing its success.

The ICT Test Bed project provides a good example. A very large investment (£34 m), relatively speaking, has been put into the provision of very high levels of ICT to 28 schools and three FE colleges in three clusters based in areas of high socio-economic deprivation, with the intention of finding out through this 'test bed' whether a technology-rich school can provide better life chances for pupils who otherwise would have almost certainly under-achieved. However, there is a tendency as the life of the project progresses for expectations to be set too high, in effect looking for levels of improvement that might have been expected in areas with average or above average socio-economic demographics. Evaluators have an important role in drawing explicit attention to the huge importance of the project's original aim, because it is central to the government's vision to raise the life chances of those children who are disadvantaged. This is both a matter of discursive construction of reporting – whether in oral or written form – and a matter that demands the collection of evidence to clarify the nature of the disadvantage that the schools are working to overcome.

For example, in one of the ICT Test Bed areas there is a highly fluid population, with immigrant families moving into and out of the area, in many cases as a result of government policy for moving asylum seekers into temporary accommodation in the schools' catchment area until permanent accommodation can be found for them elsewhere. Comparisons of the aggregate test scores of children in these schools, from year to year, cannot be taken as evidence of the impact, or lack of impact, of the process of whole-school development with ICT that is the Test Bed vision, without knowing what proportion of the children has remained in the school over the four-year life of the project and what proportion has been there for only one or two terms. It is clear that otherwise judgements of the school's achievements would be unfair and judgements of the effectiveness of the policy would be made on a false premise. There are also other lessons to be learnt which could be of great interest to policy-makers, such as whether or not ICT was used to communicate with schools in other parts of the country who receive the children as they move on. Qualitative data are particularly important in seeking out unexpected successes of this kind which may provide a better justification than improvements in test scores for the strategy of placing technology-rich schools in areas of socio-economic deprivation.

A third feature of the relationship relates to the process of bringing knowledge about the project into the public domain. This relates directly to Lauder *et al.*'s (op. cit.) call for researchers to be more proactive in the dissemination of their findings. In our experience it is beyond the scope of an evaluation team, working as we do on a wide range of initiatives, to manage this process ourselves. Moreover, we are limited by the terms of our contract in what we can report. Effective dissemination of knowledge, in a world where the media spotlight focuses on sound-bites and the message is subjected to fluctuations of spin and counter-spin, is a matter for professionals not amateurs. A welcome move on the part of Becta has been the recent appointment of a communications specialist who is working with us – for us, indeed – to get key messages into places where they will be heard. This brings its own tensions because our concern for research values of balance, fairness and judiciousness makes the language of our reports insufficiently attention catching for the general public; we also need to guard the independence of the evaluation by keeping our judgements separate from up-beat assertions that are perfectly appropriate for Becta itself, as the organisation whose responsibility it is to promote the project. We are precisely 'the nuanced voices' that Wiles (op. cit.) sees as likely to be ineffective in 'public policy debates'. However, in partnership with Becta, we have the possibility of contributing effectively to that debate. We are also, of course, drawing on the 'symbolic power' residing in the DfES and Becta, what Bourdieu (1991), quoted in Loveman (2005), calls the power to 'constitute the given'. Their press releases have recognised circulation channels, their voices command attention. Their voices are expected, legitimate voices in the public arena and exercise symbolic power through what Loveman calls 'misrecognition' (original italics) which is 'the appearance that no power is being wielded at all' (Loveman op. cit. p. 1655). Yet, we must continue to hold the tension of resisting pressures to package our research reports in discourse that fractures our core values as researchers. As intermediaries between policy and research we inhabit an exhilarating but rocky territory.

Speculative knowledge: building scenarios of possibility

Walker points out (2002) that research has a backward-looking orientation which limits researchers' ability to have forward-looking impact. This is a central feature of our community of practice (Wenger 1998), or what is alternatively called by Menchik (2004, p.194), drawing on the work of Bourdieu, 'an intellectual field' that has its own 'constraints of habitus' (ibid. p. 195). Indeed, pressures to conform to the norms of building knowledge on evidence drawn from data (traces of the past) are bound up with the identity politics of the academic world. We are engaged in what Castells (2004, p. 7) sees as the building of 'a collective identity', on-going maintenance work ensuring the secure foundations of the academic community. It is a community of practice in which playing a different kind of game by popularising research knowledge is often regarded as dubious.

I think it is time to break out of this negative enculturation and follow Walker's advice (ibid.) to build scenarios for the future. Research knowledge can be forward-facing (because explanatory) just as surely as it is evaluative. Based on what I have learnt from these various projects I have had the privilege of evaluating, I can build useful speculative knowledge to guide policy-making for the future.

So what can I say with speculative certainty?

ICT is changing the world around us. Kompf (2005) describes technology as having an uncontrolled imperative that can best be understood in terms of chaos theory. Innovative policies cannot be implemented discretely in a fully controlled manner, and require understanding of the processes by which social change is occurring in relation to technological change. Their implementation in practice is an art that requires knowledge and understanding of theories of innovation (Somekh 2007).

Starting with the wide range of people who are central to all initiatives, we can say that policies for ICT need to take into account the human context in which the initiatives will be played out. People – especially practitioners in the relevant public services – need time to develop vision. To be effective users of technology, teachers need time to 'play' with new hardware and surf the internet more than they need 'training' on how to use it.

Moving on to the institutional context for initiatives, the greatest barriers to using technology in ways that enable 'learning transformation' (Pearson and Somekh 2004) are embedded in the infrastructures of an education system that was developed for human activities dependent on previous technologies. Schools are trying to introduce the technology of the internet, designed to give individuals control over the use and creation of knowledge and information, into a curriculum divided into subjects and a timetable fragmented into short time periods. Teachers need the freedom to experiment with new pedagogies and a more flexible curriculum. Radical changes in timetabling and classroom practices are needed to allow young people to use the wide range of technology tools autonomously and creatively in their own process of learning. These tools could provide support for a new kind of schooling in which teachers and students work more as partners and some of the responsibility for students' learning is shifted away from the teacher to the students themselves. To enable ICT to transform the process of learning we need to abolish the 40–50-minute teaching period and give students the same kind of access to ICT that many adults routinely expect in their workplace: that is, we need to equip students with a digital learning companion (DLC) – a cross between a laptop, personal digital assistant (PDA) and mobile phone – which they have in their possession at all times. The relationship between students and teachers could be radically changed, devoting more of the teacher's time to teaching and less to classroom control. This might be achieved by means of learning contracts (agreed weekly and reviewed regularly) becoming the core mechanism for independent learning programmes, supported by regular small group tutorials rather than the traditional continuous routine of large-group teaching in formal classrooms. The extent of the freedom given to individual students could vary, as their teacher judges appropriate, according to their preparedness and ability to take this responsibility, perhaps measured by their products and achievements.

The examination system needs to be radically reformed so that it supports the process of pedagogic change rather than locking teaching into the established tramlines. For example, it simply does not make sense for students who use a computer on a daily basis to be asked to produce examination scripts in handwriting; and it does not make sense in a world where resources are constantly available on a DLC – and where skill in using them is the paramount requirement – for students to be tested on how they can perform without access to those resources. An alternative model of assessment would involve autonomous learners being allowed to progress at their own chosen speed, working to the learning contracts negotiated with their teachers and, with their support, entering themselves for assessment when they are ready rather than having to wait for a due date.

In terms of policy implementation we also know a number of things with certainty. First it is critically important for policy-makers to have a realistic understanding of how long it takes to procure and install new technology infrastructures. Huge undertakings of this kind, involving the spending of large amounts of money, nearly always take between a year and 18 months before they can be used by students and teachers. System-wide supply of new equipment, such as interactive whiteboards (IWBs), also takes time because, unless there is phased roll-out, shortage of expertise will lead to poor installation and faulty operation. Part-funding, for example by paying for enough IWBs for half a school's classrooms, is also likely to lead to a doubling of demand, since the half-funding will act as a pump-primer to access other funding. More realistic expectations from policy-makers at the highest level would remove the unnecessary pressure on practitioners and project managers of striving to meet impossible targets.

However, these unassimilated chunks of research knowledge are insufficient to build new policies and practices. The key to successful scenario building must lie in a new kind of partnership between researchers and policy-makers. At present the new kinds of relationships our CIPL group at MMU has been able to develop with the DfES and Becta managers of our government-sponsored evaluation studies are enabling us to feed 'theoretical insights' (Lauder op. cit.) into the policy-making process, but always our voices are filtered weakly up through the hierarchies of the civil service. What messages are actually conveyed, with what meaning, and to whom? There is a real question as to where the power lies to implement the necessary radical changes. Does it lie with government ministers? Does it lie with the media? In an education system which is strongly constructed in traditional institutional forms the process of radical change can scarcely begin to operate. To allow digital technologies to have a transformative impact on learning we need to engage collaboratively in the construction of a new educational identity. This process, as Castells (2004, pp. 6–7) describes it, 'must be distinguished from what, traditionally, sociologists have called roles and role-sets'. It is, rather, the development of a whole new set of expectations for learning (curriculum), theories and routines of practice (pedagogy), and mechanisms for recognising educational achievement (assessment). This can only be done collaboratively, through a much more fundamental integration of policy-making with knowledge production. Teachers have the expertise to support students' learning and now that they have ICT tools such as the internet they can adopt the role of co-learners with their students. They need to play a central role, alongside policy-makers, in designing new educational practices which encourage learners' creativity and independence. Children and young people, as the main stakeholders of education, often with unique knowledge and experience of using ICT creatively, should be central to this collaboration. Their voices need to be at the centre of policy-making for education and researchers can play a role in helping their voices to be heard. As Castells says: 'Although identities can also be originated from dominant institutions, they become identities only when and if social actors internalize them, and construct their meaning around this internalization' (ibid. p. 7). He goes on to note that 'the social construction of identity always takes place in a context marked by power relationships'. This is the key. Perhaps, however, this need not be an uncontrolled process in which we are powerless to bring about radical changes; perhaps those who hold power of different kinds need to engage in setting up new structures to enable collaborative identity construction.

In Castells' model of 'project identity building' (ibid. p. 8) social actors come together to use all the tools and strategies available to them, 'to build a new identity that redefines their position in society and, by so doing, seek the transformation of overall social structures'. I hope that this book may be the first step in such educational identity building.

References

Bourdieu, P. (1991). *Language and Symbolic Power*. Cambridge MA: Harvard University Press.

Castells, M. (2004). *The Information Age: Economy, Society and Culture. Volume II: The Power of Identity*. Second edition, first published in 1997. Malden MA and Oxford UK: Blackwell Publishing.

DfEE (1995). *Superhighways for Education*. London: HMSO.

DfEE (1997). *Connecting the Learning Society*. London: Department for Education and Employment.

Harrison, C., T. Fisher, K. Haw, C. Lewin, E. Lunzer, D. Mavers, P. Scrimshaw and B. Somekh (2002). ImpaCT2: the Impact of Information and Communication Technologies on Pupils' Learning and Attainment. Coventry, Department for Education and Skills. Available at: www.becta.org.uk/research/reports/ImpaCT2.

Hillage, J., B. Pearson, A. Anderson and P. Tamkin (1998). *Excellence in Research on Schools*. London: Department for Education and Employment.

House, E.R. (1974). *The Politics of Educational Innovation*. Berkeley, CA: McCutchan Publishing Co.

House, E.R. (1980). *Evaluating with Validity*. Beverly Hills CA and London: Sage.

Johnson, P. (2004). "Making social science useful." *British Journal of Sociology* 55(1): 23–30.

Kompf, M. (2005). "Information and Communications Technology (ICT) and the seduction of knowledge, teaching, and learning: what lies ahead for education." *Curriculum Inquiry* 35(2): 213–233.

Lauder, H., P. Brown and A.H. Halsey (2004). "Sociology and political arithmetic: some principles of a new policy science." *British Journal of Sociology* 55(1): 3–22.

Loveman, M. (2005). "The modern state and the primitive accumulation of symbolic power." *American Journal of Sociology* 110(6): 1651–1683.

MacDonald, B. (1974). "Evaluation and Control of Education." *Innovation, Evaluation, Research and the Problem of Control*. I. F. S. Project. Norwich, CARE, University of East Anglia.

MacDonald, B., C. Beattie, J. Schostak and B. Somekh (1988). Department of Trade and Industry Micros in Schools Support 1981–84, an Independent Evaluation. Norwich, CARE, University of East Anglia.

McLuhan, M. (1964). *Understanding Media*. London and New York: Routledge and Kegan Paul.

Menchik, D.A. (2004). "Placing cybereducation in the UK classroom." *British Journal of Sociology of Education* 25(2): 193–213.

Norris, N., R. Davies and C. Beattie (1990). "Evaluating new technology: the case of the Interactive Video in Schools (IVIS) programme." *British Journal of Educational Technology* 20(2): 84–94.

Patton, M.Q. (1986). *Utilization - Focused Evaluation*. Newbury Park, London, New Delhi: Sage Publications.

Pearson, M. and B. Somekh (2004). *Learning Transformation with Technology: A Question of Socio-Cultural Contexts?* Melbourne, Australia: Australian Association for Educational Research.

Ryan, K.E. and L.E. DeStefano, eds. (2000). *Evaluation as a Democratice Process: Promoting Inclusion, Dialogue, and Deliberation*. San Francisco: Jossey-Bass.

Scrimshaw, P. (1997). *Preparing for the Information Age: Synoptic Report of the Education Departments' Superhighways Initiative*. London: Department for Education and Employment.

Somekh, B. (1990). "The evaluation of teaching with computers." *CTISS File (Computers in Teaching Support Service)* **10**: 32–39.

Somekh, B. (2001). "The role of evaluation in ensuring excellence in communications and information technology initiatives." *Education, Communication and Information* **1**(1): 75–101.

Somekh, B. (2004). "Taking the sociological imagination to school: an analysis of the (lack of) impact of ICT on education systems." *Technology, Pedagogy and Education, Special Issue on Researching Educational ICT* **13**(2): 163–179.

Somekh, B. (2007). *Pedagogy and Learning with ICT: Researching the Art of Innovation*. London and New York: Routledge.

Somekh, B., M. Haldane, K. Jones, C. Lewin, S. Steadman, P. Scrimshaw, S. Sing, K. Bird, J. Cummings, B. Downing, T. Harber Stuart, J. Jarvis, D. Mavers and D. Woodrow (2007a). *Evaluation of the Primary Schools White board expansion project*. London: Report to the Department for Education and Skills.

Somekh, B., J. Hall and J. McPake (1999). "Serving multiple stakeholders: Issues arising from a major national evaluation study." *Education and Information Technologies* **4**(2): 1–18.

Somekh, B., C. Lewin, D. Mavers, T. Fisher, C. Harrison, K. Haw, E. Lunzer, A. McFarlane and P. Scrimshaw (2002). *ImpaCT2: Pupils' and Teachers' Perceptions of ICT in the Home, School and Community*. London: Department for Education and Skills.

Somekh, B., C. Lewin, D. Mavers, P. Scrimshaw, A. Haldane, C. Levin and J. Robinson (2003). *Evaluation of the GridClub Educational Service: Final Report to the Department for Education and Skills, March 2003*. Manchester: Manchester Metropolitan University.

Somekh, B., D. Mavers and C. Lewin (2002). *Using ICT to Enhance Home-School Links: An Evaluation of Current Practice in England*. London: Department for Education and Skills.

Somekh, B., J. Underwood, A. Convery, G. Dillon, J. Jarvis, C. Lewin, D. Mavers, D. Saxon, S. Sing, S. Steadman, P. Twining and D. Woodrow (2007b). *Final Report of the Evaluation of the ICT Test Bed Project*. Conventry: Becta.

Stake, R. (1998). "When policy is merely promotion, by what ethics lives an evaluator?" *Studies in Educational Evaluation* **24**(2): 203–212.

Stake, R.E. (2003). *Standards-based and Responsive Evaluation*. Thousand Oaks and London: Sage.

Underwood, J., S. Cavendish, S. Dowling, K. Fogelman and T. Lawson (1994). *Integrated Learning Systems in UK Schools*. Coventry: NCET (National Council for Educational Technology).

Walker, R. (2002). "Case study, case records and multimedia." *Cambridge Journal of Education* **32**(1): 109–127.

Watson, D., ed. (1993). *Impact: The Report of an Evaluation of the Impact of Information Technology on Children's Achievements in Primary and Secondary Schools*. London: King's College, University of London.

Wenger, E. (1998). *Communities of Practice: Learning, Meaning and Identity*. Cambridge UK, New York and Melbourne: Cambridge University Press.

Wildavsky, A. (1993). *Speaking Truth to Power: The Art and Craft of Policy Analysis*. New Brunswick and London: Transaction Publishers.

Wiles, P. (2004). "Policy and sociology." *British Journal of Sociology* **55**(1): 31–34.

Wood, D. (1998). *The UK ILS Evaluations: Final Report*. Coventry: British Educational Communications and Technology Agency.

Chapter 4

Exploring literacy policy-making from the inside out

Gemma Moss and Laura Huxford

Introduction

Drawing on our joint experience both inside and outside of national policy-making processes,[1] we will use this chapter to explore some of the defining characteristics of the education policy-making environment as it is currently constituted in England, and its impact on the content of literacy policy. In particular, we will look at the interactions between research and policy-making communities as they unfold over time and in relation to the policy cycle, using as our focus the contested area of phonics and its place in the National Literacy Strategy (NLS). We hope to draw out some general principles for understanding what currently shapes the relationship between policy and research, the distinctive qualities of these two very different knowledge communities and the ways in which they then work to create, defend, challenge or modify policy. In doing so we will draw on the distinction Gibbons and colleagues make between Mode 1 and Mode 2 knowledge (Gibbons *et al.* 1994).

The chapter begins by describing the recent policy-making environment in which the NLS has emerged and developed. It asks how this policy-making environment has helped shape decisions about the content of the literacy curriculum and the form literacy pedagogy should take. We argue that such an environment works in quite different ways from the environment for academic research and debate, and that a closer understanding of these differences may lead to a more positive relationship between policy-making and research communities. This chapter treats NLS as an organisation and a process of education reform as well as a sequence of policy documents.

Most academic commentary on NLS focuses on evaluating its effectiveness either as policy from a school improvement perspective (Earl *et al.* 2002) or as pedagogy within existing traditions of work on literacy (Fisher *et al.* 2002). In either case much of the emphasis falls on policy implementation in the classroom. By contrast, we want to focus in on what we are calling Tier 2 in the policy-making process, that is to say, those within the policy-making community who are involved in policy design and in steering the policy's ongoing development through adoption to implementation from the vantage point of a devolved government agency. In England, the number of such agencies has proliferated in the last decade, each taking responsibility for different aspects of education policy. So the Office for Standards in Education (OFSTED) holds responsibility for inspection; NLS, now re-grouped alongside the National Numeracy Strategy as part of the Primary National Strategy (PNS), is responsible for implementing literacy policy; whilst Becta oversees the uptake of ICT in schools. We think that the emergence and proliferation of agencies and actors working at this policy level in part accounts for the dynamic quality of the current policy-making environment in England, and indeed is one of its defining characteristics (Moss 2003). From this point of view, we treat NLS as a telling case (Mitchell 1983) which can help illuminate some of the main characteristics of the current policy-making environment in England and its relationship to the academic research community.

The NLS as an example of Tier 2 policy-making

To set this chapter in the context of the policy literature more generally, we will draw out two themes from that literature: ways of thinking about how policy develops over time, and how policy develops through different tiers of actors. In particular we want to contrast two approaches to policy development. The first is a linear, rational model of policy development, where policy emerges at the top of a hierarchical chain, fully fledged as it were, and then travels out and down into the contexts where it will be applied, much in the way an arrow leaves the archer's bow and heads for the target. By contrast the second model treats policy as something which inevitably changes over time as it passes through a range of different contexts, involving different actors who will re-shape it as it goes (Taylor *et al*. 1997). To capture this process, the second model incorporates the concept of the policy cycle, and attempts to name a sequence of stages through which any policy passes. Each sequence will involve different players and provide different possibilities for action and policy adaptation or co-construction (Datnow *et al*. 2002). These have been variously described using Bowe and Ball's concept of the policy trajectory (Bowe *et al*. 1992); Levin's four stage process of origins, adoption, implementation and outcomes (Levin 2001); or Earl *et al*.'s concept of the policy life-cycle (Earl *et al*. 2003).

In adopting the second view, that policy changes and evolves as it passes from one place to another, we want to pay particular attention to what we think is a new space, highly characteristic of policy-making in England under New Labour, that of the devolved agency with a particular remit to continue to develop policy as it is being implemented. This is our Tier 2. We think this leads to a new pattern of policy evolution in which policies are in a continual state of re-making as Tier 2 accepts the remit given to it by Tier 1 (politicians and bureaucrats involved in deciding on which policy to adopt) but then continues to monitor and adapt policy in the light of the interaction with Tier 3 (professionals and practitioners involved in implementation rather than design at local education authority [LEA] and school levels) whilst remaining accountable for any adaptation to Tier 1.

This perspective leads us to distinguish between the different structural roles different players within the policy process adopt, and the point in the evolution of policy at which they become involved. To use Levin's vocabulary, our Tier 1 players may well take the lead in the policy's *origins*, both in naming and prioritising the policy problem, as well as choosing a preferred policy solution. They may well scope the overall size of the policy through rationing resources in ways which will impact on subsequent decision-making, but they then cede day-to-day management of the precise track that policy takes to Tier 2 during the *adoption* and *implementation* phases, whilst continuing to make demands on how the policy develops through monitoring *outcomes* (Levin 2001). This sets up very fast feedback loops within the policy cycle (Menter *et al.* 2005). It is in this context that we will examine the evolution of one substantive policy strand within NLS, that which draws on phonics research.

We have chosen phonics as it is a particularly high-profile aspect of literacy pedagogy which often attracts considerable public attention and has been the focus of public campaigns both here and in the USA. Well known as a method of teaching reading which focuses on the sounds of spoken language and their representation in script, the long-standing campaign to give phonics a larger place in literacy instruction in England has taken new directions as the education policy environment itself has changed. For the purposes of this chapter we will distinguish between phonics as a body of academic research into sound-letter relationships and as an education campaign as we track what happens to this body of knowledge when it transfers into the policy environment.

The NLS in its context of origin

NLS has a particular political history within the policy domain. In many respects its origins lie in the introduction of a standards and accountability regime to the English school system. The legislative impetus for this process came from the Education Reform Act of 1988. This established a National Curriculum which defined both the content of the curriculum and the elements of progression that could be used to determine pupils' standards of achievement, measured through statutory assessment tests. Within four years of the Act, further legislation required schools both to publish their test results, and to be inspected on their performance by a newly constituted schools inspectorate, OFSTED. Taken together, these various elements of educational reform made schools publicly accountable for their pupils' performance in new ways, not least by providing an annual means of judging how well they were doing.

This combination of standards and accountability impacts on the policy agenda precisely because it makes areas of poor performance highly visible and open for public discussion. In England, a new dynamic to this discussion was also set in train as the kind of advice that Her Majesty's Inspectors (HMI) used to provide to government in private increasingly entered the public domain via OFSTED's rather different role. OFSTED's use of its Annual Report both to review the national inspection and performance data and to point up areas of particular difficulty they discovered within it signalled this change. The weakness of literacy teaching as a key policy discourse gained much of its public charge in this light (OFSTED 1996).

It could be argued that the Conservative government, despite having put this system in place, was not particularly anticipating the impact of OFSTED's role on the policy-making agenda (Jones 2003). The pattern of its legislation and the discourse around its actions at the time were mainly predicated on minimising state control and encouraging the fragmentation of a uniform education system through increasing competition between schools (Chitty 2004). The underlying assumption was that using the performance data to demonstrate the failures of state provision would encourage parents with the necessary means to opt out of local education services thus opening up more of the market to private competition (Whitty 2002). Yet as the 1990s gathered pace this kind of policy discourse began to be overtaken by another voicing increasing concern about low standards of pupil performance within the state sector and the need to do more with the system as it stood. OFSTED's public pronouncements on poor literacy attainment and the uncertain quality of much literacy teaching in inner city areas were certainly instrumental in giving this discourse weight (OFSTED 1996). Labour spotted a policy vacuum which could be used to its electoral advantage.

If OFSTED was making much of the running at this juncture in terms of naming a problem that would not go away and bringing it consistently to public attention, then Labour was the political party that acted most decisively to pick that problem up and proffer a comprehensive solution (Literacy Task Force 1997). It did so by building on the Conservative administration's first attempt to deal with the issue. Following the publication of OFSTED's controversial report on *Teaching Reading in 45 Inner London Primary Schools*, the Conservatives hurriedly funded a National Literacy Project (NLP) on a trial basis as a limited system of targeted support for 'failing schools' in the weakest LEAs. In the run-up to the general election in 1997, the Labour Party was able to promise to roll out the NLP to all primary schools and without delay if it was elected. It carried out its promise by instituting the NLS within a year of its election victory.

The NLS and the content of literacy policy

In rough outline, the account above focuses on the political space NLS came to occupy in the education policy arena. It concentrates on the ways in which a standards and accountability regime helped produce literacy as a focus for concern in the arena of education policy-making, and how literacy's emergence as a policy problem was then handled by a variety of players. This background shaped the context in which key decisions were made about the content of literacy policy. The absolute merits of the topic considered on its own did not account for the way in which literacy as a policy issue was taken up, nor fully determine what happened next. To take the discussion forward, we now look at the formation of the policy's content.

In the early stages of policy formation, the government's inspection agency, OFSTED, played a significant part in bringing literacy as a topic into the public domain. It provided some of the key personnel who helped shape the policy content as it developed through the NLP and continued to exert some influence as the policy moved into the organisation of the NLS. In all these respects the policy content emerged within rather than outside of government policy-making circles. This was not inevitable. In fact at the time that the policy was being formed, the government of the day could have chosen a variety of other solutions in order to address poor literacy performance. The intervention programme *Reading Recovery*, whose origins are quite specifically within the academic domain, had a proven record in this country (MacGilchrist 1997) and was already in use in several LEAs. *First Steps*, developed by the Education Department of Western Australia in collaboration with local universities as a method of in-service training and support for literacy teachers, was also making considerable efforts to promote itself in the UK at that time (Hofkins 1995). Indeed, elsewhere governments have shown themselves more inclined to sponsor the buy-in of this kind of package, leaving them in a position to exchange it for another if it does not yield sufficiently impressive results. The buy-in and then replacement of *Success for All* in New York State is one such example. Other governments have handed over responsibility for policy-making to key figures in the academic domain who have then been charged with policy design and implementation (e.g. Luke who took responsibility for literacy policy in Queensland [Luke 2005]; or Shanahan in Chicago [Shanahan 2003]). Neither of these routes was adopted in England.

The fact that the policy content was decided inside policy-making circles is significant. It means that the choice of content is geared to the primary aim of raising standards, not to selecting and developing a particular methodology or resolving conflicts between different methods of instruction as ends in themselves. The emphasis rests firmly on the outcomes that can be achieved by the route taken. For policy-makers in the English context, choosing the route meant in good part returning to the consensus about literacy teaching already represented by the National Curriculum and its specification of what should be taught to children when. If the inspection system suggested that low performance in literacy derived from poor teacher delivery of the content prescribed by the National Curriculum, then the policy intervention focused precisely on tightening up that delivery using a new range of policy tools. Policy-makers were confident that the desired rise in pupil performance would flow from directly addressing issues of teacher consistency and efficiency in this way (Literacy Task Force 1997). The changes in pedagogy heralded in by NLS, such as the greater use of whole class teaching structured around clear objectives, or the introduction of a clearer directional focus in small group teaching, make sense in this light, regardless of their theoretical underpinnings in a range of academic traditions (Beard 1999).

The NLS intensified the existing standards and accountability regime by tightening the relationship between the specification of a given curriculum content and the means to evaluate its delivery. In comparison to the National Curriculum, the *Framework for Teaching* (DfEE 1998) provided a much more detailed outline of what teachers should teach, laid out on a year-by-year and term-by-term basis. At the same time, the internal structure of the curriculum switched from a tripartite division based on language mode – speaking and listening, reading and writing – into one which encompassed different aspects of language structure and literacy pedagogy, described in the Framework as word level, sentence level and text level work. Teachers became more accountable for covering these three aspects of the literacy curriculum in equal depth both through the structure of the literacy hour, which laid down clear expectations of how much time should be given to each one; and through a planning regime which expected teachers to demonstrate in both medium-term and weekly plans how they were delivering on each aspect of the curriculum within each hour and over the year. Information on pupil performance generated year on year at classroom level provided a further means of monitoring progress. From the policy-makers' perspective, the strength of the accountability structures built into the policy in this way looked proportionate to the aim of achieving policy buy-in. In fact those most closely associated with the introduction of the policy initially thought that this was where some of the main political risks would lie. The package of support offered to teachers during the first phase of implementation was very much designed with this in mind (Moss 2004).

The strength of the consensus in policy circles over what should be done ensured that a confident case could be made to the politicians commissioning the policy content about this route's chances of success. Whilst this explains why the policy got taken up so strongly by New Labour at what might still be regarded as a trial period for the initial intervention in the shape of NLP, differences amongst policy-makers over key elements in the policy's content should not be underestimated. Keen differences in the relative weighting to be given to 'word level work', for example, and disputes over the prominence of the place for phonics within literacy policy are well-documented (see the *Times Education Supplement's* coverage of phonics, both in the run up to the introduction of the NLS and more recently). However, within Tier 2 and Tier 1 it is accepted that these kinds of differences will be resolved through the policy process. Once the parameters of the policy have been set, any points of disagreement will be settled through the strength of the arguments that key players inside the policy circle can muster at particular points in the policy cycle and their ability to gain and hold the relevant territory at that time.

Research evidence may indeed be brought into this kind of policy discussion. But considerations of 'what will work' in the context of implementation are also important in shaping the debate. From the perspective of Tier 2 policy-makers this may well mean thinking ahead to what will work in winning teachers over to putting any policy into action as well as what will work in winning support from Tier 1. One of the reasons why policy-makers advocating an even more prominent place for phonics within the NLS lost out in its early stages was that those opposing this solution were able to argue that it was a battle that could not be won at that time with practitioners. Forcing the issue would simply put the potential success of the

Strategy as a whole at risk. Pragmatic considerations count in this kind of context. Within Tier 2 what is tactically and strategically feasible at any one time plays a key part in deciding a course of action. As we shall see below, this is rather different from the reference points used within the academy to determine the state of knowledge within a particular field at any one time.

The NLS and the dynamics of change

The concept of the policy cycle or policy trajectory focuses attention on the way in which policy changes over time as it moves from one context to another. Policy sociologists use this concept to explain the way in which policy 'from above', designed to achieve particular ends, can nevertheless be remade by those on the ground charged with putting it into action. Within policy sociology, this becomes a means of reflecting on the relationship between structure and agency. By contrast, proponents of the school improvement and effectiveness movement use this same evidence of policy change to guide their approach to policy implementation. They may plan for the most effective ways of ensuring policy buy-in in local settings by guarding against unwarranted adaptation ('teacher capture') or alternatively by designing sufficient flexibility into policy to constructively harness local perspectives (Fullan 1993).

The structural characteristics of NLS were in many respects devised with precisely this second literature in mind. The strength of the standards and accountability structures was intended to ensure maximum uptake and resist policy 'drift' or weakening as the Strategy moved into local settings. At the same time, the policy was expected to adapt, but with responsibility for recognising when and how to adapt resting with Tier 2 rather than with Tier 3. From the policy perspective such adaptations were interwoven with the necessary pattern of support offered to teachers in line with the policy's objectives. For the Strategy's chief protagonists were quite clear that unless teachers were positively helped to improve, a standards and accountability regime would only expose not remedy failure (Barber 1996). Indeed, part of the political backing for the Strategy at Tier 1 depended upon the explicit commitment made at Tier 2 to tackling under-performance through offering active and ongoing support to teachers.

This objective explains the NLS' pattern of resourcing, and in particular the continuing spend on NLS as a Tier 2 organisation. Implementing NLS was not just a matter of rolling out the initial swathe of policy documents, it was also about providing an infrastructure of support which could steer the policy's ongoing development and thereby ensure its success. Target-setting played a key part in this process. The target of 80% of 11 year olds reaching Level 4 in statutory attainment tests four years into the policy was announced when the policy was introduced. Such a public target became the main mechanism for keeping teachers, LEAs and the NLS itself focused on the same aim as their performance was monitored year on year. In this way both Tier 3 and Tier 2 become continuously accountable to Tier 1.

In this kind of standards and accountability regime, any gap between the target and actual patterns of achievement, made visible in the annual published results, can be used as a way of analysing and then distributing resources to address particular issues that might be holding up the expected rise in results. Resources can then flow in proportion to the identified need. Externally specifying a given performance target reflects political confidence in the scheme as a whole and acts as a demonstration of the commitment to making such a system work. Internally it works as a trigger for ongoing activity. Of course it also creates political risks if results do not rise as expected.

In practice, this structural characteristic of NLS has meant that problem identification has been much more closely linked to mechanisms for creating policy solutions than was the case before. The flow of information can be managed more speedily and feed quite rapidly into policy action. In this context, the ability of players outside this particular policy loop to shape the policy agenda is considerably reduced. There are other political advantages. The fact that the organisation can continually respond to the available data with a sequence of policy initiatives that are broadly consistent with its overall aims helps its survival (Earl *et al*. 2003). The final moment of judgement on the policy's efficacy can be postponed whilst there is still more work to do.

In many ways, target setting and the associated processes of data monitoring and data analysis have driven the development of NLS. As data on pupil performance and teacher delivery have accrued, policy-makers within Tier 2 have continued to choose between a range of options about where to go next without throwing the viability of the whole scheme into question. The annual planning round has acted as the main point at which to review progress made towards achieving the targets set, and decide on future action. Actions have ranged from targeting particular groups with supplementary curriculum advice or materials (*Grammar for Writing; Early Literacy Support*), reinforcing key messages (Quality First Teaching) or even changing gear (*Excellence and Enjoyment*; Assessment for Learning), depending on the analysis of the problems faced. Any disagreements over which route to take have remained largely internal to Tier 2. They have been resolved within the policy field.

The steady flow of initiatives this process has provided has certainly ensured that the policy did not falter once early gains gave way to a more stubborn plateau in the results. But as results have stayed stubbornly short of the initial target, so answers to the question of how to improve pupil performance have seemed less certain whilst the need to act has intensified. The limits of the available analysis have been tested. In this context, managing the Strategy at Tier 2 has increasingly meant managing where to invest the money to keep going and choosing which avenue to take next, whilst continually seeking support for the new directions chosen both from Tier 3 and Tier 1. The policy space is constantly changing, whilst those in charge have inevitably found themselves steering by events. Literacy research brought into the policy field is recontextualised in line with this dynamic.

Recontextualising phonics inside the policy field

To understand what happens to research as it moves into the policy field, and how research and policy intertwine over the length of the policy cycle we turn now to look at the development of the phonics strand in the Strategy. We explore this from the perspective of policy-makers and researchers. We treat these as distinct communities whose interests and responsibilities are not the same. To analyse their different orientations to the business of knowledge making within their specific institutional settings we draw on the useful distinction Gibbons and colleagues make between what they call Mode 1 and Mode 2 knowledge (Gibbons *et al.* 1994). Their brief summary of the main differences between modes runs like this:

> In Mode 1 problems are set and solved in a context governed by the, largely academic, interests of a specific community. By contrast, Mode 2 knowledge is carried out in a context of application. Mode 1 is disciplinary while Mode 2 is transdisciplinary. Mode 1 is characterised by homogeneity, Mode 2 by heterogeneity. Organisationally, Mode 1 is hierarchical and tends to preserve its form, while Mode 2 is more heterarchical and transient. Each employs a different type of quality control. In comparison with Mode 1, Mode 2 is more socially accountable and reflexive. It includes a wider, more temporary and heterogeneous set of practitioners, collaborating on a problem defined in a specific and localised context.
>
> (Gibbons *et al.* 1994: 3)

We consider that the kind of knowledge making associated with phonics as a sub-discipline of psychology exemplifies Mode 1, whilst the kind of knowledge making that predominates in policy contexts exemplifies Mode 2. We begin by considering the kind of use that the Mode 2 policy context in England has made of Mode 1 knowledge from the phonics field.

Phonics as a field sets out to identify the optimum sequence in which a particular range of literacy skills should be taught. It conceptualises reading as phonological processing in which the sounds of the language have to be retrieved from the letter shapes. Writing is seen as the reverse process. In an orthography such as English, individual sounds within the language (phonemes) are represented by letters or groups of letters (graphemes), in particular combinations. Children have to learn this system. Once they have acquired the necessary knowledge they can then apply it to either decode or encode any stretch of language. Disputes within the field turn on the resources children bring to mastering this task; the pace and sequence in which particular combinations of phoneme/graphemes should be taught; and the kind of phonemic/graphic units that children should ideally deal with, at what stage of the process, whether through segmentation or blending. These issues are reflected in arguments over the kinds of texts that children should be exposed to as they learn.

From the policy-makers' point of view, bringing phonics into the curriculum via the Framework document does not necessitate fully settling these points of contention. The policy arena makes different demands on the research base it incorporates. Whilst it is important that any such research should be broadly defensible in its own terms, it must also be able to gain assent from a wider constituency, including teachers, parents and even the media, as well as accommodate to the general thrust and direction of the policy overall.

The version of phonics which was adopted in the Strategy is consistent with this approach. Many of the elements of progression written into the Framework document reflected the general consensus in the field at the time. Other aspects were inevitably going to be more contentious to those with specialist knowledge in the area, simply because they covered issues which were still matters of debate. For instance, by introducing phonemic segmentation before phonemic blending, and by supporting the use of rhyme as part of the resource that children could bring to bear in developing phonological awareness, the policy content became more closely allied with some strands of research in the field than others. Some of the motivation for co-opting this specific selection from the available research rested with the logic of the policy development as a whole. The initial and subsequent roles given to onset and rime (the distinction between the initial consonant cluster [onset], and the vowel and any consonants that then follow it [rime]) and rhyme within the Strategy demonstrate this.

At the time the Framework document was published, Usha Goswami's and Peter Bryant's (1990) work on phonological skills had suggested that teaching children to attend to onset and rime would help them to read and spell. Although this position was well supported by research, counter arguments were being mounted by others within the field (Hulme *et al.* 1998). From the Strategy's point of view, there were good reasons for incorporating onset and rime into the Framework before these points of contention in the research base had been fully resolved because it solved another policy problem: namely persuading those with a rather different background in early years teaching who eschewed formal teaching methods to nevertheless accept that there was some point and purpose in adopting a systematic and explicit approach to word level work, and that such work could be incorporated into the kind of structured play which such specialists favoured with this age group. Goswami's and Bryant's work was important in this respect as it could be re-read from this competing paradigm as supporting the introduction of work on rhyme with very young children. From the policy perspective, work on rhyme then became a bridgehead to work on phonics.

The policy arena is precisely predicated on working across different paradigmatic allegiances in this way rather than plumping for just one. The decisions taken are tactical and strategic in line with the larger policy purposes. Often this means that policy-makers choose from a selection of potentially relevant research which suit a particular policy purpose most, rather than attempt to resolve once and for all the differences between a range of perspectives. Fitness for purpose matters. But at the same time the pragmatics of policy action have to remain responsive to the legitimacy of the research base on which they draw. The research base changes as old questions are settled and new ones emerge, just as the tactical considerations within the policy arena move on. This ensures a continuing dialogue between research and policy, rather than a single foundational moment from which the rest of any policy can flow.

In one sense, this kind of dialogue between policy and research interests becomes visible in the succession of materials which the Strategy published on phonics in this order: the distance learning materials (DLMs); *Additional literacy support* (ALS); *Progression in phonics* (PIPs) and *Playing with sounds* (PwS). From a policy perspective, each of these has a policy purpose consistent with its place in the policy cycle. Thus the resources on phonics (DLMs) issued in the first phase of NLS were needed to convince all teachers that this kind of word level work was a necessary part of the literacy curriculum, to introduce the relevant subject knowledge required for teaching phonics, and to provide examples of teaching materials that would encourage teachers to integrate this approach into their classroom repertoire. ALS was designed to 'catch-up' those children falling behind in Year 3 (age 8) who might have missed out on phonics input in Foundation Stage and Key Stage 1 (ages 4–7), prior to the introduction of the Strategy, an omission which might dent attainment for this cohort in the target year of 2000. PIPs offered a more structured programme of phonics suitable for whole class use in Foundation Stage and Key Stage 1, and was produced partly in response to early evaluation of the NLS by OFSTED, which reported continuing poor quality phonics teaching. PwS had a more complex policy logic. It balanced a perceived need to continue to strengthen the quality of phonics teaching in the early years with the need to increase the pace at which phonics was taught and to win over a group who was still considered quite resistant to phonics teaching for young children. It was also produced at a point when external pressure on the policy was mounting from a combination of the plateau in the levels of attainment and lobbying by campaign groups with a particular interest in phonics.

These kinds of decisions about what new materials to publish when were reached in the context of the broader policy. The urgency of undertaking these tasks had to be weighed against other possible policy objectives. Whether they happened or not depended upon the consensus within Tier 2 as well as the pressure that could be brought to bear from outside. Pressure from outside, in the case of phonics, included both perceived changes in the legitimacy of the phonics knowledge base incorporated into the Strategy at the outset as well as intense lobbying from parts of the phonics community often conducted via political and media interest groups.

The complex array of factors which have steered the development of the phonics strand within NLS make this a good example of Mode 2 knowledge production in Gibbons *et al.*'s (1994) terms. They argue that in Mode 2 knowledge, 'the conceptualisation, selection and realisation of future options are beset by uncertainties or can only be ascertained experimentally in the course of doing the research' (ibid., p. 66). The way in which such communities gear to the context of application makes this inevitable. Yet importantly Gibbons *et al.* consider that whilst this may make Mode 2 knowledge production more 'error-friendly', such systems of knowledge production are also more likely to apprehend and correct errors because of their more diverse and wide-ranging means of quality control (ibid., pp. 153–4). This is part of their inherent greater flexibility.

Changing policy in line with the changing knowledge base of the phonics community

Although the principles which guide policy action have become the object of study and reflection within both the school improvement and effectiveness movement and policy sociology, the literacy research community often overlooks the policy context as a theoretical object in its own right. With the exception of those already committed to thinking about literacy in its social context, policy is treated as a largely transparent vehicle for the dissemination of the products of research. The questions posed of policy are whether the policy content is right, whether research can demonstrate its efficacy and whether the integrity of the research that policy incorporates has been preserved. The adaptation or appropriation of research within policy contexts according to policy rules may look like illegitimate interference in a proper knowledge domain. Many in the literacy research community continue to knowledge build steering by previous contributions in their own field, and often overlooking the policy domain and its exigencies. This is Mode 1 knowledge in Gibbons *et al.*'s terms (op. cit.).

Hulme *et al.*'s contribution to what they describe as the 'controversy over the role of large versus small phonological units as predictors of children's reading skills' provides a good example of Mode 1 knowledge building (Hulme *et al.* 2002). Although it was produced in the same time frame as the NLS policy cycle, the paper only indirectly engages with policy issues. The research they report was intended to settle whether Goswami's and Bryant's assessment of the salience of children's facility to distinguish between onset and rime should be harnessed to teach reading or not. This matters in the phonics field as it is part of the ongoing debate about the exact sequence of which phonemic/graphic units best facilitate learning to read. They used an experimental research design to demonstrate to their satisfaction that onset-rime awareness acts as a poor predictor of reading skill, but that the reverse is true of phoneme awareness, both in the short and long term. Although their work in some respects undercut support for Goswami's and Bryant's position and therefore, at first sight, the research base which supported the use of rhyme as a resource for word level work within the Strategy, they expressly cautioned against using their findings 'as support for the idea that phonological training for poor readers should focus exclusively on training phoneme-level skills' (ibid., p. 20) and added 'the present findings do not have direct implications for how best to improve children's phonological or reading skills'. Their research may have resolved one set of issues within their domain, but it also opens up another. As a holding position until the precise reasons 'why phoneme-level skills are so closely related to the process of learning to read' (ibid.) have been more thoroughly explored, they in fact advocate maintaining a teaching sequence which moves from large to small units. The narrowness of focus required to knowledge build in the field does not lend itself to more fully developing immediate conclusions for pedagogy or giving a clear steer for where policy should go next.

This kind of knowledge building happens in slow time of a kind the academic community both tolerates and expects. Points of settlement can be overturned, or old controversies revisited as the knowledge base continues to grow. Often this happens through a series of small steps whose relevance for practice may not be immediately straightforward. If policy-makers grow impatient with the slow speed of progress, from a research perspective it remains a methodological necessity.

Working on such relatively long timelines and with a different kind of evidence base, this kind of research is quite distinct from the process of evaluation to which the phonics strand within NLS has become subject as part of policy. In a policy context, the questions of uptake of the existing materials within the Strategy and the basic quality of teacher delivery have been at least as important as the detail of the content (OFSTED 2001). Indeed, the use of the term 'systematic phonics', rather than synthetic or analytic phonics, in most of the policy documentation that advocates more phonics instruction in literacy policy underlines this distinction. By counterpoising systematic phonics with presumably random, erratic or poorly organised phonics, policy-makers can simultaneously restate the importance of what teachers do whilst sidestepping disputes that within the phonics field matter hugely and are still largely unresolved (Ehri 2003; Rose 2005; Torgerson *et al.* 2005).

In fact, from a policy-maker's point of view, these kinds of changes in the research evidence base are relatively easy to accommodate. In the case of NLS, literature reviews have been used to track the emerging consensus within particular fields and on that basis suggest amendments to the policy detail where necessary (Brooks 2003). In relation to phonics, the order in which phoneme/graphemes are introduced within the Strategy has been modified; the pace of delivery has been increased; and the prominence of onset-rime has been adjusted in the sequence of publications put out for teachers.

But this kind of accommodation between domains, in which policy-makers appropriate what they want from one knowledge community into another as and when they see the need is not quite the story of phonics within the Strategy. On the contrary, different groups within the phonics community have increasingly organised tactically and strategically in relation to policy, appropriating and using for their own purposes the triggers for action that exist within the policy cycle. This has made the relations between these two communities much more fraught. We would argue that in part this conflict is shaped by phonics' history as an educational product, in which the research base has crystallised into commercial teaching programmes which can be bought and sold.

Phonics and the market place for policy solutions

Phonics as a knowledge domain places a high premium on tightly specifying an exact sequence in which learners should be inducted into the phoneme/grapheme relations which make up English orthography. As a field it is characterised by intense competition between each such specification. Differences between particular approaches are often heightened by commercial interests as they translate into teaching programmes, each one aiming to be a monopoly supplier. For such programmes are mutually exclusive of each other as well as of other literacy paradigms.

Accepting their role within the Strategy as one part of a broader policy poses those within the phonics field already wedded to particular models of phonics instruction considerable difficulties, not least because in its delineation of word, sentence and text level teaching objectives term by term and year by year the Strategy seems to establish a rival developmental sequence that juxtaposes or even conflates aspects of learning to read which phonics tries to keep apart.

This conflict becomes apparent in the way in which many proponents of a phonics-based pedagogy have consistently objected to the 'searchlights' metaphor which was written into the policy design in its early stages. In the Framework document, the searchlights metaphor acts as a way of articulating an underlying philosophy which makes sense of its curriculum reach. The diagrammatic representation of the searchlights metaphor identifies four different strategies that readers employ in relation to texts: phonic (sounds and spelling); word recognition and graphic knowledge; grammatical knowledge; and knowledge of context. It does not suggest an order in which these strategies should be mobilised nor ascribe their relative values. The accompanying text simply emphasises the importance of phonics as part of the literacy teacher's repertoire. The underlying proposition is that reading (or writing) will be strengthened if children have access to all of these strategies and diminished if they only have access to one:

> Applied to reading, the model aims to maximise 'redundancy' by optimising the range of cueing sources available, enabling the reader to cross-refer and mutually consolidate each. The more searchlights that are switched on, in other words, the less critical it is if one of them fails.
>
> (DfES 2003)

In a policy context this provides a rationale for bringing together into the same space different perspectives on literacy pedagogy which elsewhere might be seen to be in conflict. It also returns practitioners to the curriculum specification of word (phonic and graphic knowledge), sentence (grammatical/syntactic knowledge) and text (context) thus taking them straight back to the policy task of delivering on each of these fronts.

To some in the phonics field such a juxtaposition is an anathema precisely because it appears to confer equal value on a range of different methods for teaching reading rather than cede to phonics the prime place. Mounting an attack on the metaphor becomes a means of arguing against the Strategy as a whole. This is an argument between sellers of policy solutions, in which the buyer (the DfES) is berated for having made the wrong choice. The remedy is a different kind of policy solution. This remains the central point in the campaign by the Reading Reform Foundation (RRF).

The RRF have lobbied consistently for the replacement of the NLS with synthetic phonics teaching programmes. Data monitoring of NLS' efficacy in raising standards becomes ammunition in this campaign. The less convincingly the data appear to demonstrate the efficacy of NLS as a whole, the more convincing the case appears for replacing it with something else. Such lobbying has created political problems for the Strategy. The policy cycle has seen this argument develop both within Tier 2, as old divisions between policy-makers have opened up, and on a wider front as campaigning groups have gained political backing for their stance. In some quarters this has acted as a rallying point for opposition to the Strategy as a whole. In the end, the issue of whether synthetic phonics programmes would be more effective in the early years than the current programme of teaching organised through NLS was discussed by the House of Commons Select Committee on Education. Potential research questions about how the range of skills represented in the searchlights metaphor are most appropriately sequenced and taught had effectively been turned into political questions about the government's literacy policy.

This debate over policy has been fuelled not so much by changes in the knowledge base as by escalating competition between relatively fixed positions over who should control the policy space: those advocating synthetic phonics or those backing NLS. Each side musters the evidence that they can to support their own case and makes use of the opportunities that present themselves at particular points in the policy cycle. Their relative power to influence events depends upon the hearing they receive at Tier 1. In this case, the Secretary of State resolved this conflict by instituting the Rose Review. This took the issue out of the political terrain and reframed it in terms of government procedures. Whether the conflict abates or continues largely depends upon what happens next within the policy cycle as a whole.

Policy and research: co-existence, competition and influence

In the three interlinked narratives of phonics' development over the course of the policy cycle given above, what phonics 'stands for' varies. Its material and discursive realisation depends on the company it keeps. Phonics in the policy context is not the same as phonics within the research community or phonics as the focus for a political campaign. Although in one sense each community sees phonics as important to raising children's attainment in literacy they approach this issue in very different ways.

Outside the Strategy, those mounting a campaign to replace NLS with synthetic phonics focus their attention on who controls the policy space. For this group, sufficient research already exists to demonstrate the absolute merits of their approach and settle the issue of what any literacy policy content should be. The question is not about the adequacy of the evidence base but the political will to put phonics first. Building the political will to align policy with their part of the research field is very much about capturing the attention of those in the best position to influence events. The phonics lobby regards itself as thwarted in this endeavour by the unreasonable intransigence of the policy community which will not listen to the evidence. This analysis brings this community into direct conflict with the policy domain. The knowledge base is relatively settled. Capturing the policy space brings the promise of delivering the chosen goods to teachers in unadulterated form. A sense of certainty and continuity over this drives the campaign. This aligns this community with those who see policy as a delivery vehicle for a given content, rather than as itself an adaptive process.

Outside the Strategy and within the research community, phonics is still developing through knowledge building in slow time. New questions follow from what has gone before. As one issue is resolved so others open up. This work is relatively well insulated from the policy context, and from other literacy paradigms. It is governed by the methodological interests and intent that shape and define the phonics field as a whole. These require the appropriate conditions in which to control the necessary variables to adjudicate between competing knowledge claims. The policy context does not substantially alter the questions that are posed within the field, nor speed up the time it takes to answer them. Development of the knowledge base is ongoing and fuelled by disagreement and debate amongst community members over key issues. The nature of the policy space is largely ignored.

The development of phonics inside the Strategy depends on how Tier 2 players adapt what they do to the context of implementation, as they struggle to make literacy policy work across the various levels. Phonics and its knowledge base must here align themselves with broader considerations. Decisions over how much phonics, where and of what kind are settled as they arise in relation to the pressure points which punctuate and steer the broader reform process. These pressure points can be created internally, through the processes of data monitoring that take place within Tier 2, or externally as more general debate threatens to destabilise the policy space. Adaptations can be tracked through the ways in which phonics crystallises into a series of documents, each of which were designed with particular policy purposes in mind. These policy purposes arise in the context of the policy life cycle and its various twists and turns. This aligns this community with those who understand policy as a mutually adaptive process (Datnow et al. 2002).

The distinction we make between policy and research communities, their interests and responsibilities, in many respects maps onto the distinction Gibbons et al. make between Mode 1 and Mode 2 knowledge (see above). Their characterisation of Mode 2 knowledge fits the policy context well. Where phonics as a research field excludes extraneous information so that it can narrow its focus on tightly framed questions in controlled conditions, policy as a whole is constituted in relation to much broader flows of information. Alongside the phonics strand these also track: how many schools are fully implementing the policy; the continuing gap in performance between schools with similar intakes; which aspects of the literacy curriculum require most support; how well the last range of initiatives have done; and what lessons can be drawn from current progress for the future. The dilemma in this narrative is knowing which one of the various strands within the policy requires most attention at any particular time. This is not a given. Often the data alone cannot resolve these issues. The same evidence can be read differently through the lens of different paradigms. It is hard to see how more research would of itself help resolve these dilemmas when the problems are not couched within a single paradigm's field of reference. For instance, if boys' performance at literacy continues to lag behind girls', is this due to insufficient attention to phonics in the early years, gender stereotypes manifesting themselves in poor behaviour, a sign of continuing poor-quality teaching which girls survive but boys do not, or a product of an over-dominant performance culture which measures the wrong things? The diagnosis of the problem matters at least as much as the efficacy of the proposed solution. Moreover, arriving at apt judgements is further complicated by the relative attention such issues attract in the political domain. The campaign around synthetic phonics demonstrates this point. From a policy-maker's perspective, implementation means managing this level of uncertainty with a sure grip.

Research for policy, research about policy: ways forward?

We began this chapter with a contrast between two different ways of thinking about policy: a linear, rational model where implementation instantiates the policy as it was originally intended; and a rather different view of policy as inevitably contested, co-constructed or remade as it is enacted over time and across a range of different settings. For all their differences, both policy sociology and the school improvement and effectiveness movement recognise the difficulties associated with policy implementation in line with this second view. We have sought to add to this literature by focusing on the dilemmas faced by policy-makers who hold responsibility for the success or failure of a particular policy as it unfolds over time (our Tier 2), and who from this vantage point need continually to make sense of the feedback data they receive across a range of different dimensions and then act. We have found Gibbons *et al.*'s characterisation of Mode 2 knowledge a useful way of recognising the different demands made on this community and the distinctive ways in which they then respond. In our analysis, policy-makers at Tier 2 are not short on Mode 1 knowledge, rather they are struggling with the conditions in which Mode 2 knowledge emerges and which determine its characteristic features.

Debate over the relations between research and policy often assume that what is required is more transparent transfer of goods from one domain into the other. Researchers complain that policy-makers ignore their best advice, whilst policy-makers complain that there is not enough high-quality research that addresses their most pressing questions. In an attempt to bridge the gap between the two, a whole array of brokers have come forth to ferry policy to research and vice versa. By contrast we assume that Mode 1 knowledge will always be transformed as it moves into policy contexts which will test it in new ways. This is not a contrast between theory and practice, or research and application. It is about recognising and understanding the transformative effect that different kinds of conditions in which knowledge is produced have on knowledge itself. If Mode 1 knowledge involves narrowing the scope of enquiry to keep out the background noise and chatter that threatens to fragment or distort the empirical object, then Mode 2 knowledge involves endlessly adapting through attending to the noise of the policy context. One form of knowledge need not replace the other, but they should not be regarded as the same thing. Perhaps research needs to concentrate less on finding new content for policy to convey from one place to another, than on better understanding the opportunities, predicaments and constraints that Mode 2 contexts represent.

References

Barber, M. (1996) *The Learning Game: Arguments for an Education Revolution*. London: Gollancz.

Beard, R. (1999) *National Literacy Strategy: Review of Research and Other Related Evidence*. London: DfES.

Bowe, R., Ball, S.J. and Gold, A. (1992) *Reforming Education and Changing Schools*. London: Routledge.

Brooks, G. (2003) *Sound Sense: The Phonics Element of the National Literacy Strategy*. London: DfES.

Chitty, C. (2004) *Education Policy in Britain*. Basingstoke: Palgrave Macmillan.

Datnow, A., Hubbard, L. and Mehan, H. (2002) *Extending Educational Reform*. London: RoutledgeFalmer.

DfEE (1998) *The National Literacy Strategy: Framework for Teaching*. London: DfEE.

DfES (2003) *Teaching Phonics in the National Literacy Strategy*. London: DfES.

Earl, L., Watson, N. and Katz, S. (2003) *Large Scale Education Reform: Life-cycles and Implications for Sustainability*. London: CfBT. Available at: http://www.cfbt.com/pdf/lifecycles.pdf (Accessed 11 July 2006).

Earl, L., Watson, N., Levin, B., Leithwood, K., Fullan, M., Torrance, N., Jantzi, D., Mascall, B. and Volante, L. (2002) *Watching and Learning 3*. London: OISEUT/ DfES.

Ehri, L. (2003) *Systematic Phonics Instruction: Findings of the National Reading Panel*. London: DfES.

Fisher, R., Brooks, G. and Lewis, M. (2002) *Raising Standards in Literacy*. London: RoutledgeFalmer.

Fullan, M. (1993) *Change Forces: Probing the Depths of Educational Reform*. London: Falmer Press.

Gibbons, M., Limoges, C., Nowotny, H. and Schwartzman, S. (1994) *The New Production of Knowledge: The Dynamics of Science and Research in Contemporary Societies*. London: Sage.

Goswami, U. and Bryant, P. (1990) *Phonological Skills and Learning to Read*. Hove: Lawrence Erlbaum Associates Ltd.

Hofkins, D. (1995) "Huge gains claimed for literacy project." Article in the *TES* 4/6/95.

Hulme, C., Hatcher, P.J., Nation, K., Brown, A., Adams, J. and Stuart, G. (2002) "Phoneme awareness is a better predictor of early reading skill than onset–rime awareness." *Journal of Experimental Child Psychology*, **82**, 2–28.

Hulme, C., Muter, V. and Snowling, M. (1998) "Segmentation does predict early progress in learning to read better than rhyme: A reply to Bryant." *Journal of Experimental Child Psychology*, **71**, 39–44.

Jones, K. (2003) *Education in Britain: 1944 to the Present*. Cambridge: Polity.

Levin, B. (2001) *Reforming Education: From Origins to Outcomes*. London: Routledge.

Literacy Task Force (1997) *A Reading Revolution: How we can Teach Every Child to Read Well. The Preliminary Report of the Literacy Task Force*. London: Institute of Education.

Luke, A. (2005) "Evidence-based state literacy policy: A critical alternative," in N. Bascia, A. Cumming, K. Leithwood and D. Livingstone (eds.), *International Handbook of Educational Policy* (pp. 661–677). Dordrecht: Springer.

MacGilchrist, B. (1997) "Reading and achievement: Some lessons for the future." *Research Papers in Education*, **12**(2), 157–176.

Menter, I., Mahony, P., Hextall, I. and Moss, G. (2005) "New models of policy-making: developing a framework for analysis." Paper given at the European Conference of Educational Research, University College, Dublin, September 7–10.

Mitchell, J.C. (1983) "Case and situation analysis." *Sociological Review*, **31**(2), 187–211.

Mortimore, P. and Goldstein, H. (1996) *The Teaching of Reading in 45 Inner London Primary Schools: A Critical Examination of OFSTED Research*. London: Institute of Education.

Moss, G. (2003) Re-making School Literacy: Policy Networks and Literacy Paradigms, ESRC-Funded research proposal. Unpublished.

Moss, G. (2004) Changing practice: the national literacy strategy and the politics of literacy policy. In *Literacy*, **38**(3), 126–133. Available at: http://m1.ioe.ac.uk/content/bpl/read/2004/00000038/00000003/art00003;jsessionid=302k2dk6wubu2.henrietta.

OFSTED (1996) *The Teaching of Reading in 45 Inner London Primary Schools*. London: OFSTED.

OFSTED (2001) *Teaching of Phonics*. OFSTED. Available at: http://www.ofsted.gov.uk/publications/index.cfm?fuseaction=pubs.summary&id=1251 (Accessed 11 July 2006).

Rose, J. (2005) *Independent Review of the Teaching of Early Reading*. London: DfES.

Shanahan, T. (2003) "Research-based reading instruction: Myths about the National Reading Panel report." *The Reading Teacher,* **56**(7), 646–655.

Taylor, S., Rizvi, F., Lingard, R. and Henry, M. (1997) *Educational Policy and the Politics of Change*. London: Routledge.

Torgesen, C., Brooks, G. and Hall, J. (2006) *A Systematic Review of the Research Literature on the Use of Phonics in the Teaching of Reading and Spelling*. London: DfES.

Whitty, G. (2002) *Making Sense of Education Policy*. London: Paul Chapman.

Chapter 5

Negotiating policy space for teachers' continuing professional development

A view from the higher education institution

Hazel Bryan

Introduction

This chapter takes as its theme the evolution of teachers' continuing professional development (CPD) as a policy concern in England from the early 1970s to 2006. It goes on to discuss the implications of different policy conceptions of CPD for the role of higher education institutions as providers of CPD on the one hand and as creators – in partnership with teachers – of knowledge about teaching and learning on the other. The status, or indeed, possible value, of higher education institutions in relation to CPD is explored from the current trend for professional development capacity-building in schools, and the fact that there are numerous CPD 'providers' – the higher education institution is but one of many options from which schools (and/or individual teachers) select professional development programmes that are in line with their respective ethos, vision and professional development needs.

The author works in a university and has responsibility for the MA Framework within the Faculty of Education. In addition, the author is Programme Director of an MA in Educational Studies and as such is involved in teaching and working with other Programme Directors and tutors in responding within Masters Programmes to Government CPD policy, local authority initiatives, cluster and consortium plans and sometimes working with just one school in terms of professional development interests. Negotiating professional space in this sense involves balancing the requirements and interests of programme participants – including funding partners – with the academic requirements of a Masters degree. Developing and teaching Masters Programmes is a complex cocktail of policy considerations – both local and national, the desire to provide teachers with a professional research – using environment, the opportunity to learn from the wisdom of previous generations of educators whilst at the same time exploring and critiquing current theories and practices from home and abroad. It is about passion and it is about inspiration. It is also framed within a national policy for teachers' CPD.

The genesis of national policy on teachers' CPD in England

CPD is a concept that has its origins in the James Report (DES 1972). This report promoted sabbaticals and refresher courses for practising teachers and as such represents what we might term 'periodic and personal' post-initial professional development with a focus specifically on the individual teacher. This early conception of professional development illuminates the status at the time of initial teacher training – that is, as the main source of teachers' knowledge and skills. It also throws into relief the individual professional identity of the teacher at the time, as one who personally selected professional development opportunities. In a sense also, it hints at a time when the perception of what 'knowledge' teachers needed was perhaps rather more straightforward and easily packaged into an initial teacher training programme. Arguably, a qualified teacher at this time was perceived as 'the complete article', undertaking professional development out of personal interest or curiosity rather than the concept of a professional whose ability to undertake the role depends upon continuing development. There is a distinguished body of knowledge on the subject of teacher professionalism (Friedson 1994; Helsby 1995; Hoyle 1995; Ozga 1995; Lawn 1996; Evans 2001; Whitty 2003) and whilst it is not the purpose of this chapter to explore constructs of teacher professionalism, it is perhaps significant to highlight the fact that for other well-established professions such as law or medicine, CPD has always been central to the role.

An important dimension of the educational context of this time, in terms of professional development opportunities, is the status and work of the Schools Council. Established on 1 October 1964, the Schools Council for Curriculum and Examinations was a joint venture between local education authorities, central government and the teaching unions. Teachers and Unions were particularly influential during the 1970s, their presence and commitment shaping the Council's decision-making (Plascow 1985). The aim of the Schools Council was to fund projects which would improve practice in the classroom (Parsons 1981), and 'widen the choice of curricula and teaching methods available to teachers by delegating the generation of new ideas, methods and materials to projects' (Steadman *et al.* 1978, p. 17). In the early days of the Schools Council this seemed optimistically possible. The Schools Council generated many curriculum projects, promoting innovative pedagogical practice and new resources. Although the establishment of the Schools Council (1964) pre-dated the James Report of 1972, the contribution it made to the educational environment at the time was significant in terms of introducing individual teachers to new pedagogical and subject practices. However, the diffusion of new subject and pedagogical practices was traditionally slow in the British education system and problematic for the Schools Council, as illustrated by Jack Wrigley, Director of the Council's Research Section, 'it's fairly easy to have bright ideas; less easy in the sphere of the School's Council to see that idea to fruition' (Wrigley 1975, p. 106). On the one hand, the Council was committed to the notion of centrally funded projects, whilst the constitution, in contrast, proposed schools as autonomous units, generating their own curriculum projects. These early professional development opportunities were complicated by the relationship between the Schools Council, teachers' centres, initial teacher training institutions and in-service training (Nisbett 1975).

It is perhaps helpful to consider the wider policy context within which teachers were practising at this time. Largely framed by Circular 10/65, The Organisation of Secondary Education, was sent to local education authorities and governing bodies on 12 July 1965. A motion was passed on 21 January 1965 in the House of Commons, stating the 'need to raise educational standards at all levels and regretting the realisation of this objective is impeded by the separation of children into different types of secondary schools' (DES 1965). This circular is extremely significant. In stating this intention, government, for the first time ever, expressed not only an interest in standards, but also a wish to raise them. The Labour government of 1965 clearly saw it as its responsibility to act to raise standards, and the restructuring of the educational system was its response. However, Circular 10/65 did not simply refer to the structure of the secondary system; the design of the curriculum in the junior school, the appropriate deployment of staff to address differentiation, teaching methods, monitoring, assessment and continuity of experience between junior and senior school were all highlighted as crucial. Also highlighted as essential in raising standards were issues around transition, junior and senior school staff cooperation and a 'regular exchange of information and views between junior and senior schools' (DES 1965). This wider policy context set the scene for professional development issues at the time. Indeed, it could be argued that these are the very issues still hotly debated today and it is perhaps salutary that we are still exploring these issues some 40 years later.

The discourse of primary education at this time was shaped by a focus upon the child; it could be said that this was a period when the link between education and society was relatively disregarded, a time when the ultimate professional goal was a child-centred approach to teaching and learning, influenced by Rousseau's philosophy. Certainly, the values of a child-centred approach were promoted and celebrated in the Plowden Report of 1967. Significantly, this was a period when the government was still only partially concerned with education, in a structural sense, and the economic optimism of the times had not led governments to make an explicit link between education and the economy. Although there was a championing of the child in Plowden, not all teachers were enamoured with child-centred approaches to teaching and learning. The Black Papers, published between 1969 and 1977 represented a sustained critique of child-centred approaches to teaching and learning in Britain. The Black Papers had three central themes, namely, the decline in standards in literacy and numeracy, the danger of progressive methods including feminist ideology and the progressive's perceived resistance to industrialisation and third, indiscipline in schools which represented a perceived threat to society (Trowler 2003). Whilst the Black Papers were a vehicle through which standards in reading and writing were critiqued, the ultimate criticism within the

Black Papers was of 'progressive' methods, which, to the contributors, meant that 'children will choose to work when they are ready to do so; that children know what is best for them and should never be corrected' (Pinn 1969, p. 102). High academic standards were presented within the Black Papers as undesirable to the 'progressives': 'Never before have we been in a situation in which our schools of high academic excellence were regarded as undesirable because of their academic excellence' (Pedley 1970, p. 62).

The tensions within education at this time, the beliefs embodied within the Plowden Report which differed so greatly from those expressed within the Black Papers, should be understood within the context of the educational laissez-faire that operated in terms of government control of curriculum design during this period. This embryonic period of teachers' CPD can be understood as a patchwork of providers where individual teachers opted into courses set against political argument around the point and purpose of education.

In 1970 a Conservative government was elected and the Ministry of Education became the Department of Education and Science, led by Secretary of State for Education, Margaret Thatcher. This change from a Ministry for Education to a Department placed education at the heartland of government interest. In 1974 the Centre for Policy Studies was formed, and this, along with the Adam Smith Institute and the Institute of Economic Affairs became an 'influential powerhouse of ideas and policies for 1980s Conservatism, acting as a focus for talented intellectuals of the Right' (Baker 1993, p. 162). Although Conservative governments were developing education policy designed to relocate the locus of financial control away from local education authorities into schools between 1979 and 1997 (Welch and Mahoney 2000), the impulse for these policy initiatives can be located within these 'powerhouses' or think-tanks. Conservative education policy was thus shaped not only in terms of financial control of schools, but also in terms of the curriculum and, significantly for this chapter, the role of the teacher, the status of the higher education institution in initial teacher training, indeed, the value of initial teacher training. This is important with regards to CPD as the status of the teacher was beginning to be explored at the highest political level.

By 1976 a Labour government was back in office. Keen to have a special feature of office, Prime Minister Callaghan welcomed the opportunity to speak on education at Ruskin College, Oxford University in October of 1976. Callaghan raised four points of concern with regard to education, namely the basic teaching of the three Rs; the relevance of the curriculum for older pupils; the examination system; and further education. The Labour Party, according to Chitty (1989) and Jenkins (1995), was keen to address the perceived deterioration in teacher performance: 'while teachers in general still recognise the importance of formal skills, some have allowed performance in them to suffer as a result of the uncritical application of informal methods; and the time is almost certainly ripe for a corrective shift of emphasis' (DES 1976, para. 13). From here on, a different form of accountability can be seen to dominate political discourse and legislation, and the 'accountability movement' is generally agreed to have begun with the

Ruskin speech (Busher and Saran 1995). The 'secret garden' (Eccles 1960) was to be discussed at the highest political level, leading to comprehensivisation, Carlisle's 'A Framework for the School Curriculum' (1979), The Curriculum from 5–16 (HMI 1985) and eventually the Conservative government's radical Education Reform Act (1988). Each of these political moves brought with them professional development opportunities and increasingly, expectations.

The provision of CPD, since the Education Reform Act of 1988 up to 2001 was broadly characterised by two approaches: independent, personally negotiated, largely *ad hoc* development and training programmes to support the implementation of central initiatives which have become increasingly characteristic of the English education system. The Technical and Vocational Education Initiative (TVEI) of the early 1980s is an example of the first centrally funded 'giant programmes' (Williams and Yeomans 1993) initiated by government. Although centrally funded, the initiative was planned through localised projects, with an emphasis upon teamwork, where teachers were provided with the opportunity of taking responsibility for certain areas of curriculum development (Busher and Saran 1995). Key characteristics of the introduction of TVEI were its unprecedented speed and ambitious goals (Trowler 2003), an approach which set the scene for the introduction of the National Literacy and Numeracy Strategies (DfEE 1998). The National Strategies were launched as Secretary of State for Education David Blunkett's highest profile initiative and were presented as the vehicle through which reform in literacy and numeracy standards would be realised. The 'seamless join' (Ball 1999) between the previous Conservative education policies and New Labour is particularly evident in relation to literacy policy. Perceived low standards in literacy had been the explicit concern of government since 1976. Debate concerning whether a return to a traditional model of literacy and classroom practices, and a rejection of progressive models would be desirable had become the source of much political and academic tension.

With these issues constantly debated, the Labour Party, while still in opposition, set up a Literacy Task Force in May 1996. Chaired by Professor Michael Barber the remit was to recommend a 5–10-year programme which would raise literacy standards. In a climate of increasing criticism of literacy standards, the Interim Report, 'A Reading Revolution: how we can teach every child to read well' was published. The report made proposals for a National Literacy Strategy (NLS) which would necessitate an extensive programme of training for teachers and would have implications for Initial Teacher Training and the nature and status of English within the National Curriculum. At the same time the Conservative Party established the National Literacy Project which was underway in schools by January 1997. The National Training Programme for teachers began in the summer term of 1998. Literacy consultants were appointed. From within schools, literacy governors and literacy coordinators were to be appointed. Schools received two-day conferences for head teachers, literacy governors and literacy coordinators. Three professional training days during 1998–1999 were planned and those schools in need of intensive training were offered the opportunity of sending two teachers on a five-day course. Local authority consultants were appointed with the remit to provide five days of support per school. Government allocated £60 m per annum to fund the first three years of the NLS and a further £3,000 per school was provided for new books. Newly elected on a tide of overwhelming support, New Labour continued both Literacy and Numeracy Strategies, which encompassed specified targets, suggested teaching techniques and a model of classroom organisation in the form of a 'Literacy Hour'. These literacy and numeracy policies and the training requirements that accompanied them, arguably positioned teachers, learners and the nature of literacy and numeracy 'knowledge'. Thus, the Literacy and Numeracy Strategies heralded a new era in CPD structure, style and expectation. Literacy consultants, or 'policy drivers' (Bryan 2004), working with teachers through training materials were in a position to have a significant impact upon curriculum change, the role of the teacher in literacy teaching, and to ensure that literacy policy was driven into practice through their work.

National CPD policy today

Something new and rather different happened in 2001. The government launched a national strategy for CPD in England in March of that year: Learning and Teaching: A Strategy for Professional Development (DfEE 2001a). This was accompanied by a Code of Practice (DfEE 2001b) and by substantial funding. The following key principles were presented in the document following a consultation exercise in 2000:

- increase funding to create more time and opportunity for teachers' professional development;
- help teachers so that they can select the development activities that are likely to have the greatest impact on their teaching, and in particular which help them to learn from each other;
- improve provision, including new training for teachers with subject or specialist leadership responsibilities;
- identify and encourage good practice in professional development and spread it more widely to other schools;
- raise the expectations on heads and teachers about professional development; and
- carry out good-quality research and evaluation into professional development opportunities and their impact on teaching and learning so we can build up the evidence of what works.

These principles provided a suggested framework within which CPD should take place. It is important to stress that this was a *suggested* framework; schools were at liberty to select CPD opportunities from within the 'market' – a market consisting of higher education institutions, local authority provision, private sector companies and educational consultants. At present, funding is generated from the 'Standards Fund' and general grants (DfEE 2001) and this goes direct to schools. Whilst schools were encouraged to direct this funding towards professional development in relation to national initiatives, school foci and individual teacher development needs, there was no statutory arrangement here. As such, schools across the country presented a rich mosaic of CPD engagement which has a focus upon perceived localised need.

The 2001 strategy also carried a strong commitment to research and evaluation, and the resulting reports have given us a great deal of worthwhile evidence, summarised in Bolam and Weindling (2006) in their 'Synthesis of research and evaluation projects concerned with capacity-building through teachers' professional development'. The review was commissioned in 2005 by the General Teaching Council and Association of Teachers and Lecturers GTC and ATL, in order to assess and synthesise 20 policy-related studies, and to provide an evidence-based commentary on CPD policy design in a new policy environment (see below).

This report makes it clear that the developments both before and since the 2001 CPD strategy have been influenced by a concern to drive up standards, and a corresponding recognition that the quality of teachers' post-initial development and education is key to this. Bolam and Weindling cite three key policy documents: 'Learning and teaching: A strategy for professional development' (DfEE 2001), the 'TTA's role in the future of continuing professional development' (TTA 2005), and the TTA's response to the letter from the then Secretary of State, Ruth Kelly, setting out its new remit (DfES 2005). In essence, this approach is a policy response to the need for capacity building through CPD, which has arisen from the government's concern with pupil under achievement and a belief that a major part of the solution is to be sought in making teachers' professional development more systematic and systemic. 'Capacity building' has been defined as:

- the closer integration of CPD, performance management and school improvement as key components of effective whole-school policies on teaching and learning.
- a stronger CPD infrastructure in schools.
- schools' increased awareness and use of CPD activities that lead to significant and sustained changes in practice.
- clearer expectations of the skills, knowledge and understanding that teachers should develop over the first five years of their careers.

(DfES 2004)

The national strategy as set out in 2001 had a clear focus upon performance, school improvement, development of a CPD infrastructure and staged 'expectations' in relation to professional development. Whilst these elements present a somewhat externally determined approach to CPD, the strategy also embraced and promoted an organic, developmental entitlement for teachers. This philosophy was broadly supported by Bolam and Weindling's findings (2006):

- involving participants in identifying their needs and planning CPD was more likely to lead to their needs being met and higher ratings of the effect on their practice.
- a supportive ethos in the workplace and support from senior managers were necessary for the implementation of change arising from CPD.
- involvement in CPD increased the likelihood of further participation in CPD, perhaps promoting lifelong learning.
- a supportive culture where teachers were actively encouraged to lead initiatives within the school via processes for sharing ideas such as engagement in research activities; providing feedback through different forms of data (photographic, written, taped); a high degree of trust.
- a high degree of commitment to various forms of action enquiry and action research. It was felt that the training had contributed significantly to the work of the group and the subsequent quality of the developmental activities.

In 2005, the Teacher Training Agency was given an enlarged remit and became the Training Development Agency for Schools (TDAS); in so doing it took over the responsibility from the DfES for the strategic direction and delivery of CPD, in the context of strengthened performance management requirements and the revised Professional Standards Framework, plus a commitment to e-learning options. Therefore, head teachers have a statutory duty to realise a CPD entitlement for teachers, and CPD is now to be understood as continuous teacher learning and enquiry. OFSTED carried out a survey of CPD in 2006: 'The Logical Chain: continuing professional development in effective schools' (OFSTED 2006). This report found:

- Few of the schools evaluated successfully the impact of CPD on the quality of teaching and on pupils' achievement because they did not identify the intended outcomes clearly at the planning stage.
- Arrangements for identifying staff's individual needs were too subjective in about a third of the survey schools. These schools relied too heavily on staff's own perception of their needs and on the effectiveness of individual subject leaders to identify needs accurately.

(OFSTED 2006, p. 4)

The 'New Professionalism'

In her letter of 2005 setting out the new responsibilities of the TTA/TDAS, the then Secretary of State (Ruth Kelly) expressed a wish to establish structured CPD opportunities in line with teachers' career development. The New Professionalism is characterised by a closer association with the TDAS. New Professionalism heralds an era of stratification of CPD, and a wish by government to bring 'coherence' to the mosaic of practices that currently characterise professional development. As such CPD is positioned as a central factor in the reform agenda, the vehicle as it were, through which teachers are re-professionalised. The TDAS' remodelling website (www.remodelling.org/) states that 'the remodelling process is a proven approach that gives you the tools and techniques to meet the new challenges effectively' and will enable schools and partners to:

> identify and agree where change is necessary, facilitate a vision of the future shared across whole-school and stakeholder communities, collaborate internally and externally, with other schools, organisations and agencies, in an effective and productive way, create and implement plans for 'tailored' change in an atmosphere of consensus, embed an inclusive and proactive culture of long-term progress, and improve standards for staff, stakeholders and pupils.

Perceptions and critiques of current national CPD policy

The 2001 CPD strategy stated that 'professional development is above all about developing the extraordinary talent and inspiration, especially the classroom practice, of teachers, by making sure that they have the finest and most up-to-date tools to do their job' (p. 1, Foreword by the Secretary of State) and: 'By "professional development" we mean any activity that increases the skills, knowledge or understanding of teachers, and their effectiveness in schools' (p. 3, Introduction). These statements reflect the government position that teachers should be well equipped to undertake their roles in schools within the wider frame of the 'school effectiveness/school improvement' environment. School effectiveness essentially provides tools to capture practice and measure the attainment of pre-specified targets: sociologically based and quantitative in nature, this approach has a pedigree in American education, where external standards and measurements are applied to schools. It has been suggested that this approach was at odds with the British psyche: 'The intellectual hegemony of British educational research, with its psychologically determined paradigm as to the primacy of the individual, family and community based explanations for children's "educability" created a professional research climate somewhat hostile to school effectiveness work' (Reynolds and Cuttance 1992, p. 2). School improvement, on the other hand, essentially works from within, is fluid in nature rather than seeking to provide a snapshot of a moment in time, working with teachers towards negotiated goals. Methodologically qualitative in nature, school improvement has a focus upon leadership (as distinct from management), vision and the individual school (Stoll and Fink 1996).

The blurring of these two paradigms can arguably be seen in the 2001 CPD strategy, where a focus on centralised initiatives as well as local contextualised initiatives are to be achieved through CPD that focuses upon performance, staged development opportunities, school development needs and personal development needs or interests. As such, the 2001 strategy blends 'system-led' CPD with 'individual-led' CPD. The strategy, however, is very much framed by the wider context of a New Labour drive to develop a teaching profession characterised by a developmental stratum. In the 1998 Green Paper 'Teachers Meeting the Challenge of Change', Prime Minister Blair stated: 'We need a modern professional structure capable of achieving our goals. These are urgent national imperatives. Only by modernization can we equip our nation for the new century' (Foreword, DfEE 1998, p. 4). This extract from the Green Paper illuminates the drive in 1998 for teachers to achieve 'our goals'. This period in education can be characterised as a time when CPD policy initiatives were translated into text in a deeply 'readerly' style (Barthes 1977). Taking the NLS (DfEE 1997) – and the unprecedented volume of training materials that accompanied it into schools – as an example of the emergent robust policy texts of this time, the document presents a suggested subject knowledge and pedagogy in the form of a 'Literacy Hour'. The reification of this particular blend of subject knowledge and pedagogy and the design and suggested delivery of the training materials positioned teachers, learners and the nature of knowledge. The idea of a blank slate upon which to draw the boundaries of education is an appropriate analogy here. Smyth and Shacklock (1998) write of the existence in education from the 1990s of a '"palimpsest", a word of Greek origin which refers to the process of rubbing something smooth and then reinstating it' (Smyth and Shacklock 1998, p. 4).

It could be argued that CPD policy at this time had the potential to create the 'listening practitioner' and the 'listening school' (Gunter 1997), a compliant construct of both personal and corporate identity. Within the CPD policy environment of the late 1990s 'ordinary common sense' and 'what works' were raised up as authentic starting places for education policy (Whitty 2006). This model has been critiqued as a hyper-rationalist-technicist approach, a view which is further critiqued by Radford (2006). In the analytic reductionist view, 'educational situations and events are assumed to comprise of particular elements working together in a linear and causal relationship ... there is an assumption that schools and individual learners can improve along clearly defined trajectories towards specific targets' (Radford 2006, p. 180). Radford opposes this view arguing that schools are complex 'ecologies of practice' (Stronach et al. 2002) that do not lend themselves well to reductionist analysis, and calls for research that looks at 'the nature of information flow, and its constitutive impact on clusters of possible causes and effects' (Radford 2006, p. 177). As the National Literacy and Numeracy Strategies became embedded in school culture, professional development foci adapted to encompass performance management: a definition of CPD from the 2001 strategy suggests that CPD should 'provide opportunity for teachers to engage in individual professional development, not just system led professional development. This, however, should be framed within a "performance management process", and should have a focus upon their own school context'. The GTC at this time offered a statement on their position in relation to CPD:

- Develop a shared understanding in the profession about what professional development and learning should include.
- Influence national policy and funding.

- Raise teachers' expectations both on entry to the profession and of professional learning communities.
- Enable teachers to reflect on how they can and do contribute to the profession, collective knowledge about teaching and learning.
- Provide the basis for widening opportunities for accreditation and recruitment.
- Provide support for school leaders in making time and support available.

(GTC 2002)

These layers of professional development present a broader concept of the potential and purpose of CPD, one where teachers have agency and are viewed as players in the creation of knowledge in relation to teaching and learning (as opposed to the earlier position where they were positioned as in need of specific training). There are, of course, alternative perspectives in relation to the processes and indeed, purpose, of CPD:

> It is the process by which, alone and with others, teachers review, renew and extend their commitment as change agents to the moral purposes of teaching; and by which they acquire and develop critically the knowledge, skills and emotional intelligence essential to good professional thinking, planning and practice with children, young people and colleagues through each phase of their teaching lives.

(Day 1999)

This definition (which also appears in Bolam and Weindling's 2006 report) introduces the concept of the moral dimension to teaching and learning. Arguably, this dimension empowers teachers. Carr (2003) warns that teachers are in danger of becoming mere 'operatives of a technology of pedagogy' in the face of centralised initiatives and that engagement with one's values is central to the undertaking of teaching and learning, 'those engaged in educational activities are committed to some elaborate if not explicit set of beliefs about what they are doing' (Carr 1998, p. 80). The call for shared values at the heart of the policy-making in the education system is echoed by Alexander (2001). He argued that the 'centrally and ruthlessly policed' education system still lacked clarity in terms of a vision or clear goals, 'and this is reflected in the eclectic mix or morass of values in the government's National Curriculum for the year 2000' (Alexander 2001, p. 532).

Another dimension to CPD is presented in Extended Schools and the DfES Five Year Strategy for Children and Learners (DfES 2004) which expressed, in the Executive Summary, 'a major commitment to staff development with high quality support and training to improve care and teaching'. This statement expresses the shift in policy from a purely teaching and learning focus to a multi-agency concept of teacher professionalism, where the teacher works as part of a team in the extended school. Within the context of Extended Schools and the panoramic reform agenda of Every Child Matters, the conception of teachers' work is likely

to be challenged. The GTC, in response to Every Child Matters, whilst supporting the aim of a 'seamless universal service to all children' in multi-disciplinary
teams, states that 'the teaching profession must retain its sharp focus on educational attainment within a multi-agency framework' (DfES 2003, p. 3). Within
this evolving environment, professional practices and professional cultures are
likely to meet. The emerging CPD policy agenda has emphasis upon the New
Professionalism (determined by workforce remodelling) and the 'New Relationship
with Schools', the TTA (2005) initiative to 'bring coherence to the Standards used
throughout the school workforce' (TTA 2005, para. 3.1).

The future: alternative ways
of conceptualising CPD?

It has been argued that the efforts of past governments have 'confused rather than
enhanced the underpinning rationale for the CPD of teachers' (Patrick *et al.* 2003,
p. 237). Patrick *et al.* question whether CPD is heading for a functionalist training model, or rather, they ask, 'do we facilitate critical reflection and enquiry with
the aim of encouraging pedagogical excellence?' (p. 238). The authors are concerned that CPD will become centrally controlled and defined only in terms of
'driving up standards' and workforce remodelling, that is, as a tool for undertaking government initiatives. This concern is at the heart of their article where they
ask in what way can the purposes of CPD be understood: 'is CPD to enhance professional practice or is it to enhance performativity?' (2005, p. 239). The authors
argue that this confusion at the heart of CPD results in the 'dual ambiguity' of
'autonomy' versus 'performativity'. Central to this concern is Elliott's warning
that a national CPD strategy has the potential to establish an epistemic sover-
eignty to legitimise government's intervention policies to drive up standards'
(Elliott 1999, p. 382). This dual ambiguity in relation to teachers and to CPD has
been a feature of Labour and Conservative governments, where Conservative
governments have combined state control with market forces to position teachers.
New Labour, on the other hand, has 'increased state regulation while seeking to
"modernise" the profession and incorporate it into its own project through a new
deal for teachers based on managerialist premises and performance-related pay'
(Whitty 2002, p. 76).

A central and lasting feature of CPD policy initiatives is the way in which
teachers are positioned in an inward-looking sense in direct relation to learners
and their school culture and in an outward-looking sense in relation to external
measurements. It has been argued that the arrival of the 'market' in education as
a result of the Education Reform Act (1988) oversaw the demise of the 'modern
teacher' and heralded the arrival of the 'post-modern teacher' (Lawn 1996). This
redesignated teacher has a central focus to their work, that of 'output as the key
evaluatory rule of education' (Lawn 1996, p. 112).

Lingard (2002) calls for an entirely new dimension to the construct of teacher
professionality. He quotes Luke and Hogan (2006) in a call for 'the revisioning of

a transcultural and cosmopolitan teacher' (p. 135) in a move towards the 'deparochialisation' of education (Appadurai 2001). That is, to re-place the locus of influence from the northern hemisphere in an effort to view teachers as global citizens. This would involve a construct of professional identity that embraces global knowledges, global pedagogies and is, in essence, outward-looking. There is implication here for pan-European qualifications as set out in the Bologna Declaration of 1999, and implications for outward-looking programmes that have not just national but international currency, procedures of mutual recognition and an in-built assumption that part of teacher professional development might be in another country and at the very least, informed by practice in other countries. The Bologna Declaration, convened in 1999, was signed by representatives of 29 EU member states. It declares that by 2010 there will be a system of comparative degrees in order to ensure student mobility through the transferability of their achievements and that the European dimension will be promoted through curricula, inter-institutional cooperation and mobility schemes for students and teachers in HEIs.

Negotiating the future CPD space: the role of HEIs and resisting 'plasticity'

In the recent government policy documents relating to CPD, it is arguable that any strategic contribution from HEIs is intended to be minimal. Some would say that this has been the case for some time: 'There is hardly a whisper in "Teachers: Meeting the Challenge of Change" about the role of higher education' (Pring 1999, p. 18). This section of the chapter explores the current CPD arena from the perspective of the HEI in terms of infrastructures, structures including partnerships, expertise, possibilities of research and dissemination and evaluation and consultancy. Whilst heeding the warning that 'some educational institutions will become whatever seems necessary to become in order to flourish in the market. The heart of the educational project is gouged out and left empty. Authenticity is replaced by plasticity' (Ball 2001, p. 149), this section of the chapter represents an alternative way of conceptualising the university in relation to CPD. For the purposes of this writing, HEIs will be referred to as 'the University'.

Infrastructure

The University is likely to be physically located within easy reach for local schools and as such provides an accessible focal point. The University will be designed to offer a range of teaching and learning opportunities relevant to teachers' professional development, from large lecture theatres to smaller teaching rooms. Libraries in the University are likely to be cutting edge learning resource centres, with virtual learning places and spaces, journals and books that provide a professional context in which to consider and plan CPD. As such, the physical architecture provides places and spaces for teachers as learners. CPD is likely to be effective when learning takes place in situ (i.e. the school) but enhanced and professionalised by the support offered by the university in the form of structures and expertise.

Structures

CPD programmes within the University are likely to range from short courses through M-level opportunities to doctoral work. The structures underpinning CPD 'delivery' patterns are likely to have been carefully designed to meet the changing pattern of teacher needs. As such, remote twilight sessions that individuals attend independent of their schools are complimented by, for example, weekend or vacation study, or Masters programmes that may have been negotiated and tailor made for a particular school. Alternatively, it could be that the University has worked over a period of time to develop a Masters programme with a cluster or consortium. Both of these models contain a blend of system-led and individual-led CPD, as schools and the individual teacher are stakeholders in the venture. In such cases, teachers and schools are required to spend time in discussion with the University to develop a programme that meets all needs. Inevitably this involves compromise by all taking part, but this process enhances the professional development experience as it involves much discussion, debate and often heated argument about what is really important to all concerned. This early stage of CPD Masters development can be drawn upon to inform the early orientation stages of the programme. CPD programmes within the University are likely to have been developed with the local authority or borough, meeting the specific needs of the community and in response to specific localised initiatives. Validation documents for programmes will have been designed in all probability to facilitate flexibility in participant interests, requirements or needs and indeed, to provide opportunity for professionals from a range of backgrounds to work together. Structures are also likely to have been put in place to enhance retention and motivation. Examples of these are conferences that bring together a range of professionals in the 'big conference experience', smaller, more intimate home groups that provide a sense of membership of a group that works together over an extended period of time, varying the session locations from participants' schools to the University itself and allowing participants to determine the architecture of their CPD experiences.

Expertise

By its very nature the University will be in a position to provide expertise in terms of both subject knowledge and pedagogy from national and international perspectives. The international dimension is increasingly important, and programmes are likely to have been designed to build international perspectives into their programmes, as well as, in some cases, the physical possibility of travel to learn. The University is in a powerful position to enhance the European or international portfolio of experience of the teacher, either as an individual or indeed, as a system-led, local authority initiative. Part of the University expertise is likely to be in relation to educational consultancy and evaluation work, with a view to school improvement issues. Alternatively, the University could provide collaborative research and dissemination opportunities for individual teachers, individual schools, clusters or local authorities.

Final thoughts

Policy in relation to teachers' professional development has been seen to be an integral part of the current reform agenda and the national strategy for CPD outlines development foci. Extended Schools and the DfES Five Year Strategy for Children and Learners (DfES 2004) promise 'a major commitment to staff development with high-quality support and training to improve assessment, care and teaching' and as such, reform is clearly articulated in these policy statements. In the Green Paper 'Teachers Meeting the Challenge of Change' (DfES 1998) Prime Minister Blair stated that 'We need a modern professional structure capable of achieving our goals. These are urgent national imperatives. Only by modernisation can we equip our nation for the new century' (DfES 1998, p. 4). The Green Paper 'Every Child Matters' also outlines training and development needs for teachers in relation to extended schools and the possibilities of new working practices. These overarching reforms represent panoramic change, cutting across Key Stages and subject areas. They are at the heart of what it is to be a teacher and what it is to be a professional. From Secretary of State Estelle Morris referring to teachers' 'move towards earned autonomy' (DfES 2001, p. 6) to Secretary of State Charles Clarke stating 'we will never apologise for the directive action we took, for example, on literacy and numeracy in 1997 – it put right a national scandal of low aspiration and poor performance' (DfES 2004, Foreword), the language of policy documents has been at times confrontational and as a consequence 'repositions teachers within the educational domain' (Menter *et al*. 2004, p. 196).

Within the context of Every Child Matters and extended schools, the conception of teachers' work is likely to be challenged in a different way. The GTC, in response to Every Child Matters, whilst supporting the aim of a 'seamless universal service to all children' in multi-disciplinary teams stated that 'the teaching profession must retain its sharp focus on educational attainment within a multi-agency framework' (DfES 2003: 3). Within this evolving environment, professional practices and professional cultures are likely to meet. The terrain of professionalism (Hoyle 1995; Englund 1996; McCulloch *et al*. 2000; Whitty 2003), professionalisation (Freidson 1994; Helsby 1995; Ozga 1995; Hargreaves and Goodson 1996; Lawn 1996; Carr 2000) and professionality (Evans 2001; Whitty 2003) has been well researched over decades. However, the current panoramic reform agenda will necessitate an increased multi-disciplinary approach to teachers' work and as such has the potential to alter professional culture.

This is a complex environment within which teachers practise and make (or have made for them) professional development choices. There is a powerful agenda from central government, strong influences from local authorities, clusters, consortia and individual schools and a powerful CPD model presented by the GTC that all impact upon the professional development choices a teacher makes. In addition to these external forces, teachers have their own professional interests (Carr 1998). It is this interplay between external policy forces, teachers' own ideas of professional direction and the role of the HEI that is at the heart of this chapter, a borderland of policy texts, where professional identity is co-constructed and often contested.

References

Alexander, R. (2001) *Citizenship Schools*. London: Campaign for Learning.

Appadurai, A. (2001) *Modernity at Large; Cultural Dimensions of Globalisation*. Minneapolis: University of Minnesota Press.

Baker, K. (1993) *The Turbulent Years*. London: Faber and Faber.

Ball, S.J. (1999) "Labour, learning and the economy: a policy sociology perspective." *Cambridge Journal of Education,* **29**(2), 195–207.

Ball, S.J. (2001) "Performativities and Fabrications in the Education Economy." In S.J. Ball (ed.), (2004). *The Routledge Falmer Reader in Sociology of Education*. London: RoutledgeFalmer.

Barthes, R. (1977) *Image Music Text*. London: Fontana.

Bolam, R. and Weindling, D. (2006) *Synthesis of Recent Policy-related Research and Evaluation Projects Concerned with Teachers' Professional Development. Report to the General Teaching Council for England*. www.gtce.org.uk.

Bryan, H. (2004) "Constructs of teacher professionalism within a changing literacy landscape." *Literacy*, **38**(3), 141–148.

Busher, H. and Saran, R. (eds.) (1995) *Managing Teachers as Professionals in Schools*. London: Kogan Page.

Carr, D. (2000) *Professionalism and Ethics in Teaching*. London: Routledge.

Carr, D. (2003) *Making Sense of Education: an Introduction to the Philosophy and Theory of Education and Teaching*. London: Routledge.

Carr, W. (1998) *For Education: Towards Critical Education Enquiry*. Buckingham: Open University Press.

Chitty, C. (1989) *Towards a New Education System: the Victory of the New Right?* Lewes: The Falmer Press.

Day, C. (1999) *Synthesis of Research Evaluation Projects Concerned with Capacity Building Through Teachers' Professional Development*. London: GTC.

Department for Education and Employment (DfEE) (1997) *The Implementation of the National Literacy Strategy*. London: DfEE.

Department for Education and Employment (DfEE) (1998) *Teachers Meeting the Challenge of Change*. London: DfEE.

Department for Education and Employment (DfEE) (2001) *Learning and Teaching: a Strategy for Professional Development*. London: DfEE.

Department for Education and Employment (DfEE) (2001a) *Learning and Teaching: a Strategy for Professional Development*. London: DfEE.

Department for Education and Employment (DfEE) (2001b) *Learning and Teaching: a Strategy for Professional Development: Code of Practice.* London: DfEE.

Department of Education and Science (DES) (1965) *Circular 10/65.* London: HMSO.

Department of Education and Science (DES) (1972) *The James Report.* London: HMSO.

Department of Education and Science (DES) (1976) *The Yellow Book.* London: HMSO.

Department of Education and Science (DfES) (2001) *Learning and Teaching: a Strategy for Professional Development.* London: DfEE.

Department for Education and Science (DfES) (2003) *Consultation on the Green Paper: Every Child Matters. The Response of the General Teaching Council for England.* London: DfES.

Department for Education and Sciences (DfES) (2005) *Response to the TTA from the Rt Honourable Ruth Kelly, MP, Secretary of State (March).* London: DfES.

Department for Education and Skills (DfES) (2004) *Five Year Strategy for Children and Learners.* London: DfES.

Department for Education and Skills (DfES) (2004) *Five Year Strategy for Children and Learners.* London: TSO.

Eccles, D. (1960) *Debating the Crowther Report*, Speech delivered in the House of Commons. *Hansard*, 1960.

Elliott, J. (1999) Global and local dimensions of reforms of teacher education in Teacher Education Reforms in an Age of Globalization. Special Issue of *Teaching and Teacher Education*, p. 382.

Englund, T. (1996) "Are professional teachers a good thing?" In I.F. Goodson and A. Hargreaves (eds.), *Teachers' Professional Lives*. London: The Falmer Press.

Evans, L. (2001) *Developing Teachers: is there a New Professionalism?* Paper presented at the British Educational Research Conference, University of Leeds, 2001.

Freidson, E. (1994) *Professionalism: the Third Logic.* Cambridge: Polity Press in association with Blackwell Publishers Ltd.

General Teaching Council (GTC) (2002) *Teachers' Professional Learning Framework.* London: GTC.

Gunter, H. (1997) *Re-Thinking Education – The Consequences of Jurassic Management.* London: Cassell.

Hargreaves, A. and Goodson, I.F. (eds.) (1996) *Teachers' Professional Lives.* London: The Falmer Press.

Helsby, G. (1995) "Teachers' constructions of professionalism in England in the 1990s." *Journal of Education for Teaching*, **21**(3), 317–332.

Hoyle, E. (1995) "Changing conceptions of a profession." In H. Busher and R. Saran (eds.), *Managing Teachers as Professionals in Schools*. London: Kogan Page.

Jenkins, S. (1995) *Accountable to None.* London: Penguin Books.

Lawn, M. (1996) *Modern Times? Work, Professionalism and Citizenship in Teaching.* London: The Falmer Press.

Lingard, B. (2002) *Pedagogies of Indifference: Research, Policy and Practice.* British Education Research Association Keynote Address, 2006.

Luke, A. and Hogan, D. (2006) "Redesigning what counts as evidence in educational policy: the Singapore model." In J. Ozga, T. Seddon and T. Popkewitz (eds.), *Education Research and Policy Steering the Knowledge-based Economy.* London: Routledge, pp.170–184.

McCulloch, G., Helsby, G. and Knight, P. (2000) *The Politics of Professionalism.* London: Continuum.

Menter, I., Mahony, P. and Hextall, I. (2004) Ne'er the twain shall meet: modernising the teaching profession in Scotland and England. *Journal of Education Policy,* **19**(2), 195–214.

Nisbett, J. (1975) "The schools council: processes and prospects." In R. Bell and W. Prescott (eds.), *The Schools Council: a Second Look.* London: Ward Lock Educational.

Office for Standards in Education (OfSTED) (2006) *The Logical Chain.* London: HMSO.

Ozga, J. (1995) "Deskilling a profession: professionalism, deprofessionalism and the new managerialism." In H. Busher and R. Saran (eds.), *Managing Teachers as Professionals in Schools.* London: Kogan Page.

Parsons, C. (1981) *The Schools Council: a Case Study in Curriculum Change.* Doctoral Thesis, University of Leeds.

Patrick, F., Foorde, C. and McPhee, A. (2003) Challenging the 'New Professionalism': from managerialism to pedagogy? *Journal of In-Service Education,* **29**(2), 237–253.

Pedley, R.R. (1970) "The Destructive Element – has a trend been reversed?" In C.B. Cox and A.E. Dyson (eds.), *Black Paper Three: Goodbye Mr. Short.* London: The Black Papers.

Pinn, D.M. (1969) "What Kind of Primary School?" In C.B. Cox and A.E. Dyson (eds.), *Black Paper Two: the Crisis in Education.* London: The Black Papers.

Plascow, M. (ed.) (1985) *Life and Death of the Schools Council.* Lewes: The Falmer Press.

Pring, R. (1999) "Who should teach how to teach?" *Times Higher Education Supplement,* 25 June, 18.

Radford, M. (2006) Researching classrooms: complexity and chaos. *British Educational Policy,* **32**(2), 177–190.

Reynolds, D. and Cuttance, P. (1992) *School Effectiveness: Resarch, Policy and Practice.* London: Cassell, p. 2.

Smyth, J. and Shacklock, G. (1998) *Re-Making Teaching.* London: Routledge.

Steadman, S.D., Parsons, C. and Salter, B.G. (1978) *Impact and Take-up Project: a First Interim Report to the Programme Committee of the Schools Council.* London: Schools Council.

Stoll, I. and Fink, D. (1996) *Changing Our Schools: Linking School Effectiveness and School Improvement.* Buckingham: Open University Press.

Stronach, I., Corbin, B., McNamara, O., Stark, S. and Warne, T. (2002) Towards an uncertain politics of professionalism: teacher and nurse identities in flux. *Journal of Education Policy,* **17**(1), 109–138.

Trowler, P. (2003) *Education Policy.* London: Routledge.

TTA (2000) *The TTA's Role in the Future of Continuing Professional Development: Response to the Secretary of State.* London: TTA.

Welch, G. and Mahoney, P. (2000) "The teaching profession." In J. Docking (ed.), *New Labour's Policies for Schools.* London: David Fulton Publishers.

Whitty, G. (2002) *Making Sense of Education Policy.* London: Paul Chapman Publishing.

Whitty, G. (2003) *Making Sense of Education Policy.* London: Paul Chapman Publishing.

Whitty, G. (2006) Education(al) research and education policy making: is conflict, inevitable? *British Educational Research Journal,* **32**(2), 159–176.

Williams, R. and Yeomans, D. (1993) The fate of the technical and vocational education initiative in a pilot school: a longitudinal case study. *British Educational Research Journal,* **19**(4), 421–434.

Wrigley, J. (1975) "Confessions of a curriculum man". In M. Plascow (ed.), *The Life and Death of the Schools Council.* Lewes: Falmer.

Chapter 6

Learning from the work of the National Educational Research Forum

Andrew Morris

Introduction

The focus of this chapter is particularly on ways of improving connectivity between the three domains of policy, practice and research. This theme seems to me to be one of the most fundamental for education. Educational reform initiatives are held back, notwithstanding good intentions and expert knowledge, when policy, practice and research are at odds with one another. My belief is that connecting these three domains in live situations provides a sound basis for significant advances in education.

The heart of this chapter is a discussion of lessons to be drawn from the work of the National Educational Research Forum (NERF) in addressing this issue. Before embarking on this, however, a little biographical background will help to clarify my particular perspective. With a background in teaching and management, my starting point is the need for sound knowledge as a basis for effective professional practice.

When I began teaching in the late 1970s I felt a sense of privilege on entering one of the truly great professions, but at the same time I felt daunted by the extraordinary level of responsibility I was accepting in relation to people's lives and livelihoods. As it turned out, I found myself able to cope, largely because of the feedback students provided and the on-the-spot advice colleagues gave. From this I was able to pick up a sense of what was going down well and what was not, what mattered for learning and what mattered for examinations. I became aware of the artfulness of teaching and relished learning about it. I also began to sense some kind of method in the design of the overall process, when I first became a manager. But throughout, what I found startlingly missing was any sense of the 'science' of what I was supposed to be doing. I had anticipated being exposed gradually to the evidence upon which various approaches were based – perhaps some comparative analysis of ways of putting across my subject material or of giving feedback to students. But, after the brief period of initial training, I found very little of this occurring in practice, at least in the places I worked in that period (mostly in the post-16 further education sector). In retrospect I suppose I gradually adapted to the prevailing tradition of professional development: follow local custom, try things out raw, pick up tips from friendly colleagues.

To break out of this reliance on parochial and untheorised notions I resorted to organising development projects, trying out more systematic approaches to improve immediate, specific situations. Local projects, through which teachers (and others) could study what was happening and methodically develop better materials and methods, seemed to mark a way forward. Ultimately, however, this experience of development work brought me back again to a version of the fundamental problem I had sensed as a beginning teacher: where is the evidence upon which development should be based? I began to sense that a body of systematised research knowledge might exist somewhere but that I, by personal misfortune, had failed to connect with. I later discovered that this wasn't just a matter of personal experience, but also the common condition. An active world of educational research did indeed exist, but it seemed to be a parallel world, with which my world of practice had little connection.

Ultimately, by specialising in the management of research and development, I came to realise the procedures and resources for supporting research did not encourage a focus on key issues for the teacher or the interpretation of results for use by teachers. A systematic, collaborative approach to acquiring and utilising research evidence on the specifics of teaching was missing. However, during the 1990s, a number of publications, conferences and discussions began to suggest that interest in the role of research in providing an evidence base for decision-making in practice and policy was growing. A national report, commissioned in 1998 by Department for Education and Skills (DfES) into the state of educational research (Hillage *et al.* 1998) provided a critical and overarching account of the very problems that I had found myself encountering in my own situation. The report, even though restricted to school education, described a highly fragmented system. It recommended a series of measures to improve the linkage between research, practice and policy. The DfES, which had commissioned the report, took action on several, though not all, of them. It set up and provided core funding for research centres to focus on key policy-related issues, an evidence centre for policy and practice to develop methods and infrastructures for systematically synthesising research findings (the EPPI centre at the University of London Institute of Education) and a NERF to bring different stakeholders together to oversee the development of a coherent strategy for educational research.

At about the same time it became clear that similar ideas were developing in other public services, including healthcare, the criminal justice system and social care (Morris 2005) and that initiatives were emerging in other countries of the world – for example through conferences organised by OECD (OECD 2005) and publications from the National Academies in Washington (see for example National Research Council 2002).

It was my privilege to be able to work with one of these initiatives in England: the NERF, from 2003 to 2006. This role involved focusing on the interactions of research, policy and practice in an environment where these were considerably estranged from each other. In the following sections I consider some general aspects of these interactions and move on to the NERF experience.

Policy, practice and research

The three domains

Although much debate today focuses on the ways in which policy, practice and research interact with one another, it is instructive to remind ourselves that these three domains evolved quite separately and that the communities differ markedly from one another. The researcher, pursuing matters of concern or interest in her or his discipline, inhabits a quite different world from that of the teacher, coping with the daily demands of the classroom or the civil servant developing policy for political leaders. The purposes, motives and talents of each naturally differ. Despite this, each finds themselves acting today in a highly interdependent system in which teacher action is constrained by government policy and this in turn responds to popular perceptions of the evidence on a given issue. It is likely that professionals in each of these worlds may have little experience of interacting at a personal level with one another. An unfortunate consequence of this is that stereotypical images of each community can develop and members of any one community are tempted to blame any failure in the system as a whole on members of the others.

Research, for example, is perceived by many practitioners as something remote from their daily lives and irrelevant to their concerns. Although this perception may sometimes be borne out by personal experience, it is an increasingly outmoded view. In recent years, new centres and programmes have developed focusing on the concerns of practitioners and policy-makers, such as the *National R&D Centre for Adult Literacy and Numeracy* and the ESRC *Teaching and Learning Research Programme*. At the same time, new methods are being developed to communicate research findings to teachers such as the *Teacher Training Resource Bank* (TTRB 2006) and *The Research in Practice* website (TRIPS 2006). In the future it is possible that practitioner and policy-making bodies might see even greater need for the outputs of research and begin to raise the demand for it.

On the other hand policy development may be viewed cynically by some researchers and practitioners as having little regard for evidence. Many perceive it as driven by political or personal ambition, evidence being picked out selectively to suit particular purposes. Policy-making may be thought of as a transient affair where history is quickly forgotten and priorities moulded to suit the preferences and personalities of the present. The problem with this view is that it fails to allow for the inescapable features of policy-making resulting from the variability of popular opinion. Without adaptability on the part of policy-makers it is possible that on some key issues no direction at all would emerge from the political tumult. The research and practitioner communities have to find ways of coping with the inherent limitations of any policy-making community – its pace, its forgetting and its compromises. Without such accommodation, systematically acquired evidence cannot find its way into policy formation.

Finally, the practice community. Although frequently lauded for their devotion and ingenuity, teachers are sometimes caricatured by policy-makers as subverting the policy 'implementation' process and by researchers as ignoring the messages of research. The practitioner, however, surrounded by pressures of the immediate kind, from students, parents and employers, has limited room for picking up external messages of any kind. Professional development services that support the teacher in handling new information, including research evidence, are increasingly needed.

Their interdependence

In the light of these differences in responsibilities, accountabilities and perceptions, it is not difficult to see how primary objectives vary across the domains. For policy-makers, strategic decision-making and accountability to the electorate is paramount, in the light of unfolding events; for practitioners, the immediate and long-term needs of individual learners dominate; for researchers the creation and, in some circumstances, accumulation of empirical knowledge and theoretical understanding are the raisons d'être. What is less obvious, however, is to understand the ways in which any of these responsibilities and their accompanying traditions bear particularly on any of the others. Each has evolved independently and the people working in each of them have acquired their values, cultures, expertise and roles accordingly. In recent decades however, it is becoming increasingly clear just how interdependent the three domains are. The development of practice is increasingly happening within policy frameworks and the research community is asked to address practical questions posed by policy-makers and practitioners.

In the long run this growing interdependence could prove valuable in the improvement of educational practice. Knowledge and insight of more useful kinds could be produced and better means developed to apply these in daily practice. However, in the short term new kinds of difficulty can be created, the origins of which frequently lie in the historical disconnectedness outlined above. Examples of these occur in many areas. In planning, for example, differences in aims, timeframes, pace and project management approaches can prove disruptive. In communicating, marked differences in the mode of discourse, vocabulary and tone of discussion between the communities may cause difficulties. Even in relation to the core issue of learning itself, differences of outlook on what it is, and how to provide for it can undermine joint endeavours. These kinds of difficulty have surfaced in many of the initiatives undertaken by NERF and it is to consideration of these that I now turn.

The NERF programme

Introduction

The Forum was set up in 1999 by the then Secretary of State for Education and Employment, David Blunkett. It comprised approximately 16 people drawn from many parts of the educational world, and was chaired by Sir Michael Peckham, former director of R&D for the NHS. It discussed issues of research and its relation to policy and practice, organised working groups and seminars and published reports. It also set up a programme of projects, engaging with organisations from the different phases and domains of education. Its remit was the development of coherence across the system and it focused on the linkage between research, policy and practice. Details of what it did can be found in reports and working papers available from its website www.nerf-uk.org. In particular, a final report written in March 2006 gives an overview of its work (Morris and Peckham 2006).

NERF was conceived as a forum and accordingly its members met periodically to identify and discuss relevant issues. In addition it organised a programme of activities which included projects, seminars, events and publications. The section that follows provides a commentary on the main activities, grouped in three broad areas: planning, investigating and influencing. The hope is that this will prove of some use to those wishing to build on the work of NERF.

Planning

In the area of planning, NERF organised a number of initiatives, concerned with funding, priorities and agenda setting.

In 1999 it set up a *Funders' Forum*, comprising several dozen charitable and public R&D funders. The Forum met every few months under the chairmanship of Sir Brian Fender and addressed many issues. In relation to capacity building, it organised workshops and prepared advice; on systematic reviewing it developed guidance for funders and on other issues, such as government data sources and reform of the Research Assessment Exercise it took evidence from a range of experts. It did not however give rise, as some had hoped, to joint planning of research or coordination of funding for larger projects. What it did usefully reveal is that such coordination was unlikely to prove possible in a forum setting. One reason was that different kinds of funder have distinct or even contradictory purposes; charities, for example, may be keen to avoid funding that which government might fund. Another reason was that funders each account to their governing bodies in different ways and at different times, so that the licence to discuss cooperation around a table was strictly limited. What did prove achievable however, was to acquaint funders with one another, and to facilitate occasional bilateral arrangements. Ultimately, significant differences in needs and motivation between public sector agencies and charities and between small and large research funders made it difficult to sustain sufficient interest in the Forum. The experience was nevertheless felt to be positive by many participants and revealed an unmet need amongst research managers in funding bodies to engage together in some form of professional dialogue. In my opinion, a new, more refined structure for engaging the diverse segments of the funding community would be a worthwhile step.

A *Priorities Group* discussed ways in which a coherent national agenda for educational research might be developed. Witnesses from major educational research funding bodies provided accounts of how priorities are arrived at by particular bodies in practice. From this, based on the advice of witnesses in healthcare, a theoretical model was developed involving cost-benefit appraisals by a joint panel of researchers, funders and managers. Subsequent workshops demonstrated just how far from current practice such a model is in education and how difficult it would be for the organisations that actually set R&D priorities to plan jointly, even within a single sector (such as post-16 education) or functional area (such as leadership training), let alone across education as a whole. In the light of this, NERF work on prioritisation reverted to the preliminary task of bringing together key organisations to simply share information about their research programmes. This proved achievable and worthwhile but remains, at the time of going to press, an example of a successful initiative that needs to be taken forward.

The collapse of the Funders' Forum in 2004 and the level of interest shown in agenda-sharing activity led to the formation of a *Development Group* comprising the research leaders from most of the leading organisations in the public sector. This proved effective in stimulating discussion and action on cross-sector issues such as getting evidence to teachers. The role of NERF as independent broker, in identifying issues, convening meetings and arbitrating where necessary proved crucial. It is clear that the various bodies that wish to come together, and stand to benefit from doing so, simply do not and cannot come together unaided – a catalyst is needed to initiate and sustain activity.

Futures   A further aspect of the planning process – looking to the future – was identified as important early on by NERF. As a result it entered into partnership with a small specialist organisation, The Tomorrow Project, to study how scenarios for the future of education might impact on the agenda for research. A major consultation programme engaged participants from all parts of the educational world in assessing the effects of the drivers of change in eight identified areas, including globalisation, politics, media and technology. The discussions were well regarded by participants and the subsequent publication has aroused interest (Worsley *et al.* 2006). It outlines a number of key factors and possible outcomes, and more importantly suggests a framework for incorporating futures thinking into the various levels at which R&D interacts with policy and practice. This work needs to be taken forward now by bodies responsible for policy development, professional practice and research planning so that their constituencies become acquainted with the way 'futures' thinking can inform action in the present.

Investigating

Other NERF activities focused on the way investigations are actually conducted, in particular on proposals for programmes that combine development with research (D&R) (Stanton 2006). These, together with proposals for a National Evidence Centre for Education, formed the basis of NERF's strategic proposals published in 2003 (Morris and Peckham 2003). In essence they call for practical intervention programmes to incorporate research and development strands, in which practitioners, policy-makers and researchers interact repeatedly, informing and learning from the intervention as it proceeds. Practical action on the D&R concept was progressed through a series of workshops, and later a network, for organisations and individuals wishing to work in this way. The concept has attracted the interest of groups actively involved in both research and in developing practical solutions to specific problems. It is not easy for bodies working principally in either research or development to engage in this way, given the practical difficulties of coordinating the respective resources. Funding for each is usually the responsibility of separate organisations operating on different schedules, using different criteria. This essentially administrative difficulty may itself go some way to explaining why so few interventions effectively integrate research into their programmes of activity.

D&R network   For those interested in working with D&R, a network was formed which attracted people from both academic groups and from organisations working for practitioners (such as British Educational Communications and Technology Association [Becta] and Learning and Skills Development Agency [LSDA]). Each had experienced frustration with traditional approaches and wished to develop ways that lead to improvements on the ground as well as development of theory. Workshops organised by the network led to increasing clarity about the concept and about ways of running D&R programmes in practice. Examples include one university working with a network of local schools on developing inclusiveness; another working with local authorities and schools on a programme for able inner city students; a national organisation developing its research strategy in a D&R direction; and another coordinating Educational Psychology doctorates as a coherent D&R programme. The challenge now is to encourage leaders of intervention teams in the policy community to join up with research teams to use more sustained D&R approaches.

Behaviour D&R programme   In an effort to stimulate policy-led D&R programmes NERF set up two working groups to explore what such programmes might look like in two exemplary areas: student behaviour and physics and maths education. Both groups consulted experts to produce reports which outlined key research questions and developmental objectives. Arising from this, a programme on pupil behaviour is being planned, based on a city-wide scheme in Coventry. It will start by identifying anti-bullying strategies and testing them on the ground. The design of local actions will be informed by existing research knowledge and by feedback on their effectiveness as they proceed. The potential wider value of this project is in demonstrating ways of enhancing a local development scheme with a flexible research resource capable of responding to needs as they arise.

Physics and maths D&R programme   The second working group produced a consultation document on radical options for increasing the uptake of physics and maths. Discussions with academics, government officials, industry leaders and teacher representatives led to a commonly-held view that the problem has become particularly serious and calls for radical rethinking. However, this problem has been addressed many times over the years and has led to many local and partial hypotheses about the nature of the problem and ways of remedying it. The challenge for a D&R approach is to identify leadership that will take the long view and invest in testing out such hypotheses.

Capacity building   Work by NERF and the Funders' Forum on capacity building took the form of a series of workshops resulting in reports and proposals for both the research community itself and for the communities that need to make better use of research. Many key organisations, including Economic and Social Research Council (ESRC), Teaching and Learning Research Programme (TLRP), National College for School Leadership (NCSL), Training and Development Agency for Schools (TDA) and DfES were involved but it did not prove easy to take forward proposals in a joint manner. Some initiatives were taken forward nevertheless by some key bodies such as ESRC. It is difficult to see how a concerted programme of capacity building should be brought about across the countless organisations with an interest. There is widespread agreement about the need for it and a very large number of organisations who feel they have a part to play in it. But none feels dominant or strong or sufficiently well resourced to take a lead on behalf of all. This is a particular area in which a catalytic body, capable of inspiring and integrating efforts amongst many small players could prove helpful.

Quality   After producing an early working group report, NERF did little more itself on the issue of quality in research. However, an important study for ESRC on quality in applied and practice-orientated research (Furlong and Oancea 2005) was undertaken in preparation for the 2008 round of the Research Assessment Exercise (RAE) which has provided a conceptual framework for differing ideas about quality. The broadening out in this framework, from a single conception of quality to a range of use-related ones has proved helpful and mirrors the evolving debate on a related issue: systematic reviewing. Here, arguments about the merits of particular methods have to some extent given way to the idea of a typology or spectrum of approaches for different purposes. In yet another area, the assessment of quality of studies for inclusion in the Educational Evidence Portal (EEP) no attempt was made from the outset to define or apply a universal standard. In this case the idea of assessing quality on behalf of the user has been rejected in favour of providing a set of options to enable users to choose for themselves the kind of evidence they wish to retrieve. This trend towards empowering the evidence-user to make informed choices seems an important step forward that both exploits the potential of information technology and shifts the balance of power and control. It remains to be seen however, whether in the long run these frameworks, typologies and internet options ultimately provide the practical user with the assurances she or he needs or whether they simply add further layers of unmanageable complexity.

Influencing

Apart from activities aimed at improving research planning and research investigations NERF also focused on improving the means by which evidence influences practice and policy-making. Projects of this type are outlined below.

NERF Bulletin: evidence for teaching and learning   A bulletin was developed for teachers, originally inspired by the example of *Bandolier* for healthcare practitioners. It was conceived, funded and produced by NERF and written and researched by the company CUREE (Centre for the Use of Research and Evidence in Education). It proved a success, according to evaluations (NFER 2004), and demonstrated the potential of basing research communications around the expressed needs of teachers rather than the outputs of researchers. Researched meticulously and written expertly, it proved useful to many readers in teaching and teacher training. Unfortunately it was unable to attract sustained funding and ceased publication with the ending of NERF. However, there remain several research-based publications that reach out to teachers – produced for example by General Teaching Council (GTC), NFER, NCSL and DfES. These demonstrate that the concept has now, in many ways, been proven – the issue now is about getting these tools into routine, mainstream use. For this to happen, those responsible for teachers' professional preparation and continuing development, leadership training, institutional improvement and local management will need to exploit these communication mechanisms and to invest in expanding them.

Educational Evidence Portal   In 2003, two organisations came together with the idea of developing a portal through which practitioners of various kinds could get easy access to evidence on topics that mattered to them without having to know about and work through multiple sources. NERF took up the role of independent broker for this project and the number of interested organisations rapidly grew. The resulting consortium gained technical support from Microsoft which, in June 2006, resulted in a pilot version of a search facility – a kind of 'Google for education'. By drawing on expertise in information science, software development, project management and quality assurance from a range of organisations (including Becta, BEI, CfBT Education Trust, DfES, GTC, Higher Education Academy [HEA], Microsoft NFER, TDA and TLRP) the project has not only demonstrated the power of collaborative working but has enabled pioneering work to be undertaken that no single organisation would have done alone. The result is likely to be a tool that proves useful across all sections of education – from early years to adult learning – and empowers new groups of professionals to make use of research evidence. The process has also revealed just how urgent it has become for organisations to extend the meta-tagging (or indexing) of their educational materials. This is a necessary preliminary to any effort to organise and make accessible educational evidence on a large scale and the EEP project is engaging with the task, in conjunction with British Education Index and Microsoft. The principal difficulty in pursuing this work is not, as in some other cases, obtaining support or agreement about the strategy and funding, but in being able to determine the way ahead. In this area there are few individuals fully equipped to advise on the range of presenting problems. Up-to-date knowledge is required on information science, software development, quality assurance mechanisms and funding streams, together with high-level skills in writing, editing, graphical representation, consortium management, strategic planning and diplomacy. It is perhaps little wonder that it has taken some time for such a desirable initiative to be conceived and set in motion in education! Inspiration has come from leading examples in other fields, notably social care and public health, in which such difficulties have ultimately been overcome.

Models of Research Synthesis (MORSE)   Another collaborative project focused on ways in which evidence from research reviews could be made more useful for practitioners. The MORSE project brought together researchers, teacher trainers, teachers and policy workers in a series of workshops to identify ways in which reviews of evidence could be written up and exploited by different target groups. Examples from education and other fields were showcased and a variety of leaflets, booklets, web pages and other products compared. The workshops proved useful to those who attended and should be carried forward in the future. Arising from them it should prove possible to develop appropriate formats for getting the findings of systematic reviews to teachers through the relevant agencies. The importance of this work is that it shifts the focus of teacher attention from single studies to the overall state of knowledge on a given topic. The challenge is to engage those intermediate authorities that routinely reach teachers and policy workers systemically so that prototyping can give way to mainstreaming. Bodies responsible for professional development, initial training, leadership development, curriculum development and improvement strategies need to be working together on this to ensure that appropriate materials are developed, based on reviews, suitable for placing at the heart of practical interventions on the large scale.

Policy research interaction   A small but significant project developed as a result of observations of difficulties in the way researchers and policy workers interact at seminars and advisory meetings. This coincided with a wish by the schools directorate of DfES to develop a series of seminars at which researchers discuss their findings with policy-makers on topics of interest in current policy-making. NERF undertook a structured observation of the events organised by DfES and produced a report on how they could be enhanced. This study emphasised the need to balance the interests of both the policy worker and the researcher by encouraging the latter to set out precisely the problem upon which research evidence needs to bear. Communication difficulties in relation to language, vocabulary and tone are important factors, but much can be done to mitigate these through detailed preparation and expert chairing or mediation between the two parties. Practical suggestions for achieving this are contained in the report (Norman 2004).

This study was small, but the issues it outlined are profound and significant. Improving the interaction between those who produce and those who use knowledge is crucial for the development of better policy. The function of such seminars needs to evolve from the exchange of information to what can be, in effect, a form of collaborative professional learning. Good pedagogic practices are needed, including expert facilitation and opportunities for each party to articulate its preconceptions and to develop its thinking in the light of the information presented by the other. Equality of regard and a balance of contributions are important to encourage two-way interaction, rather than merely one-way information flow.

To achieve such a transformation in communications is not easy. For policymakers, articulating difficulties openly may be an unusual or even counter-cultural activity. Advance preparation is needed to ensure that the agenda is shaped before research findings are selected for discussion. For researchers the challenge is to respond to the actual context in which their findings are to be received rather than to simply make a presentation on their own terms. These are fundamental challenges which will never prove easy to meet. Research, often equivocal and uncertain, can only speak solidly about some things, whereas public policy, which needs to reassure and convince, may wish for evidence that simply cannot be produced. Despite this, much can be done in practice to rebalance the contributions of the researcher and the policy worker making way for a richer, two-way interaction. Finer questions of judgement about the trustworthiness and relevance of findings and of their interpretation can be more successfully handled once such a collaborative, non-adversarial process has been established.

Implications

Beyond the learning arising from individual projects within the NERF programme, there seem to me to be some observations that need to be made about the experience as a whole, particularly about the role of the mediator.

Role   In the UK, perhaps more particularly in England, 'single issue' bodies have proliferated in recent decades to cope with various functions such as teacher training, or quality improvement. Separate bodies exist for each function and in some cases (such as leadership training) parallel ones for each sector. One consequence of this fragmentation is that action that would be desired by all or many of these bodies, such as the creation of an accessible evidence base, may not in fact take place, simply because no single body is in a position to take a lead. As a result it may not happen although it may be in the interests of each one and the system as a whole.

If this is true, there remains a paramount need for an independent entity, not tied to any specific topic area, able to act as a catalyst amongst other organisations. Frequently NERF found itself having to act in this way. With the demise of

NERF, it seems important that other structures be developed to play this role. This entails identifying and working on issues that are important but for which progress is blocked because single organisations cannot act alone. The tasks are to persuade parties to engage, propose courses of action and steer the parties through the obstacles that threaten to set them against each other. Such an entity would probably need to set out some kind of vision to inspire action but would need to eschew any particular ideological or methodological standpoint so that its actions could draw impartially on whichever of these served the problem in hand.

Skills and attributes   The NERF experience also demonstrated the kind of skills and attributes demanded in the catalytic role. Effective facilitation requires high levels of empathy; the context in which policy-makers, academics and school teachers live out their professional lives needs to be understood, felt and accepted. The purposes of particular actions and the roles of each kind of partic-ipant need to be set out explicitly to minimise false assumptions. Processes need to be designed to be highly inclusive, offering attractive ways for professionals of different types and motivations to work together. For an initiative to operate effec-tively right through, from political gestation to classroom delivery, may well involve contributions from publishers and writers, software engineers and researchers, teachers and government officers – all needing to engage with the same process in order to arrive at solutions that will work. Within such diversity, partners need to develop realistic expectations of one another. Differences in con-cepts, timeframes, planning procedures and budgets will vary markedly; the role of the facilitating body is to accommodate all of these.

Method   In a multi-party project many distinct contributions need to be coordi-nated. Team working is called for in which members of the team need to con-tribute in relation to the task in hand rather than their home organisation. Skillful team facilitation is needed over and above the specialist expertise required for the job. Effective communications across the team are also crucial to the success of collaborative projects. In such collaborative enterprises there is a paramount need to exchange emerging ideas and information as work progresses. Occasions are needed in which to pause, check and communicate between the various parties. Projects easily stray from their original objectives and periodic checks are needed to counter or legitimate this tendency. In addition the external environment often changes during the run of a project; opportunities to reassess and adjust plans are needed. Cycles of iteration in which the various players come together to reassess their positions are an important feature of collaborative designs.

Where next?

The discussion so far has focused on the experience of the NERF programme 1999–2006. To conclude I turn to consideration of what needs to be done to build on this experience.

The NERF was a unique experiment at the level of a whole country. In the UK and abroad, there are many examples of initiatives being taken in relation to particular aspects of the problem: linking evidence and policy, enhancing teacher training, informing school development or changing social science methodology. The NERF experiment, rashly or otherwise, took on all of these simultaneously. In my view, though often painful and invariably slow-moving, this holistic approach is what is needed. It is ambitious, it creates tensions, it offers little short-term pay-off; but it does address the *chronic* rather than the acute condition of educational improvement. Over the long term, in many countries, it has proved difficult to achieve the scale of improvements desired, for both social and economic reasons, in education. Political aspirations have not been regularly fulfilled and high levels of illiteracy and ignorance and low levels of skill persist in important places. Given the social and economic benefits that education is thought to bring, it is of the utmost importance that policy priorities are scientifically informed, interventions robustly designed and development action in schools, colleges and universities effective. The many links from parliament to classroom must interact coherently.

For this to occur, a gradual rapprochement between the political, academic and pedagogic communities must be sustained. Structures are needed to achieve this – it cannot happen unaided. The boldness of the government intention in 1999, in setting up NERF across *all* parts of education, should be restored. It is important, but not sufficient to improve coherence across research or to enhance evidence use in government and teaching. Additional effort is needed to develop coherence *between* these nexuses, to aim for long-term programmes that satisfy the political will, but also work effectively at local level, in the interests of learners, parents, communities and employers. To do this requires active collaboration between the producers of knowledge and those who need it in practice. There are many developments taking place all the time on many of the topics raised in this chapter: synthesising what is known, getting evidence distributed to practitioners, consulting on research agendas and so on. Much of this is invisible, buried inside the processes of organisations, rarely reaching across the education sector as a whole. The challenge for the future is to work in these key areas so that they are effective across the education system as a whole and influence a much larger proportion of the workforce.

References

All NERF working papers can be downloaded from: www.nerf-uk.org/publicationsnetworks/ workingpapers/

Furlong, J. and Oancea, A. (2005) *Assessing Quality in Applied and Practice-Based Educational Research*. Oxford: Oxford University Department of Educational Studies.

Hillage, J., Pearson, R., Anderson, A. and Tamkin, P. (1998) *Research into Schooling*. Research Briefing RR7. London: Department for Education and Employment.

Morris, A. (2005) "Evidence initiatives: aspects of recent experience in England." *Evidence & Policy*, **1**(2), 257–268.

Morris, A. and Peckham, M. (2003*) NERF Strategic Proposals*. NERF working paper 3.1.

Morris, A. and Peckham, M. (2006) *Final Report of NERF.* NERF working paper 9.2.

National Research Council (2002) *Scientific Research in Education*. In Shavelson, RJ and Towne L, eds. Washington: National Academy Press.

NFER (2004) *Evaluation of the NERF Bulletin Trial*. NERF Working Paper No. 7.6.

Norman, L. (2004) *Research-Policy Interaction*. NERF Working Paper No. 8.1.

OECD (2005) CERI. *Evidence-based Policy Research in Education*. Conference series. Available at: http://www.oecd.org/document/4/0,2340,en_2649_34525_36007044_1_1_1_1,00.html

Stanton G (2006) *D&R Programmes: Concept and Practice*. NERF working paper No. 5.6.

TRIPS (2006) *The Research in Practice* website: www.standards.dfes.gov.uk/research/

TTRB (2006) The *Teacher Training Resource Bank* website: www.ttrb.ac.uk/

Worsley, R., Moynagh, M. and Morris, A. (2006) *Futures and Educational Research*. NERF working paper No. 6.5.

Chapter 7

Go-betweens, gofers or mediators?

Exploring the role and responsibilities of research managers in policy organisations

Lesley Saunders

Introduction – what this chapter is about

National policy agencies in education (including but not limited to the Department for Education and Skills [DfES]) employ between them large numbers of qualified researchers (of whom the author is one), whose roles include designing, commissioning, managing, undertaking, collating and mediating research evidence in and for a policy environment. The interventions of such people are, or ought to be, crucial to the ways in which research enters (or is detached from) the discourses of policy-making. However, not much in the literature on policy-makers' use of research refers to the role of these professionals specifically and directly, and what there is seems to rest on assumptions and assertions rather than empirical-analytical description. This chapter discusses the findings from an exploratory project undertaken with a small number of research staff known to the author. It goes on to offer the beginnings of a framework for investigating, understanding and supporting the roles, activities, professional values, status and professional development needs of people who work as research directors, managers and/or advisers in organisations with a policy remit for education.

Some personal background

It will be obvious from the brief description I have given in the book's list of contributors that I have a vested interest in this topic, and a lesser aim of writing this chapter was to understand what it is I do – sometimes on the basis of careful planning but often by intuition and making it up as I go along – with more insight and disinterest. Moreover, the chapter is written from the perspective of one who has moved from a research-producing environment (the National Foundation for Educational Research) to a research-using environment (the General Teaching

Council for England) – although these ascriptions are already a form of shorthand that distorts the more complex reality of both these organisations and the way they work. As many readers will be aware, I have continued to be intrigued by, and to voice (see, for example, Saunders 2001, 2002, 2003a, 2003b, 2004, 2005a, 2005b), the challenges of responding to the very different perspectives and priorities of policy and research. I do take seriously (personally, even) the demands and desires – articulated by, amongst others, Andrew Morris and Judy Sebba in this book – to try to align them at least to some extent, in an effort to uphold the 'rationalist ideal' of research-informed policy-making, as far as this is possible in reality and *realpolitik*. I count myself fortunate in working for an organisation that is exemplary in trying to enact this ideal.

So my intention is to illuminate one corner of the social, political and institutional environments in which research ideas, issues and evidence are, or might be, taken up and utilised – or not – for decision-making in education policy environments. I hope it makes a modest contribution to the discussion, although I am fully aware that more empirical and conceptual work is required.

My starting points

The discussion needs to be situated within the growing body of work concerned with elucidating what is meant, and entailed, by research-informed (a term I much prefer to 'evidence-based') policy-making in public sector services, particularly education. I am going to assume that readers are already familiar with much of the relevant literature, including the range of arguments supporting, elaborating, illustrating, critiquing and problematising that general agenda. In writing elsewhere about some of the issues that interest me (Saunders, op. cit.), I have pointed to the large and respectable body of scholarly evidence (in, for example, BERA 2003; Davies 2004; Davies *et al.* 2000; DETYA 2000; Galvin 2004; Hanney 2004; Levin 2001, 2003a, 2003b, 2003c, 2004; Morris 2004; Munn 2005; Nutley 2003; Nutley *et al.* 2003; Pawson 2006; Percy-Smith *et al.* 2002; Walter *et al.* 2003; Weiss 1979, 1991; Whitty 2002; Willinsky 2000, 2003) that has explored and critically discussed the complexity of policy-making processes and highlighted the challenges and opportunities for the role and associated activities of research in them. Many of the chapters in this book – as I explained in my editor's introduction – now move the debate on, through their welcome attention to specificity and nuance across a range of issues.

A key point that emerges is that publication and dissemination of research may be necessary, but is far from sufficient, for the uptake and utilisation of research as knowledge. It is now well understood that research findings – in which I include theories and concepts as well as empirically or otherwise generated data – need to be actively managed and 'brokered' with and for different kinds of policy audiences, in order to influence policy-making in an intelligent and realistic way. We know, at a general level, that this entails, amongst other things, creating processes and receptive cultures for policy advisers that enable them to engage with research at times and in formats – including possible policy implications of the findings – that are likely to be appropriate for their decision-making systems. Knowing this is, of course, no guarantee that such engagement emanates in better policy-making and policies, or even happens at all.

But who are the people with this mediating role, whether *de facto* or more formally? Many groups, including 'producers' such as university researchers, and 'users', such as government policy analysts, have a hand in research mediation at some stage of the process, but there are people whose job descriptions probably give them explicit responsibility for such activity, however conceived and enacted. If we think, for a moment, about research management and mediation in terms of encounters between persons, I think it becomes obvious that the process is very likely not just a matter of the perceived credibility, rigour and relevance of the concepts, data and inferences of the research, important though these are. Issues of the status, authority and even the personality of the research 'mediator' are probably also – at least subliminally – salient.

However, as I noted above, I have so far been able to find very little in the literature on the relationship between research and policy that refers specifically and directly to the very practical matter of who these people are, what they do, and what kinds of professional expertise, values and relationships they draw on in meeting the challenges of their work. What literature there is seems to rest more on assumptions and rather negative assertions than on empirical-analytical description; it also tends to bracket all kinds of policy staff and research advisers together and seems to assume that there is no stronger impulse guiding their work than political naïveté or expediency (see, for example, Humes and Bryce 2001; Temple 2003; Weiss 1991).

It is for this reason, as well as the fact that a great deal of policy-making in practice takes place in dynamic, oral and relatively informal cultures, that I have called for (in Saunders 2004, op. cit.) the re-instigation or further development – following earlier studies like that of Ball 1990 – of something resembling 'thick descriptions' of the events, activities, relationships, conversations and encounters that make up the observable day-to-day business of policy-making in education. The chapters in this book by Moss and Huxford, and Somekh, exemplify what I have in mind; whilst the symposium titled 'Commissioned educational research as *realpolitik*: voices and experiences from the field', convened at the British Educational Research Association annual conference 2006, offered papers by Morwenna and Tony, Anne and Olwen, and Gunter and Pat that from their different perspectives signalled a need for, and the beginning of, some further detailed exploratory work on the difficult ethical issues and organisational challenges entailed by what goes on in the processes of commissioned research.

The project: research issues and mode of inquiry

I therefore decided in 2005 to undertake a small empirical investigation that might offer some provisional understandings for others in future to work with or critique, on the role and realities of said research managers/advisers, as explained by their own accounts. (It may not be irrelevant to point out that I could not take sufficient time out from my day job to undertake a more substantial and scholarly piece of work.)

My articulation of the main research issues to be investigated was as follows (and I am indebted to Pamela Nunn for her helpful comments at the design stage):

- How do research managers/advisers see their role and responsibilities? What seem to be the main features of these roles and responsibilities? Are there any differences between respondents in different (kinds of) agencies?
- How well equipped do respondents feel for these roles/responsibilities through, for example, their previous career history and/or training?
- What criteria and evidence would they use in assessing their effectiveness? Can these be illustrated through specific examples of success and failure?
- What are their main professional 'drivers' and which professional community/ies provides a framework for them to think about such issues?
- What can be said, even tentatively, about (i) the discourses; (ii) the social practices, of research mediation in policy environments that are revealed by these responses and what issues do these raise for further research?

Of course I am mindful that not all these issues can be investigated, or investigated fully, only through people's accounts of what they do. But in order to gather some first-hand perception data, I devised a set of questions to pose to respondents as follows:

- What is the main purpose of your role?
- What other kinds of research-related post exist in your organisation? How do you fit in? (Copy of organisational chart useful, if available.)
- What job(s) were you doing before your present one?
- What is the most difficult aspect of your job and why?
- What is the most enjoyable aspect of your job and why?
- What changes in your role/responsibilities do you notice?
- What kinds of strategic, operational and/or ethical decisions do you have to make, and where/to whom do you look for guidance?
- What kinds of professional development do you seek out/receive as part of your job?
- Who do you consider constitutes your 'professional community'?
- Do you have any other comments/observations?

In the spring of 2005, I sent the aims, issues and questions to a selected group of potential respondents whom I happened to know, with a written request to participate and the option of responding in writing or by interview. The people I approached were the members of the Schools Research Liaison Group

(SRLG), a working group comprising the then heads of research, senior research analysts and advisers, at the main national educational agencies (DfES, British Educational and Communications Technology Agency [Becta], General Teaching Council for England [GTC], Learning and Skills Development Agency [LSDA], National College for School Leadership [NCSL], National Educational Research Forum [NERF], Office for Standards in Education [OFSTED], Qualifications and Curriculum Authority [QCA], Teacher Training Agency [TTA] as it then was). The SRLG was itself an innovation in terms of information sharing and mutual support initiated by Judy Sebba when she was specialist adviser for research at the DfES. The group remains active at the time of writing and meets termly on an informal basis to exchange information about research programmes, strategies and future plans, as well as discussing more theoretical ideas, issues and concerns (see White's chapter in this book for an account of the group).

The project: findings

Responses to the questions were given by a subset of SRLG colleagues (representing three of the organisations listed above); the majority of responses were in written form and one was conducted through telephone interview. Because of the offer I made to respondents about confidentiality – which most took up – I am reporting the findings in aggregate form as far as possible and anonymously throughout. I have occasionally added my reflections on my own experiences as additional data, noting where this is the case.

A general comment to make is that the responses typically indicated that postholders had already given a lot of thought to their work and its purposes and challenges; on the whole, there was a strong sense of professional fulfilment as well as a keen sense of the many challenges, as the tone of this observation illustrates:

> I enjoy the variety of work I cover and the fact that it is constantly evolving and hopefully moving forward.

Personal background and previous professional experience

Respondents came with a variety of previous experience, though the majority had worked in the education sector for some time. Several had been teachers at some point in the past, with a couple having held school or college senior management posts. Several had shifted from a policy role in one or more education policy organisations to a research role, whilst others had moved from research posts in academic or independent institutions into their current policy organisations; one had a generic background in information and knowledge management.

With such a small sample, it would have been impossible in any case to talk about a typical career trajectory – but these data raise interesting questions about career decisions and profiles, including the range and variety of backgrounds, the likelihood of progression or stagnation within the particular policy organisation, the ease or difficulty of transition to other kinds of institution, the frequency of change of jobs/roles, individual career plans and hopes, and above all whether their current post represents a particular stage in a continuing career in research or something more transitional or accidental.

Organisational structures, roles and responsibilities

Unsurprisingly, the organisational arrangements and structures for the research function looked different in different organisations: for a start, teams were of very different sizes, both absolutely (numbers given ranged between four and 30) and relative to the whole staffing complement (ranging between three and ten per cent); they also differed with respect to whether they were headed by a member of senior management or the directorate, or whether there was an intermediate layer or layers of reporting; and they consequently differed with respect to the degree of strategic influence as well as executive authority they wielded within the organisation.

Differences also emerged between a research functionality that is bounded and identifiable (in the form of a distinct team with defined line management accountabilities and/or a delegated budget, for example) and one where there is a variety of individuals/teams across the organisation who may have similar or overlapping roles (such people might comprise social researchers, economists, statisticians, operational researchers, policy advisers with a background in research, etc.). The consequences, if any, for influence on policy development of such differences are not clear, however.

Finally, there appeared to be differences in terms of accountabilities: whether, for example, respondents and the teams were responsible for all the organisation's 'deliverables' pertaining to research, evaluation and evidence activity, or for providing advice to others in the organisation who may be doing/commissioning research. In the latter case, the respondent may see it as part of his/her role to try to develop common organisational understandings and practices about good research commissioning and management.

Despite these differences, in all organisations 'evidence' was rated, at least in principle, as crucial, and there was a pervasive and explicit requirement that research findings should underpin policy and practice development in some way. Recent and ongoing structural changes had often been introduced to strengthen this, such as: the reorganisation of existing staff to try to 'embed' research in policy teams, the recruitment of additional research staff, and/or the creation of more strategic or senior posts/roles.

A striking thing is the range of roles and responsibilities undertaken by these respondents, both individually and as a group. Three had the task of creating, developing and implementing a long-term research strategy for their organisations, in pursuance of the requirement or commitment to 'research-informed' or 'evidence-based' decision-making in education.

All held operational responsibilities of the project management kind: designing, commissioning and managing projects with external contractors and/or designing and conducting or overseeing projects with an internal team:

> I make a wide range of operational decisions on a day-to-day basis, concerning people (human resource issues within the team and commissioned teams of researchers), financial resource, time, and partnership working both within and outside the organisation.

Such projects often included action research projects, and designing/populating websites, writing material for knowledge resources, offering content for Teachers TV, as well as more conventional research studies.

Respondents also tried to ensure that they were knowledgeable about the scope of, and outcomes from, major research programmes in the external environment like the Economic and Social Research Council (ESRC) Teaching and Learning Research Programme and the Evidence for Policy and Practice Information (EPPI) centre for systematic reviews in education; they thought it crucial that any studies they wished to commission themselves should take account of work already undertaken or under way; and that internal policy formation should be as informed as possible by the key messages and findings from a range of sources including but not limited to research that had been directly commissioned. This presented some problems, described below.

All had a major intellectual responsibility within their organisations which took the form of analysing, summarising, synthesising and interpreting research and evidence on an astonishingly broad spectrum of issues and topics of importance to the remit of the entire organisation; they were writing overview papers (which may also have required technical and/or statistical commentaries) and making presentations to internal and external audiences. They took primary responsibility for the technical quality of research-based evidence, but at the same time could not afford to be narrowly specialist:

> I make the key decisions about the depth and robustness of research briefings which I produce – and whether to contact "experts" from the research community for research knowledge on particular problems (and if so whom).

They were also conscious of the risks that may be associated with the wider use and application of hard-won research findings:

> I am very aware that I'm enquiring in an area where people work hard to deliver good results on a tight budget, so I'm very keen that any outcomes

from research are helpful and not ammunition to beat up on practitioners in the field.

This area of responsibility was closely connected with another major but not necessarily well-defined area of work, concerned with improving the flow of research and evidence to policy-makers (mainly but not exclusively inside the organisation), and developing a range of activities – newsletters, briefings and e-mail alerts, seminars and workshops – to support this:

> I work very much at the interface of the policy and research communities, in a "virtual team" across these communities.

> I've devised long term communications strategies for individual projects. And I put together the content of newsletters – judging what policy makers are likely to be interested in, in relation to the recently published research available – trying to balance supply and demand.

However, there was no hard and fast guarantee that this work would be used, or used in the ways intended:

> it is not entirely clear how the detailed briefing papers produced by the research team are actually used in policy work, and some further evaluation is called for.

Essentially, then, a major aspect of these respondents' role – whether or not it appeared as such in their job descriptions – could be called 'mediation', that is, the very delicate task of bringing together the different needs, perspectives, cultures and processes of policy and of research to produce outcomes that have integrity as well as intentionality:

> a big challenge is balancing the evidential needs of policy makers and politicians with the need to provide independent and unbiased advice and reporting of the evidence.

> I have to find ways of balancing the need to make a quick response to [policy] enquiries with the need to undertake more detailed and rigorous investigations.

> ethical decisions have more often than not concerned conflicting interests between funders, researchers and educational communities.

Respondents also saw themselves as responsible, through their commissioning and networking activities, for encouraging new research projects and helping to build research capacity. Perhaps by temperament, they were inclined to want to take the longer view, and talked about how to identify priorities for future research commissions that could have significant import for the educational system; they were the ones who could recommend whether – given funding constraints – to push for particular new areas of investigation to be taken forward. In this context, it is interesting to note one ethical dilemma, as follows:

> it's my responsibility to decide whether to recommend funding of unsolicited proposals – this is especially difficult when proposals are from researchers I have worked with before ...

My own take on the importance of networking with the research community in order to help identify possible future themes is that, soon after the GTC was launched in 2000, I used the *Times Educational Supplement* to put out a call for expressions of interest in the GTC's newly-devised research strategy, and I set up individual meetings with over 50 academic and private sector researchers over subsequent months. This was an invaluable exercise, and I have warmly appreciated, and in many cases drawn upon, the enduring contacts I made. For their part, a considerable number of researchers have had opportunities for directly engaging with, as well as contributing ideas and evidence to, a very receptive policy environment at the GTC.

Increasingly, it would seem, respondents saw themselves as needing and wishing to develop partnerships with other national education bodies around key topics and issues in research and evidence: this in turn was leading to a greater number of co-funded/co-sponsored projects and activities, which brought its own challenges (see below). Quite a lot of effort was being expended on setting up and/or providing input to a wide variety of steering groups, advisory bodies, working parties and so forth.

All respondents felt that their role also, at least to some extent, demanded 'thought leadership' and creative thinking. One respondent made an explicit point that seems to reflect what others implied:

> I think it is worth getting across that much of my work is about personal effectiveness and being creative, e.g. I have to a great extent built my own job description – it is about seeing a need and trying to fill a gap!

Main problems and concerns

Respondents identified some quite deep-seated concerns as well as some practical difficulties in carrying out their work. On the one hand, one respondent believed that, despite the rhetorical commitment to evidence-based education, there had actually been a failure of nerve by policy-makers coupled with a drift away from involving stakeholders in research strategy and practice: 'practitioners are angry with the failure of policy-makers to promote research'.

On the other hand, all respondents expressed – in different ways – the intrinsic problem of trying to align the needs of policy colleagues and seniors for 'insight and foresight' with the proper constraints and requirements of research.

Policy-makers and politicians may hold unexamined assumptions or unfounded expectations of the kind of influence research could or should have on decision-making, and managing those expectations was clearly a major part of the work of the respondents; so getting genuine organisational 'buy-in', as distinct from notional agreement, to the research strategy was high on the list for some. For others, it was a question of coping with institutional behaviours:

> There are a number of problems. These include short deadlines for contributing to research briefings, often compounded by requests for evidence that are broad or vague.

Second – and probably connected with this – was the sense that 'politics with a small p' played a larger role than respondents would have liked:

> I find the management of a range of relationships from different organisations an interesting challenge. This is primarily because of historical issues and the differing goals and interests represented by those organisations.

> Negotiating the internal politics of the organisation. There are SO many people who have to be consulted and have to have their fingerprints on anything. It takes a long time and can be quite dispiriting. There is plenty of external politics too, but it's easy compared to the internal stuff.

One variant on internal political issues was the strong possibility that different cultures had grown up between finance teams, who were operating to a procurement model of tenders and contracts, whilst research teams were trying to develop more negotiated and flexible ways of commissioning research that take better account of the provisional relationship between the aims and outcomes of research studies, however well designed and planned. The Social Research Association has published an excellent resource book which provides a helpful rationale for this way of working (Social Research Association 2002 and see the SRA website http://www.the-sra.org.uk/).

Another challenge is that information flows into and within the organisation, whilst critical to the 'fit' of research and evidence to policy initiatives, were hard to manage in themselves:

> policy makers would like to have access to a comprehensive schedule of all research from external organisations to be published say over the next 12 months. Some of this information is available through current systems e.g. CERUK, but it is by no means comprehensive.

> I find it difficult keeping up to date with emerging work from within the organisation, both new policy developments and research. So I sometimes find myself reinventing the wheel or not getting properly linked into work which is relevant to my own area.

For one or two respondents, there was an ongoing failure in the organisation to provide appropriate resources, including administrative support.

Finally, a feeling articulated by one respondent but evident in one or two other accounts was that it was the fate of research advisers/managers to be 'prophets not recognised in their own land'; this sense of relative professional isolation is taken up in two further places below.

Main satisfactions and successes

It is therefore interesting that, for several respondents, it was the relational aspects of the work that provided a major source of professional satisfaction and sense of purpose:

> ... the management of a range of relationships from different organisations: I enjoy working with people.

> Working and networking with external organisations on common problems. I enjoy these productive liaisons, with the opportunity to be outward looking as well as bringing back new knowledge (and practical actions) to [the organisation].

They also referred to the intellectual fulfilment they derived:

> I also thoroughly enjoy the 'thinking' part of my job – devising and communicating strategy engages parts of my brain that other parts of the job don't!

> Engaging with new and innovative projects that provide new insight ...

Their sense of effectiveness came from direct feedback on their work, both specific and general:

> Getting your work quoted by somebody else. It helps answer the nagging question "was that any good?"

> I sense an increasing interest in research from policy colleagues – noted by increasing requests for research information and positive feedback on the research initiatives we provide.

I also have an intuition, from the way in which respondents spoke or wrote about many other issues, that they were deeply engaged with their work in a way that they each found positive and sustaining through hard times. Moreover, all respondents seemed to have a personal belief in the broader significance of the work in which they were involved, that is, in the 'project' of research-informed decision-making in education. One respondent was at pains to explain his commitment to the philosophy-in-action of 'a progressively more robust and systematic approach to development in education underpinned by research'. None spoke or wrote with any cynicism about the underlying purpose of their work, even when they were frustrated by particular circumstances or sceptical about the immediate or direct effect of their efforts.

Significant changes in role

One of the evident if unstated professional satisfactions for respondents was their facility to reflect on and analyse the political environment in which they work. They all noted some changes in their roles which were related to that wider context. One said that during his tenure the whole perception of research had changed, from a view of research as a commodity that got put on a shelf to a belief in research as active knowledge for organisational learning. The assumption that the completion of a research project was signalled simply by the publication of a report was, in his view, replaced by a notion of research as influencer. This respondent contrasted a 'diminished', 'woolly jumper' view of research with a 'close to market' relationship between research and organisational development that he had '*passionately*' promoted. He believed his legacy was to be seen in the small mechanisms he had introduced which had changed the cultural default, not least the introduction of the requirement for each research study to have an 'impact strategy'.

Another respondent noted similar far-reaching changes to his work environment, which meant that he had been promoted to do a different kind of job:

> from being a project manager delivering a range of research projects, to developing and advising on policy, and developing a strategy with a national perspective and with intended national impact.

Another mentioned her increasing involvement in 'higher-level discussions' in the organisation.

A related shift in the policy environment is 'a greater awareness of, and coordination with, the work of key national partner organisations', which has resulted in some significant changes to how research is conceived, managed and funded: one respondent says that she now has responsibility for:

> managing jointly-funded projects and thus having to take account of different funders' interests: I have responsibility for managing several collaboratively funded projects with other agencies, schools and LEAs.

The most vivid description of the effect on individuals of the change in how research is valued was this one:

> The biggest change for me personally is now having a boss who understands what I'm saying, rather than one who thinks I'm weird.

Nonetheless, there is an ongoing need to investigate and understand the power relationships within different organisations that have a direct or indirect effect on how research in general, as well as the outcomes from particular projects, is received and re-interpreted.

Main professional 'drivers' and development needs

Not surprisingly, given the breadth of their remit combined with the kind of systemic changes outlined above, respondents found some aspects – intellectual, strategic and operational – of their work difficult from time to time, and they had some insightful things to say about their preferred sources of advice and guidance. Some were working within clearly defined teams and were able to refer to their line manager and/or to senior staff in the organisation. Others not thus located said they were likely to seek guidance from research colleagues in other agencies and also 'individual researcher contacts who appreciate the nature of (organisation's) work and role'.

Professional development and support took a variety of forms, including the kinds of things one might expect, like attendance at conferences and learning on the job (which can be significantly enhanced by good management support, as both the comments below make clear):

> Just reading/surfing the net I find very valuable, being an excellent way of stumbling across alternative views/approaches. Most of all, and I've recently become aware of this, having a boss who you can learn from is the best thing of all. Having had a boss I couldn't/didn't want to learn from immediately before this one has made me realise how important this is.

> I have also learned on the job. My organisation funded my MA and my line-manager at the time gave me opportunities to undertake developmental tasks e.g. critiquing research papers, managing research projects, some data analysis and interpretation (e.g. consultation responses).

Respondents also said they sought out specific and technical input, such as internally provided research methods workshops or an externally provided course on SPSS (a statistical package for social researchers) awareness and use. (I have found that subscribing to e-mail alerts from research training and development providers is a useful way of identifying possible professional needs that I might not have thought about myself.)

Because of the intellectual responsibilities they carry on the one hand and the degree of esteem they sometimes fail to command from academic researchers on the other, I think it is important to highlight the credentials and professional qualifications of the respondents and others in similar positions:

> A research background is especially important in the ... team, and many of the project managers have postgraduate qualifications.

Some respondents mentioned that they had undertaken further academic study specifically to equip them better for their job, as this one explains:

> When I started in the area of education policy/research I lacked both education knowledge and research skills. I tried to redress this imbalance by studying for an MA in Education which included a module on research methods.

One respondent was adamant that he had 'invented my own professional development' for the role he was occupying. When people are creating their own opportunities, however, time and workload are a definite constraining factor:

> There is an annual research induction programme within [the organisation]. However, I have not had an opportunity to go on this yet due to pressures of work. I am planning to go on some systematic review training in the summer and intend to share what I learn with colleagues. I am considering studying for another higher degree – but will need to balance the demands this will bring against an already heavy workload and my home life.

The range of development needs relevant to their roles was wide, including newer, policy-related skills like 'negotiating skills' and 'analytical skills that are well grounded in evidence and research but appreciate and understand government policy issues'; for those in senior posts, organisational management and leadership, and strategy development; and for many the ongoing need for research project management. Not all these needs are easily met, even the last of these:

> I think there is definitely a lack of effective research management training available, particularly since the demise of the CMPS [previously the Civil Service College] course. To this end, I am investigating the possibility of enrolling on a PhD course, focusing on the management of national social research projects in the public sector.

Since the time of collecting data, a National School of Government, hosted by the Government Social Research Unit (GSRU), has been set up: see http://www.nationalschool.gov.uk/individual_development/professions.asp. The framework of professional skills for government includes analysis and use of evidence, and the GSRU in conjunction with the Institute of Education, London, offers a part-time MSc course in Policy Analysis and Evaluation. It will be interesting to see what difference, if any, this makes to the work of specialist research staff.

Other needs were clearly emerging out of the recent changes to the functions and foci of their roles, so respondents talked about needing training and guidance on producing research briefings, for example, but would also welcome input on the strategic task of 'how we can best convert meetings and seminars into practical steps, and begin to build solutions'.

A particular concern, expressed by one respondent, was the squeeze on budgets for research across all organisations:

> I would welcome some training or examples of good practice, not just guidance on best practice at the commissioning phase but also during the life of the project especially if on-going – in which case long term priorities of the other funding organisations are an issue, when we know that all research budgets are under increasing pressure ...

Given my initial contention that staff with a research role in policy organisations constitute a largely 'invisible' group, I was interested to know whether respondents considered themselves to be part of a professional community of some kind and, if so, which. Their reactions indicated that, on the whole, the idea of a professional community was not a familiar one:

> I am not sure that I can identify a community in my recent roles ... as we sit between the research and teaching communities and civil servants. I suppose the nearest affinity I have felt of late is with other colleagues in a research role at NDPBs [non-departmental public bodies].

> At the moment I don't particularly feel I am within a community – in many ways I think I still think of myself as a teacher!

> Never really thought I belonged to one until recently. I look around the room and think "my professional community is people like this". There are others in other organisations too, I'm just beginning to meet them.

These comments suggest that it was the Schools Research Liaison Group that acted as the main catalyst in people's thinking about their affinities and sense of peer group.

One respondent was explicit about the need for a professional community, not least to counteract feelings of isolation:

> Researchers within [the organisation], research colleagues in national and local agencies, as well as researchers I have worked with over time. I think the notion of a professional community is important – I sometimes feel isolated in my job – the professional community provides mutual support and advice.

Another respondent said that he felt accountable to practitioner and policy communities on the one hand, and maintained a strong adherence to the enduring values of research on the other, but that he did not feel a close affinity with the academic research community and its structures. In practice, he too experienced a degree of professional isolation and detachment.

It seems, then, that research managers in policy organisations are in effect the ones who 'hold' the tensions between policy and research ideologies and cultures, but without experiencing professional support from either community.

Towards a closer understanding of discourses and social practices of research mediation in policy environments

This small study went only a limited way to answering some of the questions I posed at the outset, though I think the data have managed to shed some light on the issues, challenges and professional satisfactions associated with managing and mediating research for policy purposes in policy environments in England. I also think the study has raised some further questions and issues deserving of serious exploration, both conceptually and empirically. I would like to suggest the following, in no particular order of priority:

- Research managers' self-accounts are revealing up to a certain point – and to have even greater credibility, those in this chapter would need to be supplemented by interviews with a far wider range of people. Self-accounts would also need to be complemented by document analysis, for example, of 'milestone' documents like the organisations' published research strategies/programmes and their ethical guidelines for research, and perhaps also of a sample of internal papers. Ideally, these would need to be triangulated by observational data too, such as might be gathered through attending and recording a range of meetings and of less formal encounters – though I do not underestimate the methodological challenges this would entail.
- The exploration of which kind(s) of 'conceptual framework' – policy studies, sociology, politics of education, etc. – might be most able to provide a sensitive and plausible way of thinking about interactions between policy and research, and about those who manage or broker them. In particular we need to understand how to conserve an appreciation of the 'good faith' of those who work in these roles, which I think the data in this chapter vindicate, whilst also allowing for the ways in which their self-accounts are shaped by the boundaries and requirements of those roles.
- The occurrence of the metaphor of 'balancing' in research managers' accounts of their roles (for example, between the different or conflicting needs of policy and research), along with other similar tropes, deserves some discourse analysis based on larger amounts of *verbatim* interview data.
- Some exploration is needed of whether research can and should be conceived of (and flourish in practice) as an independent professional discipline within policy organisations or whether it is more usefully and pragmatically to be thought of and organised as an internal service, possibly with the full apparatus of service level agreements.
- It would be good to have more 'stories from the field', in other words, a selected case-study approach – Somekh's chapter in this book on ICT research provides a helpful analogy, I think – to some characteristic problems and pitfalls in specific encounters between research and policy, how they have been addressed and with what results.

• It would also be helpful to have an analysis of the range, direction and potency of strategies and strategic management (as distinct from programmes) of research in different national policy bodies.

Given my very vested interest in the issue, I shall look forward to suggestions from others about how best to design, conduct and fund further studies, which might appropriately be based on a collaborative approach.

Some questions about professional community and association

I want to finish on a somewhat provocative note, because I believe the account provided in this chapter – notwithstanding the small scale and avowed partiality of the data on which it is based – does not support the notion that research managers working in policy environments are either naïve or culpable or both. As represented by the respondents quoted in the chapter, they do not seem to be the kind of people who would 'considerately filter out all the politically "unhelpful" findings' (Temple, op. cit., p. 220).

On the contrary, I think these people show themselves as professionals with a sense of self-reflexivity which is rooted at least in part in the research values they have acquired through their work and/or formal training. My contention is that the views expressed by respondents about their felt connection with academic researchers 'out there' on the one hand and their lack of a sense of professional community on the other cannot but raise some questions for and about the role of professional research associations. I believe such bodies should ask themselves whether and how far their constituency avowedly includes researchers in national and local government; and whether their events and activities explicitly seek to address the professional, intellectual and ethical issues faced by such people, as well as those of academic researchers in universities. Some re-thinking of the kinds of support that could be made available from a professional association to all those employed in professionally relevant roles, regardless of institution, would, I think, be most helpful.

If some of the contributors to this book are right in their analyses, the conceptualisation of relationships between research and policy-making in future will need to take account both of the devolved and iterative ways in which policy-making is now being done (see Moss and Huxford in this book) and of a more engaged, speculative and scenario-building role for research (see Somekh in this book). I am sure that one of the things this means is that the mediating and brokerage role will need to be strengthened, and the skills, knowledge and values of the mediators and brokers will need to be thoroughly understood, supported and developed. I should like to think that professional research associations would wish to take the lead here.

But to start with the present: one obvious area of need for researchers working in non-university environments is surely support and protection over ethical issues and dilemmas: in terms of practical decision-making, these are likely to go far beyond the *über*-question of 'independence and critical autonomy' (Munn 2005), important principles though these are as a foundation. One respondent said he had to 'dig up' ethical codes from different places, and eventually found something relevant and useful on the website for a government department that deals with employment rather than education issues, the Department for Work and Pensions. A key development, in my view, would be to work towards the acceptance by sponsors and funders as well as individual researchers of the *binding* nature of an ethical code which goes beyond guidelines and is backed up by appropriate apparatus.

Some other ideas include the possibility of professional research associations hosting invitational seminars for selected people in national agencies, to assist their engagement with the research ideas and evidence on particular themes. This would follow the lead of the research teams conducting projects under the ESRC's Teaching and Learning Research Programme, who have held seminars for policymakers in the Department for Education and Skills on the key policy-related messages from their studies. Such an approach might also serve to strengthen the hand of pioneering colleagues in the national agencies who are trying out different forms of research engagement for their policy colleagues.

Professional research associations might also give some thought to how the research community could do more to ensure that research advisers are kept up to date with important research ideas, trends and generic findings: even with the help of our tiny but excellent library and information service at the GTC, I do not have time to sift through, and critically appraise, the detail of all possible relevant journal articles and books.

Individually, association members who are based in universities could acquaint themselves more fully – *via* a few clicks on relevant websites, for example (the GTC's website address is www.gtce.org.uk/) – with the research-related work of national policy organisations, and how their research strategies and efforts are evolving. We always appreciate feedback and a sense that our efforts are at least noticed, if not always commanding approval.

Finally, as Levin (2004, p. 11) remarks, 'models of dissemination and impact (of educational research) remain quite cautious'. It should concern all of us that one respondent became so frustrated with the lack of helpful materials and activities that s/he went looking outside education for ideas. I have done a bit of looking around myself: to take just one example, the Overseas Development Institute – the independent think-tank on international development and humanitarian issues – has published a handbook for researchers working in a policy context (Start and Hovland 2004), together with other materials as part of its RAPID (Research and Policy in Development) programme. Here is something really useful for the education sector to take forward collectively and with some urgency: at present, the Centre for the Use of Research and Evidence in Education (CUREE: http://www.curee-paccts.com/index.jsp) is almost alone in having as its main organisational aim 'supporting and developing the effective use of research and evidence in education'.

In summary, my data indicate that the invisible 'go-betweens' and 'mediators' (and they are definitely *not* 'gofers') of policy-relevant research need to be seen as highly qualified and experienced professionals who would like – amongst many other things – to feel more recognised and strategically supported by their professional research bodies, as well as by their policy communities, in the work they do. And I am also fairly sure that such a move could only strengthen the relationship between research and decision-making in policy environments.

References

Ball, S.J. (1990). *Politics and Policy Making in Education*. London: Routledge.

BERA. (2003). *Educational Policy and Research across the UK*. Report of a BERA Colloquium held at the University of Edinburgh, 7–8 November 2002. Nottingham: British Educational Research Association.

Davies, H.T.O, Nutley, S.M. and Smith, P.C. (eds) (2000). *What Works? Evidence-based Policy and Practice in Public Services*. Bristol: The Policy Press.

Davies, P. (2004). "Is evidence-based government possible?" The 2004 Jerry Lee Lecture, Campbell Collaboration Colloquium, Washington DC, 19 February.

DETYA. (2000). *The Impact of Educational Research*. Canberra: Commonwealth of Australia. Downloaded June 2002 from: www.detya.gov.au/highered/respubs/impact/overview.htm

Galvin, C. (2004). "The making of public policy in a digital age: some reflections on changing practice." Paper presented at Market Research Society Conference "Social Policy Research in the Information Age", London, 17 February.

Hanney, S. (2004). "Assessing the impact of research on policy: concepts, models and methods." Paper presented at a seminar, *Assessing Research Impact*, St Andrews University, 15 January.

Humes, W. and Bryce, T. (2001). "Scholarship, research and the evidential basis of policy development in education." *British Journal of Educational Studies*, **49**(3), 329–52.

Levin, B. (2001). "Knowledge and action in education policy and politics." Presentation at conference on empirical issues in Canadian education, Ottawa, November. Downloaded 24 July 2003 from: http://home.cc.umanitoba.ca/~levin/sweetmanconf_ files/frame.htm

Levin, B. (2003a). "Increasing the impact and value of research in education." *Educators' Notebook*, **14**, 1.

Levin, B. (2003b). "Increasing the impact of research." Presentation to University of South Australia, 3 March. Downloaded 24 July 2003 from: http://home.cc.umanitoba.ca/~levin/increasing_impact_ofresearch_files/frame.htm

Levin, B. (2003c). "Research, policy and the state in education." Presentation to Deakin University, 28 March. Downloaded 24 July 2003 from: http://home.cc.umanitoba.ca/~levin/deakin%20mar03_files/frame.htm

Levin, B. (2004). "Making research matter more." *Education Policy Analysis Archives*, **12**, 56. Downloaded 12 December 2006 from: http://epaa.asu.edu/epaa/v12n56/

Morris, A. (2004). "Research impact." Paper presented at Market Research Society Conference "Social Policy Research in the Information Age," London, 17 February.

Munn, P. (2005). "Researching policy and policy research." *Scottish Educational Review*, **37**(1), 17–28.

Nutley, S. (2003). "Bridging the policy/research divide: reflections and lessons from the UK." Keynote paper presented at "Facing the future: engaging stakeholders and citizens in developing public policy," National Institute of Governance Conference, Canberra, 23 April.

Nutley, S.M., Percy-Smith, J. and Solesbury, W. (2003). *Models of Research Impact: a Cross-Sector Review of Literature and Practice*. London: Learning and Skills Development Agency.

Pawson, R. (2006). *Evidence-Based Policy: a Realist Perspective*. London: Sage Publications.

Percy-Smith, J., Burden, T., Darlow, A., Dawson, L., Hawtin, M. and Ladi, S. (2002). *Promoting Change Through Research: the Impact of Research in Local Government*. York: Joseph Rowntree Foundation.

Saunders, L. (2001). "The General Teaching Council: developing a policy and strategy for research." *Management in Education*, **15**(1), 6–8.

Saunders, L. (2002). "Evidence, professionalism and values: the GTC's research agenda." *Professional Development Today*, **5**(1), 63–70.

Saunders, L. (2003a). "Becoming an evidence-based professional organisation: *en route* from research projects to organisational knowledge." Paper presented at the Market Research Society conference, *Challenges and Opportunities in Public Policy Research*, London, 12 February.

Saunders, L. (2003b). "Supporting policy with research: challenges and possibilities." Paper presented at the British Educational Research Association Annual Conference, 12 September, Edinburgh, Heriot-Watt University.

Saunders, L. (2004). *Grounding the Democratic Imagination: Developing the Relationship Between Research and Policy in Education. Professorial Lecture*. London: Institute of Education.

Saunders, L. (2005a). "Research into policy doesn't go? A response to 'Interesting times, and interested research', British Educational Research Journal Editorial, **30**(4), 475–476." *British Educational Research Journal*, **31**(1), 2–4.

Saunders, L. (2005b). "Research and policy: reflections on their relationship." *Evidence and Policy: a Journal of Research, Debate and Practice*, **1**(2), 383–90.

Social Research Association (2002). *Commissioning Social Research: a Good Practice Guide*. London: SRA. Downloadable from: http://www.the-sra.org.uk/commissioning.pdf

Somekh, B. (2005). "The interplay between policy and research in relation to ICT in education in the UK: issues from twenty years of programme evaluation." Paper presented at the British Educational Research Association annual conference, University of Glamorgan, Pontypridd, 15 September.

Start, D. and Hovland, I. (2004). *Tools for Policy Impact: a Handbook for Researchers*. Overseas Development Institute. Downloadable from: http://www.odi.org.uk/RAPID/Lessons/Index.html

Temple, P. (2003). "Educational research and policymaking: findings from some transitional countries." *London Review of Education*, **1**(3), 217–28.

Walter, I., Nutley, S. and Davies, H. (2003). "Developing a taxonomy of interventions used to increase the impact of research." Unpublished paper.

Weiss, C.H. (1979). "The many meanings of research utilisation." *Public Administration Review*, **39**(5), 426–31.

Weiss, C.H. (1991). "Policy research: data, ideas or arguments?" In: Wagner, P., Weiss, C.H., Wittrock, B. and Wollman, H. (eds), *Social Sciences and Modern States: National Experiences and Theoretical Crossroads*. Cambridge: Cambridge University Press.

Whitty, G. (2002). *Making Sense of Education Policy*. London: Paul Chapman.

Willinsky, J. (2000). *If Only We Knew: Increasing the Public Value of Social-Science Research*. London: Routledge.

Willinsky, J. (2003). "Policymakers' online use of academic research." *Education Policy Analysis Archives*, **11**, 2. Downloaded 20 February 2003 from: http://epaa.asu.edu/epaa/v11n2/

Chapter 8

Enhancing impact on policy-making through increasing user engagement in research

Judy Sebba[1]

Introduction

Background

User engagement has become part of the rhetoric of educational (e.g. Levin 2004) and social science (e.g. Nutley 2003) research, and many funders (e.g. initially the Nuffield Foundation and more recently the Economic and Social Research Council [ESRC]) expect research applications to address issues of how users will be engaged in the research process. There is little agreement on what is meant by 'user engagement', who constitutes a 'user' or a shared understanding of the assumed relationship between the engagement of users and subsequent impact on policy. The current reality of user engagement often is limited to inviting policy-makers and practitioners to discuss emerging findings and attempts to increase the accessibility of outputs.

Many writers (see, for example, Davies 2004; Davies *et al.* 2005) have suggested that increasing user engagement in research will improve the subsequent impact of the research on policy, though have themselves acknowledged that little evidence for this exists, partly because of the complexities in the policy-making process which limit the possibility of isolating the specific impact of research evidence. These writers stress the need for engagement to move beyond the established debates about improving dissemination strategies in order to increase access for users, to much more extensive and ongoing involvement of users in research. Weiss (1998), in promoting user engagement in evaluation, suggested that 'sustained interactivity transforms one-way reporting into mutual learning'. However, there remain major challenges in developing meaningful user engagement throughout the process of framing research questions, commissioning projects or programmes, data collection, analysis, reporting and dissemination. In particular, the implications for research design have been barely explored. This chapter explores and critiques these issues through the outcomes of a seminar series funded by the ESRC, *Making a Difference: Working with users to develop educational research.*

The context

Hillage *et al.*'s (1998) review of educational research reported that researchers felt that the educational research being commissioned was too skewed towards policy and practice, while the policy-makers generally thought that it focused insufficiently on these. They concluded that most educational research does not impinge much on policy and where it does so, this tends to happen in an *ad hoc* and individual way. This was noted to result partly from the complexity of the policy process and partly from the lack of a coherent dissemination strategy. The report also expressed the view that this reflected a lack of interest and understanding of research among policy-makers.

Where research did address policy issues, it was reported to be small scale, limiting its scope to be reliable and generalisable, insufficiently based on existing knowledge limiting its capacity to advance understanding, inaccessible to a non-academic audience and lacking interpretation for policy-makers. This final conclusion was noted to reflect the absence of an infrastructure for mediation of research through which research is interpreted and assimilated into actions, decision-making and practice. One of the explanations proposed for these conclusions was that research is too researcher- or supply-driven, a point later taken up in the OECD (2002) review of educational research in England. The Hillage *et al.* report also noted a mismatch in the timing of the policy-making and the research production cycles in that policy-makers were commissioning mainly evaluations that tended to be backward-looking while researchers wanted to undertake more theoretical and conceptual work that might be regarded as more likely to inform future directions.

Critiques from the research community of the Hillage *et al.* report were plentiful and assertive. Many made similar points though rarely as succinctly as Goldstein (1998), who suggested that it was inappropriate to assume that all major research was concerned with influencing policy and practice. He noted that much major educational research is methodological or theoretical, providing new perspectives on learning, teaching or policy but not necessarily of immediate relevance. Similarly, Atkinson (2000) argued that the analysis in the Hillage report, and indeed in other critiques of educational research produced around that time, was based on a strongly instrumental model. This approach assumed that a published report arising from research is the 'end-product' of the research. Instead, she argued that the research community saw:

> the published report as the 'beginning' of an essential process of discourse and debate, in which further questions are raised and the views and conclusions of the researcher are challenged.
>
> (Atkinson 2000, p. 322)

Others were less polemical in their analysis of the relationship between theoretical and applied research. A review by the Organisation for Economic

Cooperation and Development (OECD 2002) cited Stokes (1997) in arguing that research can be simultaneously both 'pure' and 'use-inspired'. In the conclusions of their report, the OECD team suggested that the English government should create a portfolio of research, in which more research would simultaneously address issues of policy (or practice) and issues of fundamental knowledge.

The need to increase the expectations and capacity of policy-makers to use research was emphasised by Mortimore (2000, p. 22) through his presidential address to the British Educational Research Association:

> ... we must learn to listen to our users—not to abdicate our own responsibil-
> ities, nor to provide 'tips for teachers' or ready-made policies for politi-
> cians—but in order to ensure that the serious business of research, such as its
> capability to create new knowledge or to challenge accepted ways of thinking,
> matters to them and not just to us.

In response to the recommendations of the Hillage report and OECD review, initiatives such as policy fora, the setting up of the National Educational Research Forum (NERF) and the Funders Forum were developed with aims that included creating a more open dialogue between researchers and users. These initiatives are described in more detail elsewhere (see Sebba 2004 and also Chapter 6 of this book). The Commission on the Social Sciences (2003) recognised the increasing involvement of academics on research steering groups, advisory groups and other work in government. Furthermore, it recommended increasing the programme of secondments in both directions between staff in academia and those in government as a means of creating greater mutual understanding and knowledge transfer.

The Teaching and Learning Research Programme (TLRP) seminar series

In this context, in 1999 the Higher Education Funding Council for England (HEFCE) decided to 'top slice' the university research funding allocation for education in order to develop a centrally determined research programme that was aimed at providing more targeted research to inform teaching and learning and build research capacity in education. The ESRC was given the responsibility for managing the programme and at the launch user engagement was specifically addressed:

> ... projects will be required to show how they will work in partnership with
> potential users of the research throughout the course of the programme and
> communicate their findings to all interested parties.
>   (Press Notice, p. 4: http://www.tlrp.org/pub/press/PhaseINov1999.pdf)

Hence, the TLRP was set up with a strong commitment to potential users of research. It also had the overarching purpose of supporting and developing educational research leading to improvements in outcomes for learners of all ages, in all sectors and contexts of education, training and lifelong learning throughout the UK. The first projects began work in 2000. By 2006, it had received around £30 m from HEFCE, the Scottish Executive, the Welsh Assembly, the Northern Ireland Executive and the Department for Education and Skills, making it the largest single research programme in education in the UK and one of the largest in Europe. The TLRP programme provided a major opportunity to interrogate the evidence of the value of educational research in making a difference.

The TLRP seminar series *Making a Difference: Working with users to develop educational research* was designed and convened by the author of this chapter, together with Professor Anne Edwards and Dr Mark Rickinson. It aimed to develop the capacity of educational research to make a difference to policy and practice through better understanding and promotion of user involvement. Five seminars took place over an 18-month period with development work continuing between them. Papers were prepared to inform the seminars and the process and conclusions were documented and are accessible on the website: http://www. tlrp.org/themes/seminar/anneedwards.html. This chapter reports on the outcomes and issues arising from the seminars. Further accounts will become available through a planned book (Rickinson *et al.* 2008) and journal papers.

In the first seminar the scope of the area was explored. The intention was to identify aspects of user engagement in examples of TLRP projects in order to begin to map the areas for future conceptual work. Three projects were presented as case studies: the Phase I network on *Towards Evidence-Based Practice in Science Education*, the Phase II project on *Learning How to Learn* and the Phase III project on *Learning in and for Interagency Working*. From the discussion of the experiences of these projects, five themes emerged:

- the purposes of user engagement;
- epistemological determinants of user engagement;
- expectation of policy-makers to relate to research;
- feasibility/practical issues of involving practitioners and policy-makers in research;
- how knowledge is used in the policy community.

The rest of this paper is structured under these five themes but with the four issues of different interpretations, different frameworks, implications for research design and implications for capacity building, addressed through the themes. Before embarking on the themes, clarification is needed of what is meant by 'users'.

Who are 'users'?

The aim of maximising user engagement in the research process assumes clarity about the definition of the user community. Traditionally, users have been distinguished from researchers, leading to assumptions about the capacity of users to engage with, and understand research findings. However, researchers themselves are of course, a key audience for the findings of other researchers and the first audience for many academics, in particular, for more theoretically focused outputs. In defining users, the issue of epistemology discussed below is relevant, since the conceptual framework for the research will influence, or sometimes be a determining factor in defining the potential users of it. In the seminar series, users were defined as including those involved in education services (teachers, local authority staff, etc.), policy-makers at local, regional, national and international levels, funders of research and other researchers. The focus for this chapter, however, reflecting the scope of the book, is on policy-makers as users of research.

The purposes of user engagement

A key question was, what are the purposes of user engagement? Initially, two purposes were identified in the seminars. The first was concerned with improving the respectability of educational research (partly a political agenda) in a climate in which repeated reports, reviews, analyses and publicity were perceived as having damaged its already-fragile reputation. Promoting engagement of policy-makers and funders was seen as a way of improving the understanding of what research was about, what realistically could be expected of it, the constraints within which it operates and the need for support from funders and other users in developing dissemination strategies.

The second main purpose of user engagement discussed was to support professionalism including the practitioner as researcher, practitioners as users of research and practitioners as users of research-informed teaching materials. Feuer *et al.* (2002) note that although the argument for greater involvement of practitioners usually focuses on the importance of practical wisdom in the design of specific interventions and evaluations, they believe that conscious integration of knowledge from the world of practice could also lead to new and improved research designs more generally.

An alternative perspective to that traditionally given on the relationship between research and practice was posed in the seminars. If practice is thoughtful action, and research is a matter of generating knowledge in particular rulebound ways, the relationship between research and practice is one of interruption. That is, research-based knowledge can interrupt practice, and practice may have the potential to interrupt taken-for-granted aspects of research. The same may apply to policy. The challenge lies in generating these interruptions. This perspective takes us from a concern simply with how research knowledge is used by different communities to an examination of two-way relationships between research and practice and research and policy which both Weiss (e.g. 1998) and Nutley (e.g. 2003) have written about extensively.

The two-way relationship was also discussed in the context of approaches to knowledge production and the relationship between research and development that ensues. The boundary between research and development was a strong element in the discussions which followed the case study on the *Learning How to Learn* project. In this case, the scale of the research design had been increased to incorporate more teachers than originally intended and the presentation led to discussions about the challenges of 'scaling up' possibilities for practitioner learning from specific projects.

Since the focus in this chapter is on policy-making, readers are referred for extensive discussion of the role of research in developing teachers' professionalism to, for example, Sharp *et al.* (2005).

Epistemological determinants of user engagement

The seminars reiterated the need to recognise that educational research is not homogeneous. There are different research approaches which generate different evidence, and have the potential to engage with policy and with practice communities in ways that respect the integrity of that approach. It was noted, as discussed extensively in the US, that the *No Child Left Behind* legislation had required any publicly funded educational provision to be informed by robust evidence, defined as being generated through controlled trials. This limits the research methodology permissible to a very narrow range, although some (e.g. Feuer 2006; Slavin 2002) believe that the benefits that this will bring to children through more rigorous research informing service provision will outweigh the difficulties. Similar debates were taking place in England (e.g. Hodkinson 2004). As Berliner (2002, p. 18) noted:

> ... to think that this form of research is the only "scientific" approach to gaining knowledge – the only one that yields trustworthy evidence – reveals a myopic view of science in general, and a misunderstanding of educational research in particular. Although strongly supported in Congress, this bill confuses the methods of science with the goals of science.

The *Scientific Research in Education* report (National Research Council 2002) in the US generated much debate about epistemological and methodological constraints being placed on educational research in order to increase central control. However, Feuer *et al.* (2002) argued that good science in whichever subject thrives on a combination of generic norms that apply to all subjects and expressions of those norms that are specific to each subject.

User engagement needs to reflect the beliefs about knowledge, its production and use that are inherent in each approach, so for the publicly funded research in the US, the engagement of users in research design is likely to be restricted. In the UK, more collaborative approaches to user engagement have been adopted, which have led to significant developments in user engagement at different stages in the enquiry process.

One example of distinct types of engagement in different stages of the research process was provided by the TLRP Science Education Network (Ratcliffe *et al.* 2003). They had analysed the phases of their research in which users had been engaged. They noted that there was no engagement in the initial writing of the proposal, but some in developing the instruments and in the data collection. While there was no user engagement in analysing the data, there was considerable involvement in validating the interpretations that emerged, disseminating the findings and suggesting follow-up activities. Furthermore, national user organisations such as the national secondary strategy teams involved in supporting large-scale reform across schools, had been involved in disseminating the findings and ideas through curricular materials, guidance and training.

One factor in considering user engagement linked to the type of research approach was whether researchers can only talk to policy-makers when they are secure in the outcomes of their research. A theory-led approach was suggested in the seminars, in which the conceptual framing of the problem area is shared during the research process. Concerns were expressed that research should not be limited to finding answers to problems of practice, though the seminar discussions acknowledged that the theory-practice distinction had been unhelpfully polemical. While recognising the value of involving users in defining the research questions, it was felt that limiting research to questions defined by them might produce a rather conservative research programme of how to do the same things better.

Time-scale was also discussed in the seminars in relation to beliefs about knowledge. The time-scale at the research-policy interface is short. Research knowledge is consequently presented as a commodity to be used. Relationships at the research-practice interface may be long-term with a potential for a slow process of trust building and co-construction of knowledge. One challenge identified (and explored by Sandra Nutley in seminar 2), related to how to build relationships of mutual trust between policy and research communities so that tentative findings and conceptual framings may be brought into conversations between the two communities.

Discussion of what users accept as evidence was also related to this theme of epistemological issues. Plausibility was regarded as an insufficient warrant for researchers, while it was reported to have its attractions for both policy-makers and practitioners. Researchers tended to aim at some explanation of causality, perhaps prediction and certainly greater understanding, though approaches and explanatory weight assigned to the evidence, would vary across types of research.

Expectation of policy-makers to relate to research

The capacity of policy-makers and practitioners to understand how they might relate to the research process was a strong theme in the seminars. There were two strands in the discussion. One strand focused on what might be reasonably expected of educational research, previously explored by Edwards (2000), who concluded that 'useful' research must extend beyond demonstrating what works and why, to the structural opportunities and constraints that operate, without suggesting that these are either totally constraining or unrealistically permissive.

The other strand explored the nature of the relationship between researchers and the practitioners who are involved in the research process.

Expectation in relation to the first strand was summarised as an issue of receptivity. It was noted, for example, that current theoretical understandings of how research is used by policy communities are poorly developed. Also, emerging from the discussions of the case studies, it was agreed that the different disciplines that are represented in education will operate with different criteria for good-quality research. That is, science educators will differ from historians, who will in turn hold different expectations from sociologists. It is therefore an oversimplification to see the policy or practitioner community as homogeneous when expecting them to value research findings.

The second strand within the theme of expectation was the role of power in the relationship between researchers and policy-makers and between researchers and practitioners, in the research process. In the case study on *Learning How to Learn* (James *et al.* 2006), there were concerns that researchers have in the past tended to operate with a deficit model of teachers and considerable efforts were made by the team to engage teachers as active participants and contributors to the research process. This raised questions about who, finally, was the more powerful, given the time spent on ensuring user engagement and the use of the research project as a vehicle for improving teacher morale in one local authority. Here the question of the responsibility of the research team for scaling up the learning that was achieved by participating practitioners was highlighted.

The next case study was *Learning in and for Interagency Working* based on a project aimed at intervening in practices to promote learning. It involved developing and testing a model of work-based professional learning needed to ensure responsive collaboration. The education and care plans of young people at risk of social exclusion or with special educational needs were used as sites. The research team produced material on professional learning, interagency working and client participation, for professional and policy communities. However, negotiating and achieving a balance between a focus on, for example, the conceptual development within the project and the expectations of the cooperating local authorities was an ongoing tension.

In both these case studies the practitioners were potentially very powerful but operating within an agenda which had at its core, other concerns than the research. The third case study also illustrated that different relationships operate with each group of users and at distinct phases in the study. For example, the ongoing relationship with the reference group within the research study informed the development of the research, while the context of local authorities meant that researchers had to offer services in order to achieve cooperation.

Researchers, too, need to manage their own expectations. Greater user involvement is no guarantee of impact either during, or after the study. Instead, attention needs to be paid to working out the conflicting interests of researchers, practitioners and policy-makers when planning the research, during the research and when there are outputs to share.

Feasibility/practical issues of involving practitioners and policy-makers in research

Issues relating to feasibility ranged from difficulties in finding practitioners willing to cooperate in a research project, to meeting the expectations held by practitioners and their employers. The strong message was that user engagement takes time to negotiate and sustain and that unless expectations are managed they may orient the project to meet the immediate needs of user communities rather than the longer term aims of the research programme. Managing the tension so that user engagement enhances the research programme seems to demand a new set of skills for researchers. One starting point may be to refocus on making explicit, the different expectations at the outset, so that feasibility can be achieved. There are additional costs involved in engaging users throughout the research process including time, travel, production costs of additional targeted papers, presentations or materials. Given the changes in research-funding allocations, these costs, which may have remained hidden in the past, have to be explicitly identified and addressed by funders if they are committed to the research influencing policy.

How knowledge is used in the policy community

In the discussion of the use of knowledge, there is an underlying assumption that informed decisions are good decisions. There is a second assumption that the quality of decisions increases with the amount of 'cumulative' evidence available. Wolter *et al.* (2004) have suggested that the first assumption leads to an underestimation of the difference between information and scientific knowledge and the importance of variety and diversity of concepts, theories and research findings. The second assumption leads to an underestimation of the basic function of politics.

A study of research outputs in Germany (cited in Wolter *et al.* 2004) reported that the correlation between the amount of external funding and the number of publications per professor is near zero, which means that many of the funded research results seem to be written for educational administration and government – perhaps only to be filed away. From a policy standpoint, one could take the view that this knowledge remains invisible as an indicator of the 'usefulness' of educational research knowledge.

Discussion in the seminars focused on how research outputs are used and on an analysis of the interaction between policy and research in the research process. This latter debate considered how research-based concepts are shaped and refined in interaction with the field and the role of mediators, which is addressed in more detail in Chapter 7 of this volume. It was noted that there was little or no research on the role of mediating organisations such as think-tanks in the UK and on how the mediation process works.

Research produces knowledge which can be applied and the involvement of users in the research process is considered to lead to stronger alignment between the priorities of funders, researchers and policy-makers. This approach can be captured in a notion of receptivity, that is, how receptive potential research users are to research outputs. The limited evidence on this issue suggests a considerable lack of receptivity. Molas-Gallart *et al.* (2000) cited a previous study (Cave and Hanney 1996) showing that only 70 out of 70,000 research projects in education in the US had a significant influence on subsequent policy or practice. They note, however, that the attempts to quantify impact are riddled with difficulties which must at least raise questions over the precision of these figures. They also suggest that social science research is more likely to make indirect contributions to policy-making by modifying the options or partly influencing decisions. This is further confirmed by Rigby (2005) who reported that policy research is rarely used in direct ways but is more likely to influence concepts, propositions, orientations, and generalisations that subsequently, over time, affect policy.

The economic and political influences on how research evidence is used are not always well understood by researchers and are likely to be at the forefront of the policy-makers' agenda. Davies (2004, p. 6) suggests that:

> policy making is not just a matter of 'what works', but what works at what cost and with what outcomes (both positive and negative). This requires sound evidence not only of the cost of policies, programmes or projects, but also the cost-effectiveness, cost-benefit, and cost-utility of different courses of action.

Traditionally, cost-effectiveness and cost-benefit analyses have not been strong features of educational research although this is changing with the growth of interdisciplinary research teams and centres (see for example, the Centre for the Economics of Education website: http://cee.lse.ac.uk/). Political influences remain a challenge. Rigby (2005) notes that policy-makers *filter research through the value-laden lens of political discourse*. Her own study of research mediators concluded that policy-makers in the US rely on three sources for information: commissions, gurus and think-tanks. She suggests that these three sources are, respectively, practical only, narrow and ideologically driven. Rich's (2005) research on think-tanks in the US further confirms that they are increasingly staffed by individuals with fewer research and more media skills but that they are increasingly influential in providing 'evidence' to policy-makers.

A clear distinction was made in the seminars between how knowledge is used by policy communities and by practitioners. While it was recognised that policy-makers need clear and well-communicated ideas and research findings in which they can have some confidence, it was also acknowledged that conceptualising user engagement with the policy community was currently more challenging than working with practitioners. This may be a matter of low levels of trust, or because policy-makers have limited experience of how different types of research knowledge may be used, or simply because too little attention has been paid by researchers to understanding that interface. It was suggested that research on the social practices of decision-making in relation to the use of research in the policy community would be helpful.

However, there were examples of how research-based knowledge is shared with policy and practitioner communities. The Association of Science Education Network and the groundwork undertaken over the last 30 years by organisations such as the Nuffield and the Gatsby Foundations were mentioned as illustrations of the investment necessary to build 'an attentive audience' for research among practitioners. Discussions of networks and the role of practitioner participants and university-based researchers in them, revealed just how much work needs to be done to conceptualise how, for example, research-based knowledge is mobilised, moved, built and shared in networks. There was a recognition that opportunities for conversations between the different communities was essential for cross-boundary learning but work needs to be done on understanding how to make the best use of these and how understandings and priorities are negotiated.

Discussion of the case studies also raised questions about the importance of lead learners and policy-makers who could operate as research activists to encourage and promote learning from research in which they had been involved. Again, the need for empirical studies of the social practices of decision-making and potential research use was considered a priority.

Assessing the benefits of user engagement

The investment needed in terms of time, funding, trust and changes in culture for researchers and users to engage in the research to policy process, itself requires justification from a stronger evidence base. The methodology for studying the impact of research, and thereby of user engagement in research, is as yet, under-developed. The ESRC commissioned Molas-Gallart *et al.* (2000) to investigate the impact of research programmes on non-academic users. They defined impact as: 'whenever a research effort results in identifiable influences on current social, policy and management practices' (p. 171). The impact of the research was assessed by 'tracing post-research activity' after the project had ended and by mapping the networks of people and flow of information to identify existing or potential applications of the research results.

From their assessment of the impact of the ESRC-funded AIDS programme of research, they found that almost half the users reported that the research had provided them with new problem-solving tools and over 75 per cent of users reported that project results had justified, confirmed and helped develop new courses of action. This very high level of application was attributed to both the topicality of the research programme and the high level of need amongst policy-makers for new information and techniques. In terms of the methodology for assessing impact on users, they concluded that both researchers and users must be involved in identifying possible impacts, these should be mapped and how users are identified will depend on the type of research. However, they noted that the effects of social science research findings were more likely to be indirect and to experience a long delay between release of findings and impact, creating even greater difficulties in identifying and assessing the impact. Further work on developing methodologies for assessing the benefits of user engagement in research would be helpful.

Conclusions drawn from the seminar series

The conclusions from the seminar series were drawn together under the headings of 'knowing what, knowing how, knowing who and knowing when'. Further thoughts on social and epistemological issues were added to these and some initial ideas for ways forward were explored and are tentatively presented here.

Knowing what

Both Rigby's (2005) and Rich's (2005) research in the US described above point to the relatively low position enjoyed by 'academic research' amongst sources of evidence used by policy-makers. In an internal survey within the English government, Davies (see Seminar 5 Summary on series website) noted that academic research was the last source of evidence considered, with 'special advisers', 'experts', think-tanks and the media much more likely to be used and somewhat more encouragingly, professional associations, which might be assumed more likely to mention research.

Davies and others concluded that researchers need to think more about sharing ideas and concepts and policy-makers need to see researchers as sources of ideas. This raises interesting questions concerning the role of research in generating ideas and the role of ideas in developing research evidence. Traditionally, researchers are not always willing or able to go beyond their data and contribute new ideas and concepts, some policy-makers are interested only in evidence about what works and an understanding of the policy process will be incomplete without a recognition of the central role of ideology alongside evidence and ideas. However, greater scope for the role of researchers working in conjunction with think-tanks and the media was considered a way potentially of improving the quality of evidence used in generating ideas.

Knowing how

A recurring theme during the seminar series was the complexity of knowledge processes within and between different user groups in education. The concluding discussions highlighted the importance of notions such as knowledge transfer, knowledge translation, knowledge brokerage and knowledge transmission. 'Knowledge brokerage' was singled out by Davies as the closest depiction of the work of government social researchers. One elaboration of this term is provided by the Canadian Health Services Research Foundation (2006, http://www.chsrf.ca/brokering/index_e.php). Other models are provided by the Research Unit for Research Utilisation (www.ruru.ac.uk).

The means by which researchers are able to meet people working in the policy realm was noted to include activities such as networking, socialising and infiltration of existing fora. The social and affective dimensions of user engagement and knowledge transfer were acknowledged from this.

Knowing who

The emotional dimensions of user engagement mean that knowing how is intricately connected with knowing who. Participants in the seminars favoured the notion of 'decision-maker' over 'user' because of its focus on helping people to make better decisions and its capacity to include groups such as students and parents as well as teachers and civil servants. It was recognised that relationships between different user communities can be very different in terms of power. For example, knowledge flows between researchers and practitioners are often less problematic than between researchers and policy-makers. Differences of this kind should have significant implications for the design of research projects.

Knowing who is an issue that is relevant *within* research teams as well as beyond them. The experience of large-scale TLRP projects and the prospects of still larger educational research projects in the future have highlighted the potential for a greater diversity of roles within project teams. Within this, there is an opportunity to recognise and take seriously the knowledge management/ boundary role within projects.

Knowing when

There was strong agreement that questions of timing, time-scales and time were central to all activities associated with working with users. The importance was emphasised of knowing when to involve users and when to focus on particular research areas in terms of identifying the emerging hot issues/topics. Identifying the moment when a senior policy person is looking for something that a researcher can provide and getting involved when ideas are being formulated is a challenge.

There were references throughout the seminars to the perennial challenges of the diverging time-scales of policy, practice and research. Dyson (see Seminar 5 Summary on website) saw this in terms of an inevitable tension between acting and understanding noting: 'It is perfectly true, as philosophers say, that life must be understood backwards. But they forget the other proposition, that it must be lived forwards' (a quote from the Danish philosopher, Soren Kierkegaard). In other words, there is always a mismatch between what we know and what we want to know.

Finding the time and space to do dissemination and knowledge transfer activities is difficult for researchers and until recently, was not included in research funding. There was hope, however, that TLRP's emphasis on user engagement will help to improve the way in which this is addressed in future proposals and enhance the emphasis on knowledge transfer skills within larger and more diverse project teams.

Social and epistemological approaches

Two different ways of thinking and talking about user engagement issues were identified: social and epistemological. The social perspective uses terms such as 'tribes', 'bridges', 'fora', 'co-location', 'mediation', 'consensus building' and 'boundary crossing'. Implicit to all of these terms is the idea that research impact is a socio-cultural problem. Researchers and users have something to offer each other but they have drifted apart and so need solutions such as bridges and mediation.

The epistemological perspective uses terms such as 'ideas', 'concepts', 'forward looking', 'different ways of thinking' and 'ideology'. These assume that the problem is not so much about two groups but about different perspectives of what constitutes knowledge. If research impact is not only a social problem but also an epistemological one, then there is a need not only for fora and bridges, but also for notions of co-configuration and co-production. In other words, policy-makers work alongside researchers to construct a third type of knowledge: a 'where do we go from here' type of knowledge.

Some initial proposals for future developments

The outcomes of the seminar series should provide the basis for new and positive future action. The following are some initial ideas explored tentatively towards the end of the series and undergoing further discussion. The author, and the two other seminar series leaders, would welcome further dialogue on them.

Generating case studies of different models of participatory and democratic research. Drawing on the issues that have arisen in the seminars, the implications for research design are around participatory and democratic models of research. Existing examples of this include research about disability undertaken by disabled people, the TLRP inclusion network and the General Teaching Council for Wales professional networks and bursaries. The proposal is to take this forward by generating further examples.

Schools and other institutions use of research. The projects to date seem to have focused on schools engaging in research through undertaking research activities. The seminar series has highlighted the importance of ensuring that schools and other institutions develop a thirst for research and that findings are accessible. A further project might usefully set up experiments in this area.

Identifying and improving mediation processes. The seminars have given rise to a number of issues about who mediates research and how this is done. The role of think-tanks, the media, teacher educators and others in mediating research has been considered. A study of these agents and the processes, thus far only completed in the US context (although Professor Adam Tickell at the Royal Holloway is currently engaged in some research related to this, personal communication), might further illuminate these issues.

Development opportunities for policy-makers and potential researchers, early career researchers, contract researchers and established researchers. The need to embed and extend current training and continuing professional development to include issues around how research is designed with users in mind, the research to practice and research to policy processes and use of evidence. A few isolated examples of Masters' courses and others have been identified but further work in this area is needed.

Possible questions around improving user engagement for researchers to consider when planning research will be generated from the seminar series. Further work could involve the testing out of the utility of these.

Research into developing understanding of the role of research by users including policy-makers. Issues such as recognising the provisionality of research conclusions, valuing uncertainty and debates about weight of evidence could be researched over time, perhaps linked to one or more of the other proposals involving 'intervention'.

Challenges ahead

The relationship between research, policy and practice is subtle, complex and changing. This relationship acknowledges that the usefulness of user engagement in research is more than a matter of enhancing the impact of research findings on policy or practice, if indeed that is happening. The aim of the seminar series was to begin to tease out that complex relationship and consider its place in the development of educational research. Much has been achieved, although there is still a long way to go in exploring the nature of knowledge transfer, the implications of user engagement for research design and the culture of the policy context.

The seminar series website: http://www.tlrp.org/themes/seminar/anneedwards. html includes relevant papers as they are published.

References

Atkinson, E. (2000) In defence of ideas, or why 'what works' is not enough. *British Journal of Sociology of Education*, **21**, 317–330.

Berliner, D.C. (2002) Educational Research: the hardest science of all. *Educational Researcher*, **31**, 18–20.

Cave, M. and Hanney, S. (1996) Assessment of research impact on non-academic audiences, Consultants' Report Faculty of Social Sciences, Brunel University, Uxbridge.

Commission on the Social Sciences (2003) Great expectations: the social sciences in Britain. London: Academy of Learned Societies for the Social Sciences. Also available at: www.the-academy.org.uk/

Davies, P. (2004) Is evidence-based government possible? Jerry Lee lecture to Campbell Collaboration Colloquium, Washington DC 19 February 2004. Accessed at: http://www.policyhub.gov.uk/downloads/JerryLeeLecture1202041.pdf#page=1

Davies, H., Nutley, S. and Walter, I. (2005) Approaches to assessing the non-academic impact of social science research. Report of the ESRC symposium on assessing the non-academic impact of research 12–13 May 2005, Research Unit for Research Utilisation, University of St Andrews. Accessed at: www.st-and.ac.uk/~ruru

Edwards, T. (2000) 'All the evidence shows…': Reasonable expectations of educational research. *Oxford Review of Education*, **26**, 299–311.

Feuer M. (2006) *Moderating the Debate: Rationality and the Promise of American Education.* Boston: Harvard Educational Press.

Feuer, M.J., Towne, L. and Shavelson, R.J. (2002) Scientific culture and educational research. *Educational Researcher*, **31**, 4–14, and 'Reply' same issue, 28–29.

Goldstein, H. (1998) *Excellence in Research in Schools: a Commentary.* On Goldstein's website at: http://www.cmm.bristol.ac.uk/team/HG_Personal/excelres.pdf

Hillage, L., Pearson, R., Anderson, A. and Tamkin, P. (1998) *Excellence in Research on Schools.* London: DfEE.

Hodkinson, P. (2004) Research as a form of work: expertise, community and methodological objectivity. *British Educational Research Journal*, **30**, 9–26.

James, M., Black, P., McCormick, R., Pedder, D. and Wiliam, D. (2006) Learning how to learn, in classrooms, schools and networks: aims, design and analysis. *Research Papers in Education*, **2**, 101–118.

Levin, B. (2004) Helping research in education to matter more. *Education Policy Analysis Archives*, **12**, 56. Accessed 29 January 07 at: http://epaa.asu.edu/epaa/v12n56/

Molas-Gallart, J., Tang, P. and Morrow, S. (2000) Assessing the non-academic impact of grant-funded socio-economic research: results from a pilot study. *Research Evaluation,* **9**, 171–182.

Mortimore, P. (2000) Does educational research matter? *British Educational Research Journal*, **26**, 5–24.

National Research Council (2002) *Scientific Research in Education.* Committee on Scientific Principles for Education Research. Washington, DC: National Academy Press.

Nutley, S. (2003) Bridging the policy/research divide: Reflections and lessons from the UK. Keynote paper presented to National Institute of Governance Conference Canberra, Australia. Accessed on 8 January 07 at: www.ruru.ac.uk

OECD (2002) *Educational Research and Development in England: Examiners' Report.* Paris: OECD.

Ratcliffe, M., Bartholomew, H., Hames, V., Hind, A., Leach, J., Millar, R. and Osborne, J. (2003) Evidence-based practice in science education: The researcher-user interface. British Educational Research Association Annual Conference, http://www.tlrparchive.org/cgibin/search_oai_all.pl?pn=1&no_menu=1&short_menu1

Rich, A. (2005) *Think Tanks, Public Policy and the Politics of Expertise.* Cambridge: Cambridge University Press.

Rickinson, M., Edwards, A. and Sebba, J. (2008) *Improving Research Through User Engagement.* London: Routledge.

Rigby, E. (2005) Linking research and policy on Capitol Hill. *Evidence and Policy*, **1**, 195–213.

Sebba, J. (2004) Developing an evidence-based approach to policy and practice in education. Discussion Paper No 5 Higher Education Academy, www.heacademy.ac.uk/embedded_object.asp?id=21593&filename=QE006D

Sharp, C., Eames, A., Sanders, D. and Tomlinson, K. (2005) *Postcards From Research-engaged Schools.* Slough: NFER.

Slavin, R.E. (2002) Evidence-based education policies: transforming educational practice and research. *Educational Researcher*, **31,** 15–21.

Stokes (1997) *Pasteur's Quadrant – Basic Science and Technological Innovation.* Washington, DC: Brookings Press.

Weiss, C. (1998) Have we learned anything new about the use of evaluation? *American Journal of Evaluation,* **19,** 21–34.

Wolter, S., Keiner, E., Palomba, D. and Lindblad, S. (2004) OECD Examiners' Report on Educational Research and Development in England. *European Educational Research Journal*, **3,** 510–526.

Chapter 9

Protecting the innocent

The need for ethical frameworks within mass educational innovation

Tim Oates

Introduction: setting the scene

Having spent 20 years immersed in the policy and development work associated with large-scale innovation and transformation of the UK education and training system, I have in recent years become increasingly concerned about three things: the rapidity of change and turnover in major innovations; the lack of transparency in the origins of innovations (mitigated only to a degree by the Freedom of Information Act); and the lack of safeguards for those learners caught up in major system innovation. Rather than these being three separate things, my involvement in policy development on mass innovations – as head of research first at the National Council for Vocational Qualifications and then the Qualifications and Curriculum Authority – forced a stark recognition that they are intimately linked. This chapter examines these linkages but places a spotlight on the ethical issues relating to safeguards for learners.

From the increasingly vitriolic exchange between 'resisters' (Oakley 2006) and 'militant empiricists' (Lather 2004) I wish to extract two concepts. From Oakley I will extract the notion of 'harm' (Oakley 2000). From Hammersley I will extract the notion of 'experimentation' (Hammersley 1997). In extracting these I am not ignoring the highly specific commitments of (i) the discourse in which they are embedded nor (ii) the specific theoretical assumptions which are associated with them within this discourse. But I do deliberately wish to depart on a tangent – a line of enquiry which will hopefully be of interest to both sets of warring parties. Whilst some may feel I am simply engaging in a minor skirmish on the periphery of the conflict, my contention is that the new evidence I present opens up a whole new front.

First, Hammersley: in education (and training) '... strict experimentation is often ruled out for practical or ethical reasons' (Hammersley 1997, p. 145). The possibility of 'experimentation' has been long contested in educational research (McCall 1923; Miles 1964; Davies *et al.* 2000). Hammersley's use of the construct in his critique legitimates its application to enquiry in social and natural science by virtue of his claim that its use is limited through 'practical and ethical' limitations, rather than on absolute (ontological) grounds. As a result, I will extract the concept of 'experimentation' and examine mass innovations in education and training (such as the introduction, in England, of the National Curriculum) against criteria which are, or can be, utilised in the regulation of experimentation. Put simply, if we can describe some actions in education as 'experiments', then we can examine their characteristics and the outcomes of different approaches.

Second, Oakley:

> Paradigm wars will not bring about social justice or justify public expenditure: The goal of an emancipatory (social) science calls for us to abandon sterile word-games and concentrate on the business in hand, which is how to develop the most reliable and democratic ways of knowing, both in order to bridge the gap between ourselves and others, and to ensure that those who intervene in other people's lives do so with the most benefit and the least harm.
>
> (Oakley 2000, p. 3)

From this I derive the key notion of 'harm'. This evokes a linkage with medical ethics, and I make this central to the analysis in this chapter. Building on the notions of 'experimentation' and 'harm', I will map a line of argument which covers:

- the legitimacy of a partial and precise analogy between education and medicine in respect of the positioning of ethical regulation of practice, asserting that 'do no harm' should be central to educational evaluation and policy-making;
- the role of realist ontology and epistemology in explaining problematic elements of the relationships between educational researchers and policy-makers, and in reforming these relationships through a more realistic and functional set of mutual expectations;
- the severe ethical defects of major evaluations of fundamental reforms within the English education and training system. Four case studies will be used to exemplify different forms of these defects.

I shall argue that there has been chronic and serious neglect of key ethical dimensions in major reforms over the past 20 years. I conclude by presenting an argument for a radical look at new arrangements for ethical regulation of both educational evaluation and of innovation in education and training arrangements.

Is 'do no harm' relevant to mass innovation in education and training systems?

The principal focus of this chapter is: how should the principle of 'do no harm' be interpreted at educational system level? But is it vital to first ask – is 'do no harm' relevant to education and training? Here, I wish to argue that an analogy can be drawn between the decisions made by teachers and educationalists on the one hand, and medical professionals on the other.

I will be precise about my focus:

- I am not dealing with the ethics of educational research and evaluation;
- I am not dealing with the ethics of educational practice (for example, ethical codes for teachers);
- I am dealing with the ethics of mass innovation – policy development and the implementation of reform.

Whatever the precise origin and etymological history of 'do no harm' within medical ethics (Friedson 1970), it has emerged as a primary driver of medical ethics. Yet, what can explain one startling difference between education and medicine – the prominence of ethical regulation of medical practice and implementation of new therapies, and the lack of prominence of ethical regulation for educational innovation? The answer cannot lie in the structure of competence in the two domains, since researchers increasingly use cross-analysis of educational practice and medical practice in order to push forward understanding of the structure of competence (Boreham 2002; Fischer 2004): See Table 9.1 below.

Table 9.1

	Examples from the practice of medicine	*Examples from the practice of education*
Practice as 'treatment'	Decisions regarding therapeutic regimes, drugs administration, etc.	Decisions regarding learning environment, adapting learning approaches and activities in order to optimise learning
Formalised, conscious procedures	Diagnostic protocols; initiating appropriate tests; operating consent and confidentiality protocols; optimising outcomes for individuals; working to targets	Deployment of teaching and learning approaches such as objective-based learning, the literacy and numeracy strategies; cognitive acceleration; within-class pupil grouping; working to targets
Underlying unconscious procedures, implicit professional rules	Adapting communication strategies to the needs of different patients; optimising personal performance in different team settings	Adapting teaching and learning strategies to the needs of different learners in different contexts; optimising personal performance in different team settings
Examples of confounding variables in securing effective outcomes	Family wealth, social background, self-medication, prior conditions	Gender, date of birth, family wealth, social background, early educational experience

If systematic application of ethical controls is a principal driver of practice, policy formation and innovation in one domain, why should it not figure in the same structural way in another domain which has many fundamental features in common?

However, I wish to draw an analogy between education and medicine in respect of one key dimension only. I am not arguing that the structure of knowledge in education is the same as in the medical arena (Sokal and Bricmont 1998) nor am I arguing that methods in educational research can or should emulate those in medical research (Cook 2003). However, I wish to analogise between education and medicine in respect of *intervention*. This follows the use of the term 'intervention' to describe educational practice in educational research work which falls into an experimental paradigm (see, for example, Fitzgibbon and Defty [2000]). However, it is clear that the concept of 'intervention' extends beyond this, into areas of programme-based educational practice, such as the English literacy, numeracy and standards programmes (see DfES 2006).

Note that I am not implying that the term 'intervention' applies only to policy of a certain form or that all interventions follow a top-down approach – interventions can follow highly collaborative and negotiated forms (Stenhouse 1985; Elliot 1999). However, I am arguing that policy oriented towards change (in systems, in pedagogy, in pupil outcomes) can be characterised as 'intervention', that is, an attempt to affect the trajectory of development in systems and individuals.

Is there a seamless join between a national policy directed at change and the guidance of the teacher, supporting a learner in the day-to-day exchange of a learning setting, or are they different in type? I would argue that – in one key respect – they are the same. Even if viewed from a hardline constructivist position, the exchange between teacher and learner can be theorised as a common attempt to facilitate learning – that is, to extend learners' conceptual frameworks and schemata; to change the condition of the learner (most simply, from unknowing to knowing; unskilled to skilled; non-competent to competent) (Whitebread 2003). Learning necessitates change (Geber 1977; Mayer 1977) – and change can be construed, with validity, as involving *intervention* in things as they are, in order to make them something else. In supporting learning, a teacher or instructor faces decisions about what they say and do to support the learner and when; they exercise judgement (Walter 1981). This can be construed as 'intervention' – inputs/actions which cause learning to occur more effectively than if that support was absent. It can also be construed as 'treatment' – not only are there decisions about whether or not to support a learner directly, there are decisions about *appropriate* actions – there are choices in respect of what to do. Ignoring the connotations of passivity and one-way power relationship in the idea of a 'therapeutic regime', teachers and instructors *are* concerned with setting up 'learning milieux' – where all elements of the learning context are configured to produce beneficial learning (Stenhouse 1983). I am suggesting that this is analogous to 'medical treatment'. In this I am not arguing that a state of 'unknowing'– for instance, not knowing a set of mathematical operations, or not knowing the distinction between 'sex' and 'gender' – is an illness or pathology and that 'knowing' is a state of health. What I am arguing is that managing learning settings such that a learner can understand these things, can acquire knowledge and skill, etc., involves complex choices (Walter 1981) and these can be characterised as a choice of 'treatment'.

Definitions of 'treatment'

care by procedures or applications that are intended to relieve illness or injury

the management of someone or something; "the handling of prisoners"; "the treatment of water sewage"; "the right to equal treatment in the criminal justice system"

>   http://wordnet.princeton.edu/perl/webwn?s=treatment

A treatment is a specific combination of factor levels whose effect is to be compared with other treatments

>   http://www.itl.nist.gov/div898/handbook/pri/section7/pri7.htm

Given the power relationships which obtain in early years education and compulsory schooling (Biken and Pollard 1993) – and the power relations implicit in the requirements of a national curriculum (Tapper and Salter 1978; Aldrich and White 1998; Salter and Tapper 1981) and its assessment – there is a moral imperative associated with decision-making relating to choice of 'educational treatment' (Peters 1970; Bottley 2000). This invokes the analogy with medical treatment – an analogy strengthened by the conceptual commitments of the increasing number of teachers' codes of ethical practice which are emerging around the world. From New Zealand:

Commitment to learners

The primary professional obligation of registered teachers is to those they teach. Teachers nurture the capacities of all learners to think and act with developing independence, and strive to encourage an informed appreciation of the fundamental values of a democratic society.

Teachers will strive to:

a)   develop and maintain professional relationships with learners based upon the best interests of those learners,
b)   base their professional practice on continuous professional learning, the best knowledge available about curriculum content and pedagogy, together with their knowledge about those they teach,
c)   present subject matter from an informed and balanced viewpoint,

d) encourage learners to think critically about significant social issues,
e) cater for the varied learning needs of diverse learners,
f) promote the physical, emotional, social, intellectual and spiritual wellbe-
    ing of learners,
g) protect the confidentiality of information about learners obtained in the
    course of professional service, consistent with legal requirements.

http://www.teacherscouncil.govt.nz/ethics/code.stm

In England, the General Teaching Council has produced an analogous statement:

GTC statement of professional values and practice for teachers:

Teachers place the learning and well-being of young people at the centre of their professional practice.

Teachers respond sensitively to the differences in the home backgrounds and circumstances of young people, recognising the key role that parents and carers play in children's education.

Teachers see themselves as part of a team, in which fellow teachers, other professional colleagues and governors are partners in securing the learning and well-being of young people.

Teachers entering the teaching profession in England have met a common professional standard.

http://www.gtce.org.uk/shared/contentlibs/
92511/92572statement_of_values.pdf

Such codes assert the ethical basis of practice – that is, that ethics are not a contingent consideration but are intrinsic to practice. This mirrors the work on the centrality of ethics within competent professional practice (Eraut 1994; Boreham 2002; Oates 2004). A key to my analysis here is the commitment to principle b) in the New Zealand code above: '... base their professional practice on continuous professional learning, the best knowledge available about curriculum content and pedagogy, together with their knowledge about those they teach ...'.

These ethical considerations relate to transformation of practice – with a focus on the relationship between individual teachers and groups of learners. But in terms of magnitude of responsibility and power of effect, if ethical considerations apply at this level they surely must, by implication operate with even greater force at the level of system review and revision. 'Do no harm' is thus justified as a constraint on policy and mass innovation. But before examining a number of initiatives against this principle, an excursion into the philosophy of science is necessary.

Understanding the status of knowledge which is generated through educational research and evaluation – putting in place more realistic expectations of 'useful knowledge'

The extended debate regarding the putative reductionism in commitments to implement education policy based on 'what works' (Chalmers 2005) has skirted only loosely around the issue of the nature of knowledge in social science. Yet this is fundamental. If policy-makers and politicians are encouraged to rely on knowledge generated by educational research (Davies *et al*. 2000; Sebba 2004) they have a right to know the status of that knowledge – and I contend that this issue has been grossly neglected, leading to frustration on the parts of both researchers and of those in the policy community.

The US National Research Council's influential *Scientific Research in Education* (National Research Council 2002) contains a crucial error. The authors assert strongly the credentials of educational research, and that accumulation is both desirable and possible. Unfortunately they argue for the status of social enquiry on the basis that there is no distinction between the knowledge-creation processes of natural and social science (pp. 28ff). Ironically, this infringes the very principle of accumulation that they avow and to which they aspire. They have overlooked the key contribution of realist theory to social science – namely that there is an absolute distinction between natural and social science (Bhaskar 1979), which will be an underpinning principle for this chapter. In reaching their (flawed) conclusion regarding the commonality of natural and social science, they failed to include realist theory in their 'accumulations'.

Bhaskar's realist ontology (Bhaskar 1975, 1979) is essential to an adequate understanding of the status of knowledge generated in social science in general, and educational research in particular. I will contend that it helps to re-cast the relationship between the research and policy communities. Paradoxically, it better cements relationships by showing the necessarily conditional nature of the knowledge emerging from enquiry into social/educational systems – that is, that this knowledge is more provisional and less certain than the knowledge yielded by natural science. Realist perspectives thus hold the potential for placing this relationship on a more *realistic* footing – rather than one side (policy-makers) having over-ambitious expectations of the knowledge created by the other side (the researchers). In this chapter I wish to redefine what we mean by 'useful knowledge' (Davies *et al.* op. cit.) and try to lay the foundation for a redefined relationship between policy-makers and researchers. But I also wish to explore the extent to which a failure to characterise accurately the nature of educational research and of policy activity is accompanied by a serious omission of procedure: the failure to erect a set of ethical principles regulating innovation and experimentation, and the allied need for careful and impartial evaluation. I will offer four case studies which illuminate different aspects of this failure, and argue that innocents have been placed at risk.

Bhaskar's original texts (op. cit.) are dense – but the implications can be sketched simply: in physics, no matter what you feel about gravity, things will carry on falling at the same rate. You can run different experiments on gravitational forces, get angry that some do not work as you wanted them to, feel a warm glow as the results come up as expected. A given theory may prove right or wrong – in other words, our view of the world may be correct or defective – but meanwhile gravity will simply carry on doing what it always does: keeping my coffee cup neatly on the table and terrifying me when I go rock climbing.

But social science is *fundamentally* different. It is a science which has a different relationship with the world. The theories we have about the social world affect how that world operates. If I have a theory that certain social groups are better at certain activities, or that females are better at certain activities than men, then that affects how my relations with those groups actually operate. In other words, the social theories I have affect the social world in a way in which theories about the natural world do not affect the processes which operate in that world. So social theories are a part of the social world – their translation into beliefs and behaviours influences the way the social world operates.

Bhaskar gives us an excellent example of this important perspective on social theory: the one pound coin. It is a round piece of metal which costs a great deal less than one pound. But it is worth one pound. Why? Because a group of people share a common belief that it is worth a pound. It is of course really useful that these shared beliefs operate in the social world. In this instance, they enable the whole banking system, indeed the whole economy, to work. The example shows us that beliefs play a central role in the operation of important social systems. And it brings home some political truths, such as the fact that these systems do not operate independently of human action, contrary to what is suggested by phrases such as '... natural operation of the market ...'.

But while social theory and social research can be very good at explaining things – why certain social groups behave in certain ways, what's going on in a specific community – Bhaskar's analysis asserts that social science will of necessity lack the capacity to *predict* events. High on explanation and low on prediction again shows a critical difference between social and natural science. Natural science has high predictive power (such as predicting the temperature at which water will boil when taken to 6,000 metres, or the gauge of copper electrical cable which is needed to safely run a large piece of industrial plant of a certain power consumption).

The fact that social theory is part of the system which it seeks to explain means that social science falls over repeatedly when it comes to prediction. And when we come to the implementation of social policy it just gets worse. This is exemplified in the model of 'planned failure'. At the Third International Conference of Learning at Work in Milan, June 1994, Frank Achtenhagen outlined a model of 'planned failure' in social policy. This linked the ontology of realist theory to social policy. He argued that if you fail to adequately understand the nature of the problem you are tackling, you formulate policy which half-engages with the problem – but at the same time, putting the policy in place changes the nature of the system you are dealing with, giving you a whole new set of problems which you no longer understand at all. This is the principal causal mechanism behind the increasingly mentioned 'unintended consequences' of policy.

It is also the mechanism through which Goodhart's Law (Goodhart 1984) and the 'Texas Test Effect' operate (Wiliam 2001). In line with Bhaskar, there is reflexivity between measures and the system – the system adapts to the indicators. The weak correlation between performance indicators and performance itself is not evidence of the distance between them, but of the way in which they are entwined.

Inflated expectations of the predictive power of knowledge from educational research and evaluation poses problems for a well-grounded relationship between the research and policy communities. This is a key problem: the provision of knowledge which has adequate power – knowledge in which decision-makers at national level can have confidence. In other words, knowledge which makes clear what is going on, why it is happening, and whether revised arrangements offer an improvement over existing arrangements (particularly in terms of better use of public money). Despite their limitations, this issue was confronted in both the Tooley report (1998) and the Hillage report (Hillage *et al.* 1998). Both reports highlighted acute and chronic problems in educational research and the research-policy relation in respect of: a failure to generate/fund research knowledge which engaged sufficiently with practice; paradigm conflicts within research which militated against knowledge accumulation; and contradictory findings from broadly parallel studies – often derived from defects in method (see, for example, Goldstein 1991; Goldstein and Blatchford 1998). These problems formed a starting agenda for the ill-fated National Educational Research Forum (NERF) (NERF undated; and see Chapter 6 of the present book), and were also confronted in the US National Research Council's influential reference report on educational research (op. cit.).

But two distinct arguments were conflated in these discussions: (i) the contingent argument that researchers tended to focus on esoteric areas unrelated to practice; and (ii) the more fundamental issue of confidence which could be placed in the findings and thus their utility for policy formation. The former has, notably, been addressed in the revised Economic and Social Research Council's (ESRC) arrangements for contracting and directing research within the Teaching and Learning Research Programme (TLRP) programme (TLRP undated). I will not deal with this area. Rather I am focusing on the second issue, and examining the relationship between the structural form of knowledge in enquiry in education, the nature of the confidence which we can have in such knowledge, and the effect that inappropriate understandings of this have had on the researcher–policy-maker relation.

Far from pouring oil on troubled waters, the implied or inferred centralism in the NERF arrangements fuelled oppositions in the research community (for example, Ball 2001; Hodkinson 2001). Hodkinson subsequently re-entered the still-raging debate on paradigm wars in educational research and the research-policy relation by asserting that the necessary multiplicities of theory and discourse in educational research suggest absolute relativism in knowledge of complex social systems (Hodkinson 2004). Hodkinson's ontological and epistemic commitments – and those of others who take a similar position – imply that knowledge accumulation, indeed meaningful communication, is not possible in educational research, nor can knowledge accumulation support more effective policy-making in education. The plea for 'useful knowledge' which emerged in the wake of Hillage looked as though it was being ruled out of court on principle. But the burgeoning internal contradictions of Hodkinson's argument causes it to collapse under its own weight. Not least, just as Samuel Beckett's plays heralding the death of meaningful human communication relied on absolute precision in staging in order to communicate this message (Worth 2001), Hodkinson relied on assertion of explanation through conventional discourse in order to dispute the explanatory power of conventional discourse. This contradiction did not escape either this author or Hammersley (Hammersley 2005).

Bhaskar's realist position suggests that whilst research enquiry in social systems cannot possess high levels of predictive power and thus is to be differentiated from natural science, it does possess high levels of causal and explanatory power – and thus qualifies as science. This position on the status of the object of enquiry also suggests that some theories and enquiries will yield higher quality knowledge than others (using causal power and explanatory power as criteria). Contrary to Hodkinson's relativist position, knowledge located within different paradigms can be related one with another, since they relate to the same (real) object – social systems and their operation. All theories are not equal, and discussion, dispute and accumulation is thus not ruled out. Hodkinson's implied 'get your tanks off my lawn' position in respect of policy-makers is thus replaced with a shared, common concern: deriving the most powerful understanding of the mechanisms at play in education and training systems.

But it is worthwhile spending a little more time on the implications, for policy and research, of realist theory. Bhaskar argues that the power of explanation in social science are at their highest under conditions of *ceteris paribus* – all other things being equal (Bhaskar 1979). But this argument in respect of *ceteris paribus* is of critical importance, not least in that in respect of complex systems such as educational systems, all other things usually are *not* equal. That is, the educational attainments of individuals are determined by a range of factors, some of which are outside the control of the formal educational system, such as family wealth (or lack of it), culture, economic drivers, and so forth. Improvement in educational outcomes may derive from changes in these factors rather than from policy impacting on the form of education and training. Often neglected in explanations of educational performance, the linking of social, economic and educational policy is seldom effected in system reform and development (recent notable exceptions being

SureStart [Sylva *et al.* 2004] and Excellence in Cities [DfES 1999]). Under this form of fragmented policy management, *ceteris paribus* is startling in its absence – that is, the additional variables which will determine the success of a focused policy are not attended to; all things are not equal, and there is no attempt to affect the additional variables which make this the case. In addition, complex social systems such as education systems evolve unpredictably as individual human actions shift the underlying relations which make up those systems – actions motivated by subtle shifts in individuals' operational theories of the world ('... I'll try this slightly different approach to managing my class ...', which shifts the nature of the social dynamic in the class, the behaviour of pupils and thus the teacher's perceptions of the pupils, which demands another shift in class management approches and so on ...). As stated above, unlike in natural systems, theory in the social domain *is part of that domain*.

All this impacts adversely on the ability of educational researchers to generate 'certain' knowledge. As outlined above, this contingent lack of 'all things being equal' combines with an absolute limit on definitive predictive power. Bad news for the researcher who is asked an apparently clear and simple question by a minister – '... but will it definitely improve standards ...'? Researchers with Hodkinson's ontological and epistemic commitments would be bound by principle to say '... this is not a reasonable (or even recognisable) question ...'. For funders of research and evaluation, for policy-makers and developers, indeed, for teachers interested in innovation, this is not a response which is welcomed. By contrast, the realist educational researcher would say '... all other things being equal, this innovation is likely to produce a particular set of tendencies in the system (for these particular learners, and possibly with these unintended consequences) ...'.

This hints at the nature of a key difference between policy-makers' and (realist) researchers' views of knowledge of educational systems. Policy-makers require knowledge which gives clear direction and clear analysis of outcomes (explaining what has happened and what has caused it to be the case). A realist researcher would assert that the necessary limits on prediction in social (educational) systems lead us to conclude that it is possible to:

- generate explanations for events and outcomes;
- generate causal explanations (x caused y);
- generate knowledge of likelihoods and tendencies.

In addition, that, despite falling necessarily short of the forms of knowledge that can be created in natural science, this is an adequate base for the formulation and evaluation of innovation in education and training systems.

Under these conditions, knowledge from different communities of researchers can be accumulated (even though different paradigms may be in play, they are being deployed on the same, real object of study: features of complex social systems), and can comment on the effectiveness of innovation and on promising ways forward. But researchers and policy-makers should recognise that research should not try to meet too high a burden of proof (Minister: '... will this innovation *definitely* improve standards?...'). Rather, we should characterise the application/utilisation in policy of the outcomes of educational research as 'the integration of adequate knowledge of tendencies'. Minister: '... will this innovation definitely improve standards?...'. Researcher '... on the basis of these five qualitative and quantitative studies it is the most likely initiative to raise standards, given that factors x, y and z in the surrounding context do not change radically ...'. This is not an ineluctable descent into relativism, nor is it an assertion of infallible knowledge. It is a realistic statement of the kind of 'useful knowledge' that educational research can contribute to policy formation and policy evaluation (Pawson and Tilley 1997). Too high a burden of proof is not justified – it leads to the paradox of 'the descent into the irrational due to the rejection of "acceptable uncertainty"'. That is: policy-maker: '... if you can't give me a definitive and absolute answer to whether this innovation will definitely improve standards then I'll just go with my gut feeling and the fact that my son/daughter/nephew/niece/neighbour enjoyed this new qualification ...'.

Avoiding this paradox is vital: research and evaluation must generate useful knowledge; policy-makers must have realistic expectations of the status of this knowledge (its true limits as well as its true power). The case studies which now follow show how the relation between research/evaluation and policy/innovation has been both defective and dysfunctional. I am suggesting that the ethical dimension is vital both for understanding the nature of these defects and for considering the way in which an ethical framework for regulating innovation might contribute to (i) avoiding such serious problems in the future, and (ii) better protecting learners.

Case study #1

Ethics and 'ownership of innovation': the handling of adverse evaluation findings from Curriculum 2000 (C2K)

The problem of 'ownership' of innovation was the subject of extended discussion following the author's presentation at the dissemination conference for the ESRC-funded research project, *Education and Youth Transitions in England, Wales and Scotland 1984–2000*. From the audience of senior researchers and educationalists there emerged a strong sense of unease with current evaluation arrangements relating to mass innovation. Critically, the timing of evaluations of major innovations and programmes are most usually out of synch with the political cycles created by general elections, the duration of ministerial office, and so on. The timetable for review, development and effective evaluation of a new or revised qualification or learning programme will extend well beyond a typical four- to five-year electoral period, and certainly well beyond the period of office of a set of education ministers (Lea 2002). The revision of A levels and GNVQs (the latter into Applied A level) following the Dearing Review of 14–19 Qualifications is typical:

1994	Commissioning of the Review of 16–19 Qualifications.
1996	Report of the Review of 16–19 Qualifications.
1997	Consultation on 14–19 reforms.
1999	New form of qualifications developed for introduction from September 2000.
2000	Revised qualifications implemented.
2001	Report of Qualifications and Curriculum Authority (QCA) Research Team interim first year evaluation of revised two-year qualification.
2002	First full report of QCA Research Team review of operation of two-year qualification.
2003	Second full report of QCA Research Team review of operation of two-year qualification.

Restricted reporting by QCA to Government in 2001 was the first indicative feedback on the effects of the changes (based on a 100 per cent sample of post-16 centres). The first report of evaluation of the full operation of the two-year qualifications was possible only in late 2002. Learning programmes and assessment arrangements only begin to settle to some degree after one two-year cycle of operation (Kingdon and Stobart 1988). Teachers may adapt programmes and refine administrative arrangements before this, in response to emerging problems, and implement these in the intake year for the next cycle (the start of year two of implementation). But the outcomes of a full implementation of a two-year qualification are obvious only after the completion of the full two years of operation. In the light of changes which practitioners are likely to implement, it is also probable that further significant shifts in practice or evidence of stability in practice will only emerge after three or four years of operation of a two-year qualification.

In the case of GNVQ revisions under Curriculum 2000 (C2K), the initial proposal to review preceded the emergence of comprehensive evaluation findings by eight years. This period had seen five Secretaries of State for Education: John Patten (Conservative 06.07.92–20.07.94), Gillian Shephard (Conservative 21.07.94–01.05.97), David Blunkett (New Labour 02.05.97–07.06.01), Estelle Morris (New Labour 08.06.01–23.10.02) and Charles Clarke (New Labour 24.10.02–16.12.04).

It is clear from this that a government minister in receipt of problematic evaluation findings from an innovation may have had no responsibility for the implementation of the innovation, let alone for the commissioning of the review which led to the proposal for, and design of, the innovation. Eight years can easily span three governments, with similar issues of continuity and discontinuity in strategy and policy 'ownership'.

This is not a claim that there is no continuity in policy direction over considerable periods of time. Far from it, some elements of policy remain highly enduring – for example, (i) the commitment to a National Curriculum; and (ii) the commitment to accountability arrangements based on assessment of every child at the end of each key stage (nominally at seven, 11 and 14 years of age). These have remained commitments of successive Conservative and Labour administrations over two decades. Rather, this is a claim that the use of evaluation data for the avowed purpose of policy revision is typically out of synch with the timings of political cycles.

A ministerial team can thus be faced suddenly with a report of adverse findings for a major element of the education and training system which was neither conceptualised nor initially implemented under their 'watch'. I will not here analyse the full range of problems to which this can give rise (but see Hodgson and Spours 2004) – which include obvious effects such as premature rejection of innovations on the basis of 'not invented here' and inappropriate modification of programmes which distort original aims and objectives; and also include counterintuitive results such as re-invention of defective programme structures due to poor 'policy memory' (Higham and Yeomans 2005). Instead, I will examine the events around the reaction in December 2002 to emerging adverse evaluation findings on C2K, approximately 18 months after the initial implementation of the C2K programme. Note that this was some six months before the so-called 'A level crisis' or 'A level meltdown' of summer 2002, which featured unprecedented press scrutiny of both Advanced level qualifications[1] and the C2K changes, led to the rapid resignation of the Chair of QCA, Sir William Stubbs (on 27 September 2002), and was a contributing factor in the subsequent resignation of the Secretary of State for Education and Skills, Estelle Morris (on 23 October 2002).

Again, it is important to note my purpose of examining this case study: that is, to establish the extent to which the ethical basis of reforms was attended to during key periods of decision-making and handling. In the case of C2K and its evaluation, a serious breakdown occurred in the winter of 2001. Government had requested a report from QCA on the progress of C2K; concern had been growing as a result of the problems during awarding of the first AS (Advanced Subsidiary) qualifications in the summer of 2001, particularly in mathematics. The QCA report submitted to DfES in December 2001 took the line that problems were superficial, essentially 'bedding in' issues. There was confidence that with persistence and support, the innovation would achieve its objectives, and quickly (QCA 2001). But behind the scenes, QCA researchers were deeply troubled that the report had failed to include a series of observations from a comprehensive and ongoing survey of all post-16 centres. This survey started prior to the implementation of C2K and allowed sensitive analysis of curriculum and assessment issues (UCAS/QCA 2003) emerging in the first three years of C2K implementation; elements of the survey have continued to 2007. It involved both centre and student analysis, and included systematic combination of data from a variety of agencies, using a data-sharing protocol (Oates 2001). The observations from the survey contained indications of serious structural weaknesses and problems.

In essence, the reports from the evaluation suggested that the fundamental aims of C2K were not being met. This was fully supported by evidence. After submission of the Christmas summary report, concerned researchers approached the Chairman directly in March. After this closed briefing, a summary report was taken by the Chairman direct to senior DfES officials and the findings aired at the Education Select Committee.

In essence, the report suggested that of the three main aims of C2K, 'breadth', 'depth' and 'progression', both 'depth' and 'progression' were heavily compromised. Following years showed that they remained so. In particular, the bulk of higher education institutions continued to emphasise 'three good A level grades' as the basis for entry. Very seriously, enrichment activities remained a casualty of C2K implementation, and a growing number of voices could be heard to say 'assessment treadmill', 'assessment overload', etc. (BBC 2001; Tait *et al.* 2001; ATL 2002; Tomlinson 2004; Hodgson *et al.* 2005)

Breadth and progression

Positive outcome: The UCAS/QCA national survey showed 58 per cent of year 12 students taking four AS qualifications, with 2.8 per cent taking five or more. Using matched candidate data from examination entries, 105,067 (53.4 per cent) out of a total of 196,570 year 12 students in 2001 took four AS subjects.

This can be compared with around 25 per cent taking combinations of four or more A level and/or old AS qualifications prior to C2K. Therefore, as a result of C2K there was a substantial increase in students taking four subjects in their first year of study.

Underlying issue: however, when researchers looked in detail at the subjects which students were studying, they tended to take for their fourth AS a subject related to, rather than contrasting with, their three 'main' AS qualifications. The inspection report by the Office for Standards in Education (OFSTED) characterised this as 'bulk rather than breadth'. There were exceptional centres which had implemented a curriculum philosophy based on breadth but they were indeed exceptions. The numbers taking vocational qualifications at advanced level (AVCE) remained static, at around 12 per cent of the cohort taking any advanced level qualifications. On the basis of the national survey of centres, the numbers of students mixing academic and vocational qualifications (for example, A level students doing the 3- and 6-unit ACVEs) remained more or less static (at around 22 per cent of those doing advanced qualifications).

Significant problem: There was a near-universal view from schools and colleges contacted in the national evaluations that higher education institutions in general did not changed their admissions policy and practice in the wake of C2K. The messages from the majority of these institutions to students, schools and colleges continued to emphasise 'three good A level grades' as being the principal target for students.

Breadth – attainment of Key Skills

Significant problem: Key Skills remained very unpopular amongst students; the percentage of students which centres expected to enter for certification in three key skills dropped from 56.2 per cent in autumn 2000 (the number entered for the Key Skills qualification) to 20.2 per cent in autumn 2001 (the number entered for three Key Skills).

This headline figure for entry contrasted with much lower completion figures. Amongst case study centres committed to Key Skills and offering coherent provision, they typically had found it hard to keep students' attendance to reasonable levels, and amongst students who had actually attended provision only low percentages completed the tests; fewer still completed their portfolios.

Admission tutors in higher education institutions made it clear to schools and colleges that Key Skills were far less significant than high grades in three main subjects. When pressure increased in their programmes, students understandably placed less emphasis on Key Skills.

Progression from level 2 and within the vocational segment of the system

Underlying issue: Prior to C2K, progression from level 2 GNVQ post-16 provision to level 3 GNVQ was emerging as an established progression route for young people, often those with prior attainments other than five or more GCSEs at grade C or above.[2] Following the introduction of AVCE,[3] schools and colleges emphasised to the national evaluation teams that this progression route had been adversely affected by: change of assessment regime and backwash into learning styles; increasing entry requirements for VCE in the wake of the changes to the qualifications; and centres expressing concern that vocational GCSE would be perceived by post-16 students who have done less well in GCSEs at 16 more in the nature of a 'GCSE resit' than the motivating vocational alternative provided by Intermediate GNVQ.

It was clear that looking only at the impact of C2K on those taking advanced qualifications obscured the importance of the progression routes needed for those working at level 2 post-16.

Breadth – curriculum enrichment activities

Underlying issue: through the UCAS/QCA survey, schools and colleges reported a decrease in enrichment activities in the first two years of Curriculum 2000 (See Table 9.2 overleaf). This category included a wide range of activities, including those which were extra-curricular in a formal sense and those which broadened teaching and learning through such means as field trips and visits, visiting speakers, debates and many others.

Table 9.2

	Percentage	
Response	Nov 2000 Y12	Nov 2001 Y12
Increased	7.2%	10.3%
Decreased	38.4%	32.6%
Remained the same	50.2%	57.1%

Whilst it was clear that resource utilisation (e.g. teaching room usage) had improved as a result of C2K, survey work indicated that enrichment activities had decreased in over 30 per cent of schools and colleges for two years in a row.

'Bedding down' versus fundamental change

Underlying issue: there were indications throughout the Universities and Colleges Admission Service and Qualifications and Curriculum Authority (UCAS/QCA) survey data that centres were learning from the first year's experiences and adopting more robust approaches to timetabling, teaching, etc. However, with higher education strongly reinforcing 'three good grades at advanced level', movement away from Key Skills, and static numbers in vocational options, there was little to suggest that there would be any significant movement from the status quo. There were no strong drivers or incentives to stimulate substantial change.

(Evidence base for the analysis: 20 case study centres regularly visited by the QCA Research Team; 100 schools regularly visited by OFSTED; 40 case study centres regularly visited by team from Institute of Education; bi-annual questionnaire sent to all post-16 centres by UCAS and QCA; Learning and Skills Development Agency (LASDA) evaluation reports, information collected through focus groups and centre visits; Association of Colleges (AoC) evaluation reports, information collected through AoC members; data from the FORVUS matched candidate data set; DfES Analytical Services; QCA Statistics and Information Team.)

By December 2001 it was clear from triangulated evidence that major structural problems were apparent in the implementation of C2K and that the key policy objectives were unlikely to be met. Interestingly, the feed-in from the QCA research team included warnings regarding grade aggregation for AS-A2. This was prescient, and the potential problems highlighted in March 2002 became a stark reality in the summer awarding session.

But what of the relation between these policy events and ethical frameworks? Although the research group took corrective action which sidestepped the blockages in 'normal channels', I contend that the failure to incorporate the evaluation findings in the initial report to Government constituted an ethical breakdown. 'Do no harm' – or, as here, do not introduce innovation which is retrograde in student outcomes – was contravened in a number of respects: there was a failure to report an innovation which was not and would not be likely to meet its objectives; failure to quantify the true relationship between benefit and effort/cost; a lack of analysis of the opportunity costs and educational impact of the severe erosion of enrichment activities and of the significant problems with key skills; and a failure to put in place strategies to deal with assessment and awarding problems. By ignoring the research, 'bedding in' became the dominant message (QCA op. cit.), which understated dramatically the risks to the educational welfare of the learners exposed to the innovation. Crucially, the failure to anticipate and ameliorate problems through piloting was all too evident, and would clearly breach an educational analogue of medical ethics.

I contend that using an ethical framework to guide the evaluation of the initiative would have increased the likelihood of avoiding this breakdown, by placing the welfare of learners exposed to innovation in educational 'treatment' at the heart of the policy process.

The seriousness of the exposure of young people to untrialled 'treatment' was subsequently highlighted by the education select committee:

Government admits failing to pilot new A-level

Polly Curtis

The government has owned up for the first time to failing to sufficiently pilot Curriculum 2000, a mistake which has been widely blamed for last year's A-level crisis. In written evidence submitted to the education select committee, published today, the Department for Education and Skills says: "The AS was piloted before its introduction as QCA recognised that it was a new qualification and that a new standard would need to be established. The possibility of piloting the A2 exam was not contemplated at the time. We accept that this would have been desirable."

The admission comes after the select committee took the unusual move earlier this month of rejecting the government's first submission as "unsatisfactory" after they failed to respond to the charge that failure to properly pilot Curriculum 2000 led to last year's A-level crisis.

Barry Sheerman, chairman of the committee, said the new evidence was "eight of ten" for effort. "The original was four out of ten – we said it was so poor that we sent it back and told the secretary of state he had to stay in after school and write a new one."

"They have come back and said there will never be another exam without proper piloting. That puts our minds at rest," he said.

The failure to pilot the A2 exams in Curriculum 2000 is understood to have masked the fact that better results at AS would inevitably lead to grade inflation in the overall A-level and the problems of last summer.

(*Guardian Unlimited*, Wednesday July 23, 2003)

But a key question remains: a reassurance may have been given during a period of political exigency, but where in public institutions around and within education are the formal ethical safeguards which regulate policy development and implementation effort?

Case study #2

Ethics and 'concealed continuity' – the renaming fallacy: successive versions of vocational training for young people

Windscale did not become safer by virtue of being renamed Sellafield, although it did remove the immediate association with the 1957 accident which sent radioactive material into the UK atmosphere (Crabtree 1959). Youth training 1980–2006 appears to have undergone the same process of superficial change of identity but not of underlying form.

The 20-year period saw:

> WEEP (Work Experience on Employers' Premises) (1976)
> UVP (Unified Vocational Preparation) (1977)
> YOP (Youth Opportunities Programme) (1978)
> YTS (Youth Training Scheme) (1983)
> YT (Youth Training) (1989)
> Modern Apprenticeships (1994)

The initial schemes attracted favourable comment from evaluators, welcoming the structure and curriculum focus of the programmes (Evans *et al.* 1983). However, from late 1980s, commentary became more vocal and critical (Wolf 1993, 1995; Hyland 1994; Steedman *et al.* 1998; Winch 2002), and concerned at: the failure of successive governments to erect a high-quality, high-volume vocational route of reasonable esteem (Hodgson and Spours 1997); the outcomes of the schemes for individuals (Robinson 1997); and the economic insignificance of the output for the economy (Wolf 2002). The constant changing of name and re-casting of programme content concealed an underlying continuity in the fundamental structural forms of the programmes:

- short-duration training oriented towards attaining minimum competence for labour market entry;
- an emphasis on outcomes-based learning rather than professional 'formation';
- no tie-in to any adjuvant policy (for example, a licence to practice) which shifted labour market incentives and drivers both for young people and for employers (Oates 2005).

In particular, without an attempt to engage in the last of these, it was inevitable that volumes would be likely to remain constant, and little improvement would be obtained in esteem, outcome and progression.

The introduction of Advanced Modern Apprenticeship heralded a break with this, and was welcomed by critical commentators such as researchers at the London School of Economics (LSE) (Steedman *et al.* op. cit.). Advanced Modern Apprenticeships began to gather momentum (25,000 in 1996 to 135,000 in 2000 'in training') (source: DfES) and included more robust curriculum requirements and a commitment to longer duration, formation-oriented work-based learning (Oates op. cit., Unwin and Fuller 2003, DfES and LSC 2004). However, as numbers at Advanced level began to plateau in 2000, the 'renaming effect' kicked in once again. Official participation figures celebrated the dramatic increase in Foundation Modern Apprenticeship: 'in-training' figures up from 28,000 in 1999 to 90,000 in 2001. But while the increase in Advanced Apprenticeship represented a substantial improvement in flows into youth training, the Foundation Apprenticeship figures increased only as a result of the apparent reduction in numbers on 'other' government-funded training. In fact, lower level (levels 1 and 2) programmes of this kind were being designated as 'Foundation Apprenticeship'; a clear substitution effect.

This case study is intended to exemplify another breakdown in ethical regulation of policy. Learners and the public were being told that fundamental transformation of the vocational route was under way, whereas in fact the lower level route was simply replicating the structural form of previous programmes. The chances of substantial enhancement of progression for those participating in the programmes (the 'return on investment' to individuals, in particular), and improvements in participation (returns to the state and the economy, in particular) were therefore remote. A form of educational 'treatment' was thus perpetuated, participants were not informed of the fact that innovation had *not* occurred. In one sense, 'do no harm' had been upheld: there had been no substantial improvement in provision, but no significant withdrawal or deterioration either. But by analogy, it could be considered to be a successive placebo effect: change had been championed but in fact no change had taken place. The key ethical issue here would seem to be consent and information. The 'renaming effect' was misleading: policy innovation promised change in outcomes and effects but with no proven mechanism for yielding such changes (a case of 'false hope'?). In addition, learners were not informed of the true nature of the educational treatment which the 'revised' programmes actually offered.

Case study #3

Ethics and protection against risk – the implementation of the National Curriculum

This case study is brief. The ethical issues I wish to engage with are stark and reasonably simple to analyse, despite the scale and gravity of the National Curriculum 'experiment' in England (Aldrich and White 1998; Colwill undated); and indeed the scale of comment upon its form and effects (Chitty 1993; Osborn et al. 2000).

Ethical argument for 'no pilots' version 1: during the mid-late 1980s, Department of Education and Science (DES, as it then was) officials repeatedly stated that to test out a full prototype national curriculum offer with a selected group of pupils would be ethically unjustified. Their reasoning was that education is so fundamental to an individual's life chances that it is unjustified to 'experiment' with a small group. This sentiment/rationale remained in place for a considerable period: it was evident in the input of DES officials to the discussions in the mid-1990s of GNVQ piloting referred to earlier in this chapter.

Ethical argument for 'no pilots' version 2: however, a researcher interviewed by the author who was at that time at the National Curriculum Council (NCC) stated that other senior officials offered a very different rationale for 'no pilots'. They stated that '... the National Curriculum is clearly of such benefit to learners that its deployment should not be delayed by piloting ... large cohorts of children could lose out as a result of these delays ...'.

The first ethically based argument outlined above is deeply flawed and contradictory. The practical implication of the position is to bring about a situation where, rather than a contained experiment with a small group, all pupils become part of a grand national experiment. 'Experiment' is, of course, an inappropriate term, since the introduction of the National Curriculum was not structured as an experiment. It was an innovation which was treated as 'must succeed', and this despite the high level of innovation involved in specifying subjects as outcomes, developing assessment approaches, and so on. The ethical principle enshrined in the argument that pupils should not be exposed to undue risk since 'education is so important to each individual' is in fact grossly contravened by exposing all pupils to risk. Not only were individuals potentially compromised, but the whole system was reconfigured to deliver the national curriculum which, without piloting, was of unknown benefit and possessed unknown effects.

The second ethically based argument is flawed to a similar degree, but in a different way. Without piloting, the balance of benefits of the national curriculum was simply not known.

After more than a decade of operation, the benefits of the national curriculum have been comprehensively catalogued (Chitty op. cit.; Colwill op. cit.). They include help with pupil transfer in the system (Dobson and Pooley 2004; Ewans 2005); balanced subject coverage in primary phase education (Sammons *et al.* 2003); content which encourages enhanced performance by girls in areas such as mathematics (Elwood and Comber 1996); and enhanced development of skills (SCAA 1997). However, the balance sheet of benefit and deficit also includes a long list of serious matters such as acute curriculum overload (remedied in part by Sir Ron Dearing's first review of the national curriculum); overbearing assessment apparatus (Wiliam 2001); adverse impact of assessment on teaching and learning approaches (Wiliam op. cit.; Osborn *et al.* op. cit.); reduction of curriculum innovation (White 1997); and marginalisation of certain subjects in the 'battle for room' (Rawling 1999).

The urgent and successive revisions to content and assessment (reported in *the Guardian* 2004) hint at the problems which were caused by a failure to pilot the national curriculum. Changes were hastily formulated in the face of teacher boycott of national tests in 1993 (Alexander *et al.* 1996). Duncan Graham's autobiographical account of the development and implementation of the national curriculum provides the sole reference for the decay of public accountability

mechanisms around the development work, is itself devoid of explicit consideration of the ethical dimension of mass innovation, yet includes tantalising glimpses
of concern at the direction and pace of change: '... it can be argued that many of
the 1988 reforms were already in place without some of the prescription and
detail which was to plague the introduction of the national curriculum. There is,
therefore, a valid case for saying that in 1988 the need for a national curriculum was
less urgent than it had been in the early 1980s ...' (Graham and Tytler 1993, p. 5).

From an ethical standpoint, the national curriculum constitutes a mass innovation with inadequate ethical controls in relation to risk to students, and indeed in
respect of the risks to the integrity of the education system as a whole. The seemingly ethical argument deployed against piloting can be seen to have the form of
legitimation deriving from utility frameworks rather than ethical frameworks.

Case study #4

Ethics and temporal discontinuity between evaluation and policy formation – the peculiar case of the GNVQ, a 10-year-old qualification which never made it out of it pilot phases

The history of the GNVQ is extremely peculiar. It was designed by six people,
including the author, as a result of policy analysis which suggested that a vocational qualification designed for delivery in full-time educational settings was
needed both to provide a government-sanctioned, high-status vocational route,
and to protect the existing national vocational qualifications (NVQs) from an
increasing tendency towards delivery in colleges of further education rather than
workplaces. The original formulation in fact predated the government invitation
to develop the qualification. The design process at the National Council for
Vocational Qualifications (NCVQ) was well under way before an interested political administration sought to embrace the initiative as a government-sponsored
innovation.

The design initially included some highly unusual features:

- the qualification was fully modular/unit-based, in line with NVQ criteria.
  However, the number of units was determined by an intention to articulate
  with academic A levels (see above). The 12-unit Advanced GNVQ was designed
  to occupy two-thirds of a full-time programme, allowing a single 6-module
  A level (the dominant model for A levels), or a cluster of GCSE resits to be
  taken with the GNVQ. This was the first general vocational qualification
  designed explicitly to articulate with A level programmes and qualifications;
- the original assessment model centred on teacher-based assessment, with
  evidence assembled on a continuous basis in portfolios;
- the assessment was mastery based; the qualification was ungraded;
- the qualification required attainment in six key skills as a condition of completion;

- the qualification was to be available only at Advanced level (equivalent to A level) and Intermediate level (equivalent to GCSEs). It was felt by the designers that lower level qualifications would not provide sufficient competence to allow progression to technically demanding employment, nor allow progression to advanced Further Education (FE) and Higher Education (HE), a key requirement. It was also felt that GNVQs would never be delivered in Key Stage 4 (14–16 education) due to the then-overbearing size of the national curriculum requirements.

Of the key features, only the 6-unit building block structure survived the first months of complex negotiation. With government commitment lined up behind the GNVQ – necessary to release adequate funding for the development – political expectations and scrutiny increased. In order to ensure sufficient system-wide support, governance arrangements were set up with wide representation: the NCC, the Schools Examination and Assessment Council (SEAC), the DES, the University and Colleges Admissions Council, the Further Education Unit, Her Majesty's Inspectorate for Schools (HMI), the Further Education Funding Council and representatives from agencies for Northern Ireland, Wales and Scotland. The power relations in the policy discussions led to constant erosion of the innovative elements of the assessment model and qualification specifications. Reluctant to let these elements be diluted and the original commitments abandoned, NCVQ developers elaborated the assessment model rather than transformed it (QCA undated).

The reluctance to abandon innovation in assessment totally and move to a model which replicated A level and GCSE assessment meant that no parties in the development process felt comfortable with the emerging models (Wolf 1997). This led to constant incremental change in both assessment and the qualification specifications (NCVQ 1995; Wolf op. cit.): an issue which dogged the entire history of GNVQs.

This case study becomes relevant to the issue of ethical regulation of innovation when the details of the initial pilot are laid out.

As outlined above, the original model was anathema to key members of the first formal governance groups, particularly the DES, HMI, and SEAC. They demanded immediate changes in the assessment model. This was implemented extremely rapidly, since pilot schemes loomed. NCVQ stated that a two-year pilot phase was necessary. This was immediately rejected by ministers and senior DES officials. They stated that 'the most senior levels of Government' – assumed to be the Prime Minister – had instructed that a one-year pilot would be entirely adequate. NCVQ developers, aware of the implications, were appalled at the decision. The reality of the timeframe was as follows.

To ensure that specifications would be re-written in the light of the pilots and be ready for full implementation in September of the following year, they would need to be presented for accreditation by Easter. They would then be sent to schools at the start of the summer term, to allow adequate preparation for September starts. To allow re-accreditation by Easter, the units would need to be re-drafted in January–March. This allowed one school term for pilot work, for a two-year qualification. Remember also that this is a unit-based qualification where the units may be taken in any order. This meant that not only was there only one term in which to review the realities of implementation of the units, a term in which schools would be coming to terms with a highly innovative assessment (and learning) model, but some units might in fact not be taught in any schools by the end of the first few months.

NCVQ was aware that this was likely to lead to ill-conceived alterations to the unit specifications and the assessment approaches, in effect replicating Achtenhagen's 'cycle of planned failure'. However, the degree of political attention and general public interest in GNVQs – fanned not least by the running down of the Technical and Vocational Education Initiative and its extension (Merson 1992; Yeomans 1996; Stanley 2005) – made it realise that it would have to conform with Government requirements. This might not have been a disastrous situation. However, the 'battle for the heart of GNVQ' ensured that it was. As outlined above, NCVQ developers were deeply committed to maintaining the original functions and models at the centre of the GNVQ. Other key agencies within the governance of the qualifications were equally committed to abandoning these functions and models and adopting more conventional approaches. NCVQ developers gave ground only slowly and with great reluctance. The effect of this was to condemn the qualification to constant modification. Each modification was undertaken in the same compressed time schedule as the original pilot. On each iteration, solutions to half-understood problems led to changes which themselves only partially addressed the original problems (such as consistency of teacher judgement, management of student portfolios, consistency of awarding body practice, and so forth) and gave rise to new and unanticipated problems. What is striking is that the nature of the centralised and confrontational political dynamic meant that the cycle of short-term change became entrenched.

This had very serious consequences. There could be no accumulation of evaluation information, since re-design invalidated prior information and invalidated precise findings. Evaluation data were always grossly incomplete due to the compressed evaluation timescales. Despite the best intentions of evaluators, they simply could not keep up with the frequency and scale of changes. Successive changes were over-determined by sectional interests rather than valid evaluation information. In addition, the nature of the contested territory (learning and teaching, qualification structure, and assessment models) led to an increasingly complex qualification. One thing became increasingly clear as the evaluations rolled on: teachers were increasingly frustrated and confused by the changes. In this tortured development cycle, four remarkable things emerged: the GNVQ candidature continued to increase (albeit driven to a significant degree by the funding arrangements of the Further Education Funding Council; see Hodgson and Spours [1997]), distinctive learning styles were established (driven by the grading criteria) and were favoured by candidates (Fitzgibbon and Meagher 1995); a highly effective progression route into higher education was opened up from Advanced GNVQ (Oates and Hillier 1997); and a third 'technical route' of reasonable volume and status opened up in the system (Hodgson and Spours op. cit.).

But despite the gains, the history of the development of GNVQs shows acute and repeated failure at an ethical level. The evaluation-development cycle was essentially out of control, yet persisted for nearly 10 years. At no point could learners be assured of evidence-based modification of the qualification. The versions are shown in Figure 9.1, below.

At one point (1996) in the life of the qualification, three versions of the same qualification (for example, Advanced Level GNVQ in Business) were being taught by teachers to different groups in centres, with some of the version differences being substantial (QCA undated).

Two significant failings at an ethical level are clearly present. First, the original pilot was highly innovative in form, yet no consents or compensatory mechanisms were in place. Second, as a result of the almost complete and extended breakdown in the evaluation/development cycle, the effects of each revised 'educational treatment' deriving from the modified qualifications were and remained essentially unknown.

As a footnote to the history of GNVQs, one can only wonder at what might have been achieved if developers had been given 10 years to move from design to a fully operational mass qualification, including access to all the resources which were in practice mobilised for the successive revisions which took place. In stark contrast to the national curriculum and C2K – which were mass innovations without pilot – the GNVQ was destined to forever struggle to escape continuous piloting and indefinite revision.

| 1991 | 92 | 93 | 94 | 95 | 96 | 97 | 98 | 99 | 2000 |

model 1
pilot

model 2 adv int

foundation

model 3

model 4   model 7   AVCE
capey pilot   qual for success

model 5   model 5   model 8
part 1   revised part 1   revised part 1

Figure 9.1 The development of GNVQs – a qualification always in pilot?

Where to now?

The DfES recently has strengthened its policy in respect of ethical approvals and regulation of research. Alongside this, the Government Social Research Unit has, in 2007, produced guidelines for the ethical assurance of Government social research. (www.gsr.gov.uk/professional-guidance/ethics.asp). I am arguing for a gross extension of this: that is, for consideration of the ethical dimension of mass innovation. In implementing a mass innovation, it would appear incumbent to meet one or more of the following criteria (and avoid infringing any of them):

Criterion 1

Offer an improved performance/experience for a significant number of learners, without significant reduction of the performance/experience for any individuals or learner groups.

Criterion 2

Reduce inequalities by raising the achievement/improving the experiences of disadvantaged individuals and groups.

Criterion 3

Encourage increased participation which results in a greater supply of knowledge and skills to the individual, society and economy – in other words, offers individual, social and economic benefit.

Criterion 4

Replace existing systems with systems which offer at least the same quality of learning experience and outcomes but which offer improved system performance, for example, at a reduced cost. Performance/experience is here construed as including: the immediate experiences within learning programmes; attainments/outcomes; outcomes with currency for progression.

Medical professionals would infringe professional ethics if they changed practice knowing that it reduced beneficial outcomes (Friedson 1970; Bonell *et al.* 2003) or replaced a known therapeutic regime with a regime with unknown characteristics or outcomes. I am arguing here that educational policy-makers possess the same duty of care towards learners as medics do to patients – particularly those individuals of age 5–16 who have had their liberty withdrawn by law and are required to attend compulsory schooling (Tapper and Slater op. cit.; Lawton 2006) – and they should not replace elements of existing systems of a known level of performance with new practices which give a lower level of performance or have unknown characteristics or outcomes. This is the hub of the case for ethical regulation of practice, policy formation and system development.

This then raises the question of how to undertake experimentation and development in education. Again, practice in the medical arena provides a critical lead. There are three key elements:

1   Obtain consents and provide means for individuals to withdraw from experimentation and development work.
2   Put in place adequate safeguards to protect participants in experimental work, including cessation of experimental work if unduly poor outcomes become evident.
3   Provide compensatory arrangements if participation in experimental work compromises the outcomes of individuals participating in the study.

This chapter is not intended to present what a framework of ethics for regulating educational policy and its implementation in practice – and particularly the management of innovation – might contain in detail. What it attempts to provide is a strong argument for the existence of such a framework and its pre-eminence in controlling innovation, that is, to lay down a legitimation for the central role of such a framework in policy-making in education. I believe that the problems which I have highlighted through case study examples are serious, and have resulted in exposing large numbers of learners to substantial risk. Innocents have not been protected. I believe that my arguments have answered the first of the following questions with a robust 'yes'. The others remain open for further public discussion.

•   Is there a need for an ethical framework regulating mass innovation in education and training?
•   Who decides on the content?
•   What are the mechanisms by which such a framework would be enforced?
•   How can innovation be managed in an education and training system with powerful accountability measures – particularly when participation in innovation might compromise individual practitioners' and education/training providers' standing in the performance tables etc.?

And finally, the case studies have revealed that the temporal problems of the evaluation-policy cycle are acute. One implication of my analysis is that the timing of political cycles and the timing of ethically regulated and fully evaluated mass innovation are irreconcilable. In answer to the third question immediately above, it may be that bold moves to take mass educational innovation out of single-term politics may be required – perhaps an educational version of the Bank of England's Monetary Policy Committee?

References

Aldrich R. and White J. (1998) National Curriculum: beyond 2000 the QCA and the aims of education. Institute of Education, University of London.

Alexander RJ., Willcocks J. and Nelson N. (1996) Discourse, pedagogy and the National Curriculum. *Research Papers in Education* **11**(1): 81–120.

ATL (2002) *Work, work, work; students'perceptions of work/life balance under Curriculum 2000.* London: Association of Teachers and Lecturers.

Ball SJ. (2001) "You've been NERFed!" Dumbing down the academy: National Education Research Forum: "a national strategy – consultation paper: a brief and bilious response". *Journal of Education Policy* **16**(3): 265–271.

BBC (2001) New exams 'stress out' sixth formers BBC News 11 04 2001 British Broadcasting Corporation. Available at: http://news.bbc.co.uk/1/hi/education/1272225.stm

Biken SK. and Pollard D. (1993) *Gender and education.* Chicago: National Society for the Study of Education.

Bhaskar R. (1975) *A realist theory of science.* Brighton: Harvester.

Bhaskar R. (1979) *The possibility of naturalism: a philosophical critique of the contemporary human sciences.* New Jersey: Harvester.

Bonell C., Bennet R. and Oakley A. (2003) *Sexual Halth Interventions should be subject to Experimental Evaluation.* In Stephenson JM, Imrie J and Bonell C (eds.) *Effective health interventions: issues in experimental evaluation.* Oxford: Oxford University Press.

Boreham N. (2002) *Work process knowledge.* London: Routledge.

Bottley M. (2000) *Education, policy and ethics.* London: Continuum.

Chalmers I. (2005) If evidence-based policy works in practice, does it matter if it doesn't work in theory? *Evidence and Policy* **1**(2): 227–242.

Chitty C. (1993) *The National Curriculum: is it working?* Harlow, Essex: Longman.

Colwill I. undated *What has the national curriculum ever done for us?* London: Qualifications and Curriculum Authority.

Cook TD. (2003) Why have educational evaluators chosen not to do randomized experiments? *Annals of the American Academy of Political and Social Science* **589**: 114–149.

Crabtree J. (1959) The travel and diffusion of radioactive material emitted during the Windscale accident. *Quarterly Journal of the Royal Meteorological Society* **85**: 362.

Davies HTO., Nutley SM. and Smith PC. (2000) *What works? Evidence-based policy and practice in public services.* Bristol: The Policy Press.

DfES (1999) http://www.standards.dfes.gov.uk/sie/eic/

DfES (2006) NLS intervention programme http://www.standards.dfes.gov.uk/primary/faqs/literacy/702497/?subject=S_899187

DfES and LSC (2004) 21st Century apprenticeships, end to end evaluation of the delivery of Modern Apprenticeship. Department for Education and Skills, Learning and Skills Council.

Dobson J. and Pooley C. (2004) *Mobility, equality, diversity: a study of pupil mobility in the secondary school system.* University College London.

Elliot J. (1999) *Action research for educational change. Milton Keynes:* Open University Press.

Elwood J. and Comber C. (1996) *Gender differences in examinations at 18+.* Institute of Education, University of London.

Eraut M. (1994) *Developing professional knowledge and competence.* London: Falmer Press.

Evans K. and Bennett R. (1983) Innovation in continuing education and training in the United Kingdom: a report prepared for the European Centre for the Development of Vocational Training. University of Surrey Department of Educational Studies.

Ewans D. (2005) *Moving home and changing school – widening the analysis of pupil mobility briefing*. London: Greater London Authority.

Fischer M. (2004) *European perspectives of workplace knowledge*. Luxembourg: Office for Official Publications of the European Commission.

Fitzgibbon C. and Defty N. (2000) *How effective are interventions designed to help under-aspiring pupils?* http://www.pipsproject.org/renderpage.asp?linkid=30325012

Fitzgibbon C. and Meagher N. (1995) *Analysis of learning styles in GNVQs – ALIS data*. London: National Council for Vocational Qualifications.

Friedson E. (1970) *Profession of medicine: a study in the sociology of applied knowledge*. New York City: Dodd Mead and Co.

Geber B. (1977) *Paiget and knowing*. London: Routledge and Kegan Paul.

Goldstein H. (1991) Better ways to compare schools? *Journal of Educational Statistics* **16**(2): 89–91.

Goldstein H. and Blatchford P. (1998) Class size and educational achievement: a review of methodology with particular reference to study design. *British Educational Research Journal* **24**(3): 255–268.

Goodhart C. (1984) *Monetary theory and practice: the UK experience*. London: Macmillan.

Graham D. and Tytler D. (1993) *A lesson for us all: the making of the national curriculum*. London: Routledge.

Guardian (2003) Government admits failure to pilot new A level 23 07 2003 http://education.guardian.co.uk/alevels2003/story/0,,1004337,00.html

Guardian (2004) The SATs story http://education.guardian.co.uk/sats/story/0,,1289880.html

Hammersley M. (1997) Educational research and teaching: a response to David Hargreaves' TTA lecture. *British Educational Research Journal* **23**(2): 141–161.

Hammersley M. (2005) 'Countering the "new orthodoxy" in educational research: a response to Phil Hodkinson.' *British Educational Research Journal* **31**(2): 139–155.

Higham J. and Yeomans D. (2005) Policy memory and policy amnesia in 14–19 education: learning from the past? Nuffield review of 14–19 education and training Nuffield.

Hillage J., Pearson R., Anderson A. and Tamkin P. (1998) Excellence in research on schools. Research Report RR74 Department for Education and Employment.

Hodgson A. and Spours K. (1997) *Dearing and beyond*. London: Kogan Page.

Hodgson A. and Spours K. (2004) 14–19 education and training in England: a historical and systems approach to policy analysis. Institute of Education, University of London.

Hodgson A., Spours K. and Waring M. (2005) Higher Education, Curriculum 2000 and the future reform of 14–19 qualifications in England. *Oxford Review of Education* **31**(4): 475–495.

Hodkinson P. (2001) NERF strategy proposals: a major threat to academic freedom. *Research Intelligence* **74**: 20–22.

Hodkinson P. (2004) Research as a form of work: expertise, community and methodological objectivity. *British Educational Research Journal* **30**(1): 9–26.

Hyland T. (1994) *Competence, education and NVQs dissenting perspectives*. London: Cassell Education.

Kingdon M. and Stobart G. (1988) *GCSE examined*. London: Falmer Press.

Lather P. (2004) *The disciplining of education: new languages of power and resistance*. Stoke on Trent: Trentham Books, pp. 21–36.

Lawton D. (2006) *Education and Labour Party ideologies*. Abingdon: Routledge Falmer.

Lea R. (2002) *Education and training – a business blueprint for reform*. London: Institute of Directors.

Mayer R. (1977) The sequencing of instruction and the concept of assimilation to schemata instructional science. *Springer* 6: 369–388.

McCall WA. (1923) *How to experiment in education.* New York: Macmillan.

Merson M. (1992) The four stages of TVEI: a review of policy. *British Journal of Education and Work* **5**(2): 5–18.

Miles MB. (1964) Innovation in education. Bureau of Publications Teachers College Columbia University.

National Research Council (2002) *Scientific Research in Education. Committee on Scientific Principles for Education Research.* Washington, DC: National Academy Press.

NCVQ (1995) *GNVQ assessment review (Capey Report).* London: National Council for Vocational Qualifications.

NERF undated National Education Research Forum http://www.nerf_uk.org/bulletin/

Oakley A. (2000) *Experiments in knowing gender and method in the social sciences.* New York: The New Press.

Oakley A. (2006) Resistances to 'new' technologies of evaluation: education research in the UK as a case study. *Evidence and Policy* **2**(1): 63–87.

Oates T. (2001) *Data-sharing protocol for inter-agency Curriculum 2000 evaluation.* London: Qualifications and Curriculum Authority.

Oates T. (2004) The role of outcomes-based national qualifications in the development of an effective vocational education and training (VET) system. *The case of England and Wales Policy Futures in Education* **2**(1): 53–71.

Oates T. (2005) The role of outcomes-based national qualifications in the development of an effective vocational education and training system: the case of England and Wales. *Policy Futures in Education,* **2**(1), 2004.

Oates T. and Hillier J. (1997) Both a cause and an effect – parity of esteem between academic and vocational qualifications. *British Journal of Curriculum and Assessment* **7**(3): 40–44.

Osborn M., McNess E., Broadfoot P., Pollard A. and Triggs P. (2000) *What teachers do: changing policy and practice in primary education. Findings from the PACE Project.* London: Continuum.

Pawson R. and Tilley N. (1997) *Realistic evaluation. London*: Sage Publications.

Peters RS. (1970) *Ethics and education.* London: Allen and Unwin.

QCA undated The story of GNVQs. Qualifications and Curriculum Authority http://www.qca.org/610_1807.html

QCA (2001) Curriculum 2000 review: QCA's report on phase 2. http://www.qca.org.uk/2586_1841.html

Rawling E. (1999) Geography in England 1988–98 – costs and benefits of national curriculum change. *International Research in Geography and Environmental Education* **8**(3): 273–278.

Robinson P. (1997) The myth of parity of esteem: earnings and qualifications. Discussion paper no. 354. Centre for Economic Performance London School of Economics.

School Curriculum & Assessment Authority (SCAA) (1997). *Looking at children's learning: Desirable outcomes for children's learning on entering compulsory education.* London: Qualifications and Curriculam Authority.

Salter B. and Tapper S. (1981) *Education, politics and the State: the theory and practice of educational change.* London: Grant McIntyre.

Sammons P., Taggart B., Smees R., Sylva K., Melhuish E., Siraj-Blatchford I. and Elliot K. (2003) *The early years transition and special needs project.* (EYTSEN). London: Department for Education and Skills.

Sebba J. (2004) *Developing evidence-informed policy and practice in education.* In Thomas G and Pring R (eds.), *Evidence-based practice in education.* Maidenhead: Open University Press.

Sokal A. and Bricmont J. (1998) *Intellectual impostures: postmodern philosophers' abuse of science.* London: Profile Books.

Stanley G. (2005) *Operational selection policy OSP31 Post 16 Education 1974–1988.* Richmond: The National Archives.

Steedman H., Gospel H. and Ryan P. (1998) *Apprenticeship a strategy for growth.* Centre for Economic Performance. London: London School of Economics.

Stenhouse L. (1983) *Authority, education and emancipation: a collection of papers.* London: Heinemann Education.

Stenhouse L. (1985) *Research as a basis for teaching: readings from the work of Lawrence Stenhouse.* London: Heinemann Education.

Sylva K., Melhuish EC., Sammons P., Siraj-Blatchford I. and Taggart B. (2004) The effective provision of pre-school education (EPPE). Technical paper no. 12. The Final Report DfES. Institute of Education, University of London.

Tait T., Frankland G., Smith D. and Moore S. (2001) *Curriculum 2000+1 Preparing for year 2 of the new advanced level general and vocational qualifications.* London: Learning and Skills Development Agency.

Tapper T. and Salter B. (1978) *Education and the political order: changing patterns of class control.* London: Macmillan.

TLRP undated Teaching and Learning Research Programme http://www.tlrp.org/

Tomlinson M. (2004) *14–19 Curriculum and Qualifications Reform.* London: DfES.

Tooley J. and Darby D. (1998) *Educational research: a critique – a survey of published education research.* London: OFSTED.

UCAS/QCA (2003) UCAS/QCA report on Curriculum 2000. QCA http://www.qca.org.uk/7496.html

Unwin L. and Fuller A. (2003) Learning as apprentices in the contemporary UK workplace: creating and managing expansive and restrictive participation. SKOPE Research Paper, Universities of Oxford and Warwick.

White R. (1997) *Curriculum innovation: a celebration of classroom practice.* Buckingham: Open University Press.

Wiliam D. (2001) *Level best? Levels of attainment in national curriculum assessment.* London: Association of teachers and lecturers.

Walter GA. (1981) *Experiential learning and change: theory, design and practice.* New York: Wiley.

Whitebread D. (2003) *Teaching and learning in the early years.* London: Routledge Falmer.

Winch C. (2002) Work, well-being and vocational education. *Journal of Applied Philosophy* **19:** 261–271.

Wolf A. (1993) *Assessment issues and problems in a criterion-referenced system.* London: Further Education Unit.

Wolf A. (1995) *Competence-based assessment.* Buckingham: Open University Press.

Wolf A. (1997) GNVQs 1993–1997 *A national survey report.* London: Further Education Development Agency.

Wolf A. (2002) *Does Education Matter? Myths about education and economic growth.* London: Penguin Press.

Worth K. (2001) *Samuel Beckett's theatre.* New York: Oxford University Press.

Yeomans D. (1996) Constructing vocational education from TVEI to GNVQ. Post 14 Research Group Research Paper, University of Leeds.

Notes

Introduction

1 Clarke was responding to criticism of the utility of the social sciences in general, made in the report by the Commission on the Social Sciences (2003). He went on to suggest that the prominence of think-tanks in the policy-makers' and public consciousness reflected badly on the universities.
2 See the work of Nutley and colleagues for a set of well-developed concepts, arguments and frameworks discussing the impact and use of research across different policy sectors (selected articles given in references below).
3 'Both the degree in which consent is attainable among those who are prepared to accept the discipline of inquiry and to follow the argument where it leads and the extent to which the method is applicable in current matters of public concern have had a highly encouraging demonstration in the experience of PEP [the Political and Economic Planning research institute, later to become the Policy Studies Institute]'. Leading article in *The Times,* 25 January 1943. Cited by Young (1981, p. 94) in Pinder (ed.).

1 Education(al) research and education policy making: is conflict inevitable?

†Inaugural Presidential address, BERA, University of Glamorgan, September 2005.
1 NERF was disbanded in March 2006.
2 Appointed Secretary of State for Education and Skills in 2004, replaced by Alan Johnson in 2006.
3 The Assisted Places Scheme was introduced by the Conservative government under the 1980 Education Act to provide public funding to enable academically-able children from poor homes to attend the country's elite academically selective private schools. It was abolished by New Labour in 1997.
4 Reading Recovery is a school-based intervention designed to reduce literacy problems within an education system. It is an early intervention for children, giving those who have particular difficulties in reading and writing after their first year at primary school a period of intensive, individual help.
5 Though note criticisms of similar provision to enable teachers to undertake research by the then Teacher Training Agency through its Teacher Research Grant pilot scheme – for example, the suggested poor quality of some of the projects undertaken through this scheme (Foster, 1999).

2 Schools research in the English Ministry of Education: an inside view

1 The views expressed here are those of the author and not necessarily those of the Department for Education and Skills.
2 See Chapter 6 in the present book for Andrew Morris's account of NERF.

4 Exploring literacy policy-making from the inside out

1 Dr Gemma Moss has conducted an ESRC-funded study of policy-making in England called, *Re-making literacy for schools: policy networks and literacy paradigms*. The study was based at the Institute of Education, University of London and involved interviewing a range of policy-makers and members of the academic community who had either been directly involved in literacy policy-making, or who had written about aspects of literacy with relevance to policy within the timeframe 1996–2003/4. Laura Huxford was directly involved in policy-making in the NLS via her role as Director of Training. We draw on these two frames of reference in this paper.

8 Enhancing impact on policy-making through increasing user engagement in research

1 The author wishes to acknowledge the contributions to the ideas and issues contained in this chapter of Professor Anne Edwards and Dr Mark Rickinson, joint leaders of the ESRC seminar series on which this chapter is based.

9 Protecting the innocent: the need for ethical frameworks within mass educational innovation

1 Advanced level examinations in England are taken in post-compulsory upper secondary education; AS is the Advanced Subsidiary qualification, typically taken at the end of the first year of advanced study; A2 is the qualification typically taken at the end of the two years of advanced level study, the outcomes in the A2 being combined with the AS outcomes to yield an overall A level grade.
2 The benchmark for 'good' achievement at the end of compulsory schooling, around age 16; GCSE = general certificate of secondary education.
3 Advanced Vocational Certificate of Education, the revised title for GNVQs at Advanced level. Vocational GCSE replaced the level 2 (Intermediate) and level 1 (Foundation) GNVQs.

Index

Academies programme 8–9
accessibility, research 13, 21, 31–3
accountability, NLS 61–2
Adams, Carol xiii
Applied Educational Research Scheme 15
assessment: *see also* quality; RAE 15; research 14, 15
assumptions: policy xvi–xvii; research 4
attainment characteristics, National Pupil Database 22

BERA *see* British Educational Research Association
Black Papers, CPD 76–7
Blunkett, David 2, 7
Bolam, Ray xxiii
British Educational Research Association (BERA): activities 1, 4; aims 14–16; debate xiv
Bryan, Hazel xxi
budgets/budgeting, research 5, 22
burdens, research 25–6

C2K *see* Curriculum 2000
capacity building: CPD 80; NERF 99
case studies, specific: 'concealed continuity' 162–3; Curriculum 2000 (C2K) 155–61; ethics 155–70; GNVQ 165–70; National Curriculum 163–5; 'ownership of innovation' 155–61; renaming fallacy 162–3; risk protection 163–5; user engagement 140; vocational training 162–3, 165–70
Centre for ICT, Pedagogy and Learning (CIPL), ICT 46–9
centres, research 21, 29–30
change dynamics, NLS 61–2
change management, ICT 49–52

CIPL *see* Centre for ICT, Pedagogy and Learning
Clarke, Charles xiv, 2
classifying, research 21–2
CPD, *see* continuing professional development
codes of practice, ethics 148–9
commitment to learners, ethics 148–9
'concealed continuity', case study 162–3
conflict: between policy-making and research 1–18
congeners xiii–xiv
constraints, research 25–6
continuing professional development (CPD) xxi, 74–91; Black Papers 76–7; capacity building 80; conceptualising 85–6; critiques, current 82–5; entitlement 80–1; *Every Child Matters* 84–5, 88; expertise 87–8; funding 80; future 85–8; genesis 75–9; HEIs 86–8; infrastructure 86–7; James Report 75; *Learning and Teaching: A Strategy for Professional Development* 79–81; Literacy Task Force 78–9; national policy today 79–81; New Professionalism 81–2; NLS 78–9; perceptions, current 82–5; 'plasticity' 86–8; Plowden Report 76–7; process 84; purpose 84; research managers 118–20; Schools Council 75–6; structures 87; TDAS 81–2; TVEI 78
'culture lag', ICT 38
current situation, research 30–1
Curriculum 2000 (C2K): adverse evaluation 155–61; case study 155–61; ethics 155–61
Curriculum, National 163–5

D&R *see* development with research
Department for Education and Skills
    (DfES) 19–34; approval, research
    24–5; burdens, research 25–6;
    composition, research 20–2;
    constraints, research 25–6;
    'Excellence in Research in Schools'
    see Hillage Report 20–1, 28–9, 38;
    funding 20; Hillage Report 20–1
    see Excellence in Research in
    Schools; national context, research 23;
    priorities, research 23–5; purpose,
    research 20; RAC 24–5; research
    19–34; response rates, research 25–6;
    Star Chamber 25–6
Development Group, NERF 97
development needs, research managers
    118–20
development with research (D&R), NERF
    97–9
DfES *see* Department for Education and
    Skills
diversity, research 3–4
drivers, professional, research managers
    118–20

Economic and Social Research
    Council xv
EDSI (Superhighways) evaluation, ICT
    42–3
education/medicine, ethics 146–8
education research *see* research
Educational Evidence Portal (EEP),
    NERF 99, 100–1
engagement, user *see* user engagement
environment, policy-making 55–62
epistemological approaches, user
    engagement 140
epistemological determinants, user
    engagement 132–3
EPPI Centre *see* Evidence for Policy and
    Practice Information and Coordinating
    Centre
ESRC *see* Economic and Social Research
    Council
ethics 144–74; case studies 155–70;
    codes of practice 148–9; commitment
    to learners 148–9; Curriculum 2000
    (C2K) 155–61; education/medicine
    146–8; experimentation 144–5; future
    169–70; GNVQ 155–6, 159, 165–70;
    harm 145–50; innovation 144–74;
    National Curriculum 163–5;

'ownership of innovation' 155–61;
    policy-making 165–70; professional
    values/practice 149; renaming
    fallacy 162–3; risk protection 163–5;
    setting the scene 144–5; values/
    practice statement 149; vocational
    training 162–3, 165–70
evaluation, Curriculum 2000 (C2K)
    155–61
evaluation projects, ICT 46–9
Every Child Matters, CPD 84–5, 88
evidence-based policy xv–xviii
Evidence for Policy and Practice
    Information and Coordinating
    Centre (EPPI Centre), research
    21, 29–30
experimentation, ethics 144–5

Framework for Teaching: literacy
    policy 60, 64; policy-making 60, 64
Funders' Forum, NERF 96
funding: CPD 80; DfES 20; research 5, 20
future: CPD 85–8; ethics 169–70;
    innovation 169–70; NERF 97, 103–4;
    user engagement 140–1

GNVQ: case study 165–70;
    ethics 155–6, 159, 165–70; policy-
    making 165–70
Gorard, Stephen 8–9
government xx-xxi, 1, 4, 38–9, 43, 76
guidelines: NTRP 26; research 26

harm, ethics 145–50
HEIs, CPD 86–8
higher education institution, *see* HEIs
Hillage Report: *see* Excellence in
    Research in Schools criticism 38;
    research 20–1, 28–9, 38; useful
    knowledge 152; user engagement 128
Huxford, Laura xxi,
'hyperrationalisttechnicist' approach,
    research 6

ICT *see* information and communication
    technology
impact, policy-making 127–43
ImpaCT2, ICT 44–6
implications, research 12–14
influencing policy-making 13–14
information and communication
    technology (ICT): barriers 50; change
    management 49–52; CIPL 46–9; 'culture

lag' 38; EDSI (Superhighways) evaluation 42–3; evaluation projects 46–9; ICT Test Bed Evaluation 46–9; ImpaCT2 44–6; Micros in Schools Schemes of 1981–84; 40–2; National Grid for Learning 44–6; policy-making 35–54; research 35–54; speculative knowledge 49–52; transition, new relationships 43–9

innovation: case study 155–61; ethics 144–74; future 169–70; 'ownership of innovation' 155–61

intermediaries, research 26–33

James Report, CPD 75

Kelly, Ruth 2, 9–10, 12
knowledge: policy community 135–7; useful 150–5; using 135–7
knowledge making, Mode 1/Mode 2 knowledge 63, 65–6

Labour, New, research 4–7
Learning and Teaching: A Strategy for Professional Development, CPD 79–81
Levin, Ben 10
literacy policy: accountability 61–2; change dynamics 61–2; co-existence 69–71; competition 69–71; content 58–61; *Framework for Teaching* 60, 64; influence 69–71; Literacy Task Force 78–9; NLS 55–62; phonics 57, 63–71; policy-making 55–73; RRF 69; standards 61–2; ways forward 71–2
Literacy Task Force: CPD 78–9; literacy policy 78–9

managers, research *see* research managers
mediation, research, research managers 121–2
medicine/education, ethics 146–8
Micros in Schools Schemes of 1981–84, ICT 40–2
ministerial views, research-policy relationship 2
Ministry of Education, English *see* Department for Education and Skills
Mode 1/Mode 2 knowledge, policy-making 63, 65–6
Models of Research Synthesis (MORSE), NERF 101
Morris, Andrew xxi–xxii
Moss, Gemma xxi

national context, research, DfES 23
National Curriculum: case study 163–5; ethics 163–5; implementation 163–5
National Educational Research Forum (NERF) xxi–xxii, 92–105; attributes 103; bulletin 100; capacity building 99; D&R 97–9; Development Group 97; domains 94–5; EEP 99, 100–1; Funders' Forum 96; future 97, 103–4; implications 102–3; influencing 100–2; interdependence, domains 95; investigating 97–9; learning from 92–105; method 103; MORSE 101; planning 96–7; policy 94–5; policy research interaction 101–2; practice 94–5; Priorities Group 96–7; programme 95–103; quality 99; research 5–6, 29, 94–5; role 102–3; skills 103; user engagement 129
National Grid for Learning, ICT 44–6
National Literacy Strategy (NLS): accountability 61–2; change dynamics 61–2; context of origin 57–8; CPD 78–9; literacy policy 55–62; Ofsted 57–8; policy-making 55–62; standards 61–2; Tier 2 policy-making 56–7
National Pupil Database, attainment characteristics 22
National Teacher Research Panel (NTRP) 21; guidelines 26
NERF *see* National Educational Research Forum
New Labour, research 4–7
New Professionalism, CPD 81–2
NLS *see* National Literacy Strategy
notes 175–6
NTRP *see* National Teacher Research Panel

Oates, Tim xxii–xxiii
OECD *see* Organisation for Economic Cooperation and Development
Office for Standards in Education (Ofsted): CPD 81; NLS 57–8
Organisation for Economic Cooperation and Development (OECD): research xxii, 23, 27; user engagement 128–9
'ownership of innovation', case study 155–61

phonics: changing policy 66–7; co-existence 69–71; competition 69–71; influence 69–71; literacy policy 57,

63–71; materials 65; Mode 1/Mode 2
knowledge 63, 65–6; policy solutions
68–9; recontextualising 63–6; RRF 69
planning: NERF 96–7; research 32
Plowden Report, CPD 76–7
policy assumptions xvi–xvii
policy community, knowledge 135–7
policy, evidence-based xv–xviii
policy-making: *see also* literacy policy;
    conflict 1–18; CPD 74–91;
    environment 55–62; ethics 165–70;
    expectations, research 133–5;
    Framework for Teaching 60, 64; GNVQ
    165–70; ICT 35–54; impact 127–43;
    influencing xix, 13–14; literacy policy
    55–73; market place 68–9; Mode
    1/Mode 2 knowledge 63, 65–6; NLS
    55–62; practical issues 135; research
    1–18, 26–33, 35–54, 133–5; research-
    policy relationship 35–54; speculative
    knowledge 49–52; Tier 2; 56–7; user
    engagement 127–43
policy, NERF 94–5
policy research interaction,
    NERF 101–2
policy-research relationship 35–54;
    initiatives xviii; insights from analysis
    37–40; ministerial views 2; reflections
    on practice 40–3; SIG xiv–xv
practice, NERF 94–5
practitioners: practical issues 135;
    research 26–33
priorities: DfES 23–5; research 23–5
Priorities Group, NERF 96–7
professional association, research
    managers 122–4
professional community, research
    managers 122–4
professional values/practice, ethics 149
pure research 21–2

quality: *see also* assessment; NERF 99;
    research 3, 13, 14, 27–8

RAC *see* Research Approvals Committee
RAE *see* Research Assessment Exercise
Reading Recovery 10
Reading Reform Foundation (RRF),
    literacy policy 69
relevance, research 3
renaming fallacy, ethics 162–3
research: abuse 2–4; accessibility 13, 21,
    31–3; aims 4; Applied Educational

Research Scheme 15; approval 24–5;
assessment 14, 15; assumptions 4;
attainment characteristics 22;
budgets/budgeting 5, 22; burdens 25–6;
centres 21, 29–30; characteristics 3;
classifying 21–2; composition, DfES
20–2; conflict 1–18; constraints 25–6;
current situation 30–1; DfES 19–34;
diversity 3–4; of education 15–16; for
education 15–16; EPPI Centre 21,
29–30; 'Excellence in Research in
Schools' 20–1, 28–9, 38; funding 5, 20;
guidelines 26; Hillage Report 20–1,
28–9, 38; 'hyperrationalisttechnicist'
approach 6; ICT 35–54; implications
12–14; intermediaries 26–33; national
context 23; National Pupil Database
22; NERF 5–6, 29, 94–5; New Labour
4–7; NTRP 21, 26; OECD xxii, 23, 27;
planning 32; policy-making 1–18,
26–33, 35–54, 133–5; policy-research
relationship 35–54; practitioners
26–33; priorities 23–5; pure 21–2;
purpose, DfES 20; quality 3, 13, 14,
27–8; RAC 24–5; RAE 14, 15;
relevance 3; research centres 21,
29–30; response rates 25–6; SCIE 30;
sociologists 38–40; speculative
knowledge 49–52; spend 23; Star
Chamber 25–6; TRIPS 27; uptake 21,
31–3; use/misuse 4, 7–12; usefulness
26–33; users 26–33
Research Approvals Committee (RAC)
24–5
Research Assessment Exercise (RAE)
14, 15
research-based teaching 11–12
research managers 106–26; concerns
114–16; CPD 118–20; development
needs 118–20; discourses 121–2;
drivers, professional 118–20; findings
110–20; mediation, research 121–2;
mode of inquiry 108–10; organisational
structures 111–14; personal
background 110–11; previous
professional experience 110–11;
problems 114–16; professional
association 122–4; professional
community 122–4; research issues
108–10; research mediation 121–2;
responsibilities 106–26; role 106–26;
role changes 117–18; satisfactions
116–17; successes 116–17

research mediation, research managers 121–2
research-policy relationship 35–54; initiatives xviii; insights from analysis 37–40; ministerial views 2; reflections on practice 40–3; SIG xiv–xv
response rates, research 25–6
risk protection, ethics 163–5
RRF *see* Reading Reform Foundation

Schools: achieving success (DfES, 2001) 8
Schools Council, CPD 75–6
SCIE *see* Social Care Institute for Excellence
Scientific Research in Education report: flaw 150; user engagement 132–3
Sebba, Judy xxii
SIG *see* special interest group
social approaches, user engagement 140
Social Care Institute for Excellence (SCIE), research 30
sociologists, research 38–40
Somekh, Bridget xx–xxi
special interest group (SIG), research-policy relationship xiv–xv
specialist schools programme 8–9
spend, research 23
standards, NLS 61–2
Star Chamber, DfES 25–6

Teachers' xx–xxi, 11, 51, 74; Teaching and Learning Research Programme (TLRP) xvii; seminar series xviii; user engagement 129–40
teaching, research-based 11–12
Technical and Vocational Education Initiative (TVEI), CPD 78
The Research Informed Practice Site (TRIPS), research 27

Tier 2 policy-making 56–7
TLRP *see* Teaching and Learning Research Programme
Training and Development Agency of Schools (TDAS), CPD 81–2
treatment, defining 148–50
TRIPS *see* The Research Informed Practice Site
TVEI *see* Technical and Vocational Education Initiative

uptake, research 21, 31–3
use/misuse, research 4, 7–12
useful knowledge 150–5
usefulness, research 26–33
user engagement: benefits 137–8; case studies 140; challenges 141; conclusions 138–40; context 128–9; epistemological approaches 140; epistemological determinants 132–3; future 140–1; Hillage Report 128; identifying users 130–1; knowing how 138–9; knowing what 138; knowing when 139–40; knowing who 139; NERF 129; OECD 128–9; policy-making 127–43; purposes 131–2; *Scientific Research in Education* report 132–3; social approaches 140; TLRP 129–40
users, research 26–33
using knowledge 135–7

values/practice statement, ethics 149
vocational training: case studies 162–3, 165–70; ethics 162–3, 165–70; GNVQ 165–70

Warner, Marina xiii
Weindling, Dick xxiii
White, Victoria xx
Whitty, Geoff xix–xx